C000062841

De̲.̲._____

"The spirit of learning is about developing practical approaches towards the integration of life enhancing attitudes, universal values, and creative, holistic techniques across the curriculum and into all learning domains."

Dawn Emelie Griggs Founder/Director Soul of Education author of "Spirit of Learning."

I dedicate this book to this beautiful soul who left our world in tragic circumstances in India, March 2004.

Thank you Dawn for your vision, your passion, your exquisite humanity and for creating the Soul of Education especially in Australia.

" Keep me away from the wisdom which does not cry, the philosophy which does not laugh and the greatness which does not bow before children."

Kahil Gibran 2001

Acknowledgements

This book has been helped and assisted by many people. The most important ones I would like to acknowledge are all the students I have taught who in turn taught me and all those of any age who have visited me professionally over the last fifteen years. Your stories have shaped the words on these pages so much as together we searched for the truth that sets us free.

My next thank you is to the parents and teachers who have encouraged my work, and inspired me to share it on a wider stage. An especial thank you to all those educators who contributed "magic moments" in this book. They created a global circle that empowers all teachers to step forward once again in their career to make a positive difference in the lives of students.

To the wonderful team who help me self publish. My amazing editor Janney Wale who tightens my text and tames my verbosity! To my proofer, Liane Shavian who picks up typos and spelling mistakes sometimes at very short notice. To Katharine Middleton my friend and virtual secretary who creates my manuals, diagrams, type sets and has created my book cover at short notice. I so appreciate having such beautiful people in my life who never let me down - a heartfelt and sincere thank you to each and every one of you.

A sincere thank you to my special inner circle of people who support me, encourage me and love me unconditionally, including my four spunky sons. Finally, a thank you to Steve, my patient and supportive husband who walks beside me every step of the way. My creative juices sometimes flow at strange times in strange places and he embraces it all with an unconditional acceptance and positive regard. For this I am blessed. Thank you all.

Contents

Introduction

Chapter 1   The Background

Chapter 2   Nurturing Young Hearts and Souls

Chapter 3   Emotional Intelligence Unplugged

Chapter 4   Emotional Distress, Overwhelm
Wounding in Children

Chapter 5   Helping Children to Heal

Chapter 6   Building Intuition and Inner Guidance

Chapter 7   The Gift of Imagination

Chapter 8   The Healing Potential of Creativity

Chapter 9   Encouraging Character in Children

Chapter 10   Boys and Emotional Literacy

Chapter 11   Spiritual Intelligence Unplugged

Chapter 12   Making The Sacred Welcome in
Our Children's Lives

Chapter 13   The Power of Prayer

Chapter 14   Nurturing Kids Hearts and
Souls in Our Schools

Chapter 15   Magic Moments: Inspirational
Stories from Around the World

Conclusion

References and Bibliography

Resources

How to Nurture Kids' Hearts and Souls

❖ *Be as real and honest as possible*

❖ *Be there*

❖ *Remember their names and their birthdays*

❖ *Teach them to laugh and cry openly*

❖ *Celebrate life's special moments -create rituals*

❖ *Let music be a part of their lives*

❖ *Encourage and help them build friendships*

❖ *Share your parenting with others*

❖ *Be a storyteller and tell stories that teach gently*

❖ *Create family or classroom magic moments*

❖ *Demonstrate a gratitude attitude to life*

❖ *Model a positive lifestyle as often as possible*

❖ *Take your kids into nature often*

❖ *Practice random acts of kindness*

❖ *Encourage the uniqueness of each child*

❖ *Have a generous heart*

❖ *Respect people of all ages*

❖ *Believe in a creative power or force*

❖ *Show your love through touch as well as words*

❖ *Smile with your eyes and your heart*

❖ *Sow a seed of hope in your children's souls*

❖ *Believe in dreams*

❖ *Believe in yourself*

Maggie Dent 2002

Introduction

"We have failed a generation of
children and continue to do so."

Dr George Halasz. Melbourne, Aust.

It was 2001 and a beautiful little five-year-old girl was brought to see me. She was very sad. Her mother told me how the little girl did not play with the other children at pre-school. The doctor wanted to put her on antidepressant medication but her parents were hoping I might be able to help so that they could avoid medication. This little one, who I will call Cindy, began to draw me an intensely black picture, even though I had given her a collection of brightly coloured textas with which to draw. As she drew she asked, "Maggie, how can you die if you want to?" I asked Cindy what she meant. She responded that sometimes when she woke up in the mornings she closed her eyes and tried to die. Her eyes were sad; there was no sparkle or light in them. My heart tugged deeply within me. I explored in my mind where this deep despair could be coming from - both her parents were concerned and loving. What had gone so wrong?

Cindy's parents were professional people. They had decided to give Cindy the 'best opportunity to be successful in life' by promoting the development of her intelligence. Fantasy and the imaginary world were considered to be a distraction to her development. So Cindy had grown up with no tooth fairies, no Father Christmas, no Grimm Brothers fairy tales and certainly no opportunities for imaginary play or dress ups. Unknowingly, these caring parents had starved Cindy's emerging imagination and sucked the life out of her young spirit. They were not aware of the protective role the imagination can play in a young child's life.

Recognising this, we were able to immediately bring wonder and creativity back into Cindy's life. Fortunately, Cindy had a Montessori-trained pre-school teacher who was willing to support us and Cindy wore fairy wings every day for a month. When I saw her next her eyes were shining, she had a beautiful smile and was accompanied by two very happy parents. Cindy is now full of life and energy with her mind, body, and heart and soul all well.

Interestingly, only the week after I first saw Cindy I met another pre-schooler who had a similar story. She too responded quickly to opportunities to play, experience imaginary games and stories and have fun time with her parents. These two little girls came into my office and helped me explore the positive influences that play and imagination have in young people's lives. I am deeply grateful to them for showing me this and the impact a deficit has on healthy mental and physical development. I liken these children to the canaries that were kept in the bottom of the mines in days gone by as a way of alerting the miners to the presence of toxic gases. The girls alerted me to a modern danger for children, and to our future adults, one that can be averted with commonsense rather than medication.

I believe much of the chaos in our homes and schools is the result of the changing from an old paradigm to a new more modern one. Up to the 1970's the following things were considered to be true:

The Past - The Old Paradigm

❖ Unquestioned power of teachers and parents
❖ Unquestioned power of doctors and lawyers
❖ Unquestioned respect of authority figures especially those With financial and material power
❖ Politicians were valued and respected

- Focus on importance of the intellect/cognitive intelligence, rational thought
- Male dominance in work, government and business
- Lack of respect for indigenous peoples and cultures
- Lack of interest and respect for the natural world
- Corporate and capital punishment for wrong doers
- Strong religious power and influence in society
- Problematic approach to solution finding
- Low divorce rate and larger families
- Traditional systems and little change
- White Australia policy and fear of other cultures
- Blame and litigation getting more and more common

In this the twenty first century there has been a shift towards:

Now and The Future

- Authentic power now based on integrity and respect
- Doctors and lawyers now being questioned
- Politicians questioned and seldom trusted
- Personal responsibility for own health and wellbeing
- Less respect for materially wealthy people
- Less striving for financial wealth more for quality of life
- Less male dominance in work, government and business
- More balance between male-female, head-heart, flow-effort, resonance -balance, synchronicity-timing.
- Growing respect for indigenous people and cultures
- Growing concern for the environment and preservation
- No more corporate or capital punishment in Australia
- Less influence of traditional religions and drifting away from same
- Solution focus to solution finding away from problems
- Strong shift to non urban life styles – sea/tree change
- High divorce rate, single parent families, smaller families
- Shift to multi cultural society, more accepting of other cultures
- More authentic, holistic and open focus

❖   Cooperative rather than competitive
❖   Frequent change and fluidity in the world

Confusion has occurred on many levels with these social changes. In the last century children were not so much raised as 'happened" with parents with little spare time because there were so little time saving devices like microwave ovens, automatic washing machines and driers. With no distractions like TV, videos, DVD's, CD's Mobile phones and other gadgets kids ran pretty free in safe communities. As times were often tough, simple food was appreciated even dripping sandwiches and left overs! Kids were expected to help around the place and jobs and chores were the norm, or no dinner!

The technology-consumerism juggernaut then happened and kids became exposed to the seductive and insidious pressure of advertising. A recent report suggested that more money is spent on trying to capture the consumer mind of children under four than is spent on children's cancer research! Thus was born the "I want" and the "I need" culture of modern life. The mod cons' gave parents more time to invade their children's lives with pressure, things and too much direction and talking! The competitive parent was created. Old ways of discipline no longer work – threats, physical abuse and shaming. Instead these things cause deep resentment, mental and emotional disability and disconnectedness. The new way of managing our children requires caring guidance rather than overt control, it requires respectful cooperation and sharing, and it requires calmness, space and enormous strength to resist the pressures of the disease called modernism. On Radio National recently a representative from the national body of optometrists reported that there has been an almost 60% increase in short sightedness in children under twelve. This was mainly due to the early and excessive use of "screens" in young children making the eyes lazy. It reinforces the research that recommends "no computers before ten years of age." It is an unnatural way for the growing brain to develop –they need real environments and not virtual ones. Today's parents are being challenged more than ever before.

As Steve Biddulph writes

> "Almost from the minute you first cradle your baby in your arms, you are at war" with the world.
> (Parenting with Spirit, Jane Bartlett, foreword)

Our modern world diagnoses more children with emotional disorders, learning disabilities and mental illnesses than ever before. Why is this?

Dr George Halasz is a Melbourne psychiatrist who has worked with children and adolescents for over 25 years. He explains that the number of psychiatric diagnoses for childhood conditions has soared in the last two decades, increasing from about 70 conditions to more than 400. What this means is that "what was once considered within the bounds of normal is now treated as an illness requiring a cure, which more often than not comes in the form of medication". Dr Halasz also believes that this situation

> "has created a paradox in our society where we fight to keep our kids off illegal drugs, yet put pressure on parents to give similar drugs to youngsters when they are supplied by a doctor." (Sunday Morning Herald, May 15th 2005, p30).

'Social medication' is also a concern, where parents dose their children with over-the-counter medications to calm them down or make them more manageable. Just a spoonful of an anti-histamine medication and peace returns to the home front!

As we become more and more a part of a faster world we have begun to label and diagnose children with "problems" that previously were seen as a normal part of childhood. Poor listening skills, inattentiveness, low literacy, hyperactivity, the capacity to be emotionally overwhelmed, shyness and delayed development in speech and fine motor skills have been around forever. They were seen as a normal part of childhood. Extra help and encouragement was given to the child so that he or she could develop in these areas of weakness. Maybe we are focusing on the "pathology" of our children rather than on their strengths. While we can focus on an ADHD child's inattentiveness, we could be focusing on the exuberance and energy that they have. With a quiet shy child, maybe we could focus on their gentleness and ability to enjoy their own company. Maybe we could relax a little, and change the adult focus until after they start school to the things that they have mastered and the joy that they bring to our lives.

In today's competitive world children are pressured to perform to the highest level and their development and education is measured against prescribed benchmarks. This has created the notion that if a child does not measure up to that benchmark there is something wrong that needs to be fixed, by experts or with medical intervention. This is now seen as 'competitive parenting". Yet children are all different, they are each unique. Their growth and development is seldom a linear process that can be directed by following one recommended pathway. Children develop and grow through a complex interplay between nurture and nature, between their genes and what happens in the environment in which they grow. Culturally and socially children have different influences that help shape their development. Yes, some are delayed in their development and some will struggle with literacy and numeracy, yet we have the notion that all kids need to be achieving at the same level, behaving the same as each other and be easy to manage. They never have been and never will be. We must stop pushing kids towards our consumer driven view of "excellence" and allow them to be children.

"Parents don't want a good enough child. They want a child that gets all the prizes and beats everyone."

Ruth Schmidt Neven, Director of the Centre for Child and Family Development, Melbourne, Parents Magazine November 2004, p18.

We are all shaped in different ways to become our own unique selves. Highly spirited children can be hard to handle. Children with poor literacy struggle with school work and get easily frustrated. Who are we to judge that these children have or do not have the talents and abilities they require to make a positive difference in our world? Exploring the high incidence of attention deficit and hyperactivity disorder (ADHD) in today's children, Victoria Carlton, who is the director of the International Centre for Excellence in Perth, warns that "we are medicating against brilliance". What would have happened if we had medicated Einstein? He had Asperger's Syndrome. Victoria believes that "these kids are very, very bright and so very interesting". (Conscious Living Magazine Issue 70, June 2005, p42).

When we see childhood through the eyes of the educated mind we miss so much. Children want to feel they belong and that they are loved. They want to feel they are important, unique and that they have friends and can experience joy and fun. Children grow and develop – no matter what their weaknesses or strengths are. Building emotional and social competencies help all children in all corners of the world to become the best person they can be. This is not necessarily the 'best person in the world' but it is the best expression of them, what true potential is all about.

There is much written about the "new children" who are arriving on earth, some known as Indigo children. While I am very mindful of the detrimental effects of labels of any kind for children, there are many characteristics that today's children have in common. They are different and they see the world differently. Often their problematic symptoms in terms of conduct and attention, of being "out-of –control" disappear when they are with adults who respect and love children, and who have no agenda to control or advise them on who they should be. This is being "in attunement" that will be discussed. They are often very bright, exceptionally fast learners who are easily frustrated with "old" systems of learning. They also have a high sense of social justice from an early age and will stand up to anyone who may be acting out of integrity or truth. Many of these challenging children are reacting against old systems that no longer work, are invalid or are prejudiced in some way.

My favourite definition about Indigo children goes something like this: "They need lots of love, choices, guidance, fair boundaries and very little parenting." Isn't that what all children need?

A key part of realising true potential in ourselves and our children is the ability to form loving lasting relationships. Without emotional intelligence and social awareness this is very difficult. Let's build pathways to emotional stability and competency in our children. Let these pathways improve their ability to connect positively to themselves, their families and friends. As they grow they can also connect with their community and to the global world. We risk losing more and more of our young people to loneliness, disconnection and dis-eases of the heart and soul if they do not gain intrapersonal and interpersonal life skills. The preventative approach is so much more important and essential than applying a curative approach once problems begin surfacing, perhaps in mid to late childhood. Creating positive change in adolescence and early adulthood is much more difficult and expensive.

Let's make the first seven years of a child's life as healthy and positive as possible. Let's avoid the unintentional damage of our greatest assets. Let's get more informed. Let's have more fun and laughter with our kids so that they can look back on childhood with a smile. Let's allow our children more freedom and space to grow without trying to control them so much. Let's get the love and bonding in place BEFORE the pressures of the world distract us and them. Remember that children are gifts and miracles and that being given a child to raise is a privilege of the highest order.

Maggie Dent

Chapter 1

The Background

"The greatest terror a child can have is that he is not loved, and rejection is the hell he fears. I think everyone in the world has felt rejection. And with rejection comes anger, and with anger some kind of crime in revenge of the rejection, and with the crime guilt – and that is the story of mankind."

John Steinbeck. East of Eden, 1952.

Contemporary Australia: from 1970 to the 2000s

Influences which disorganise developmental processes of childhood

> ❖ Patterns of family work - excessive hours reducing parental commitment
> ❖ Disengaged and inconsistent parenting
> ❖ Violence - close, regular, long standing - with particularly negative effects
> ❖ Family mobility
> ❖ Few social supports
> ❖ Impacts on child development strongly influenced by local community factors which collectively support child rearing From: Professor Fiona Stanley. Telethon

Institute for Child Health Research, September 2004.

The health and wellbeing of our children is of deep concern to me. Their emotional and mental health impacts on their physical and cognitive growth during their developmental years and has enormous social repercussions. Any negative consequences influence the potential for a child to grow into an adult with attributes that allow them to live a life that benefits both themselves and our world in some way.

Long-term challenges are set up when young adults are caught up in poverty, dependency on welfare, exposure to chronic mental illness or socially deviant behaviour around alcohol and drug abuse. In the twenty years that I have worked with children and teenagers the gaps in character development, emotional literacy and social morality have grown steadily worse and worse for a significant proportion of them. A decline in manners, etiquette and respect for themselves, other people and property is matched only by the increase in aggression, juvenile crime, emotional instability and behavioural unpredictability. Schools are struggling with children who are simply 'unreachable and unteachable'; many parents the world over are challenged with children who are unmanageable and confronting to them from an early age.

> "Our world is becoming increasingly violent. Social and political initiatives everywhere are seeking to counteract escalating trends of suicide, aggression, crime, destruction of the environment and ultimately war."

James W Prescott PhD. How Culture Shapes the Developing Brain and the Future of Humanity

Enormous numbers of children are on medication for hyperactivity, aggressive behaviour, sleep deprivation, depression and mental conditions that were seldom diagnosed in children so young prior to the twentieth century. Our medical systems are struggling to meet the demands of this wave of illness. Waiting lists for child development and mental health professionals, speech therapists, audiologists and other allied professionals are long, particularly in rural areas. Autism and allergies have risen exponentially. My concerns are that the Western world has experienced such a rapid expansion in technology and consumerism that our children are being damaged by the very same changes that are meant to make our lives easier. The increased opportunities for both parents to work, the pressure to consume more, to eat more refined quick-to-prepare foods and goods, and the fast pace of life have all added to the decline in our children's health. Instead of trips to the park on weekends for picnics or to play, families drag their children around huge shopping centres or the children are stuck in front of televisions or computers to entertain themselves. The portrayal by sensationalist media of our communities as unsafe has curtailed the free play activities of generations of kids. Play equipment that involves any risk has been removed. Yet play is hugely important for the healthy mental and emotional development of growing children.

Social shifts create less time with our children - less time to nurture their emotional growth and to instil the firm boundaries needed for the healthy growth of a moral and social code that help in later life. The reality of less time also influences a child's perception of feeling connected, being valued and of belonging. Inconsistencies are often to be found between child care as practised in the family home, in childcare facilities and at school. These differences confuse children as they do not know what is appropriate and acceptable. A plethora of parenting information comes from TV, magazines and books; yet, as the world speeds up, parents have less time to read the information or to participate in parent seminars. Another area of concern is the number of celebrity parenting experts who do not have a child over 10 years of age! You have no idea how effective your parenting is until your children are young adults, no matter how wonderful your intentions!

The purpose of this book is to explore ways of nurturing the hearts and souls of our children, as well as their physical and intellectual growth. Emotional intelligence and the many different ways of developing competencies are introduced and explored. From there we move on to the growth of spiritual intelligence and nurturing of the human spirit. The intent of this book is to be rich in information, practical, and an inspiration for parents, teachers and the carers of our children, a balance between the head and the heart, between theory and practice and between knowledge and passion.

My approach is holistic, embracing transpersonal psychology, research and a deep practical knowledge that I have gained from working closely with children, teenagers and adults as they move through major life changes and emotional and spiritual crises. May my humble book be a tool to help us and our world raise children who are emotionally competent, socially aware, responsible, resilient and capable of experiencing happiness. It is my highest vision that tomorrow's children will be free to have childhoods that allow them to grow on all levels – mind, body, heart and soul - so that they may enjoy positive relationships with themselves, others and our world. I hope you can share this dream with me.

"What a child really needs is good, positive emotional relationships with parents and others. They don't need a thousand activities. Children can learn facts and gain external skills at any time. But they only gain relationship skills when young."

Ruth Schmidt Neven, Director of the Centre for Child and Family Development, Melbourne. Parents' Magazine, November 2004, p18.

Key Points

❖ Declining emotional and mental health impacts socially in our communities

❖ Declining emotional and mental health impacts negatively on the physical and cognitive growth of our children

❖ Children are medicated more than ever before

❖ Increases in the incidence of autism and allergies in children are a concern for the medical world

❖ The fast-paced world negatively impacts on our children's health

❖ Time constraints negatively influence family lives

❖ A holistic approach builds healthier children, on all levels

❖ Emotional and spiritual wellbeing have lifelong consequences

❖ Positive relationships with self, others and our world are a sign of a healthy, resilient child or teenager

A group of students were asked to list what they thought were the present Seven Wonders of the World. Though there were some disagreements the following received the most votes.
1. Egypt's Great Pyramids.
2. Taj Mahal.
3. Grand Canyon.
4. Panama Canal.
5. Empire State Building.
6. St. Peter's Basilica.
7. China's Great Wall.

While gathering the votes the teacher noted that one student had not finished her paper. She asked the girl if she was having trouble with her list. The girl replied,
"Yes, a little. I couldn't quite make up my mind
because there were so many". The teacher responded "Well, tell us what you have, and maybe we can help. The girl hesitated, and then read that she thought the Seven Wonders of the World to be to:

1. see;
2. hear;
3. touch;
4. taste;
5. feel;
6. laugh; and
7. love.

The room was so quiet you could have heard a pin drop. The things we overlook as being simple and ordinary and that we take for granted are truly wondrous!

A gentle reminder --
that the most precious things in life cannot be built by hand or bought by man.

Source: the World Wide Web.

Chapter 2

Nurturing Our Kids' Hearts and Souls

A five-year old to her Daddy,
"Daddy do you know why children are sent into the world?"

"No tell me," Daddy replied.

"To teach them to think in their hearts so everything goes right. Otherwise they think in their heads and life is hard," she replied.

Tobin Hart PhD. The Secret Spiritual World of Children pxx.

We have all read in newspapers about mass murders that have occurred in America where teenagers took to shooting their peers and teachers; these reports sent shivers of shock and concern through schools and homes globally. The same feelings were experienced years ago in Australia with the Port Arthur murders where a troubled young adult systematically murdered over 30 people on a Sunday in May. Many concerned adults ask what could have happened to these people to have them create such tragedy. One can see the perpetrators as being emotionally illiterate and socially inept, but how does this occur? A study on some of the American teenage murderers found many things in common among them. The teenagers had little opportunity to play when they were children and were largely ignored by those around them. They felt ignored, or even ridiculed, in their homes and at school and the emotional wounding and scars these experiences left on their sense of self value was obviously deep. Compounded with a fascination for violent movies, guns and weapons, there was little possibility of a positive solution to any conflict that occurred in their lives.

The final straw that breaks emotional restraint is often small and relatively insignificant. A traumatised young person may perceive that the only solution to their continued pain is to take drastic revenge for every painful experience they have ever been through.

Gayle Gregory, an educational consultant from Ontario in Canada, found the following characteristics present in the US student murderers. They were:

- ❖ ignored as children
- ❖ deprived of play activity as children
- ❖ of average age 13 to 14 years
- ❖ typically very bright
- ❖ usually overweight or underweight
- ❖ in a poor relationship with Dad or he was absent
- ❖ unable to lose
- ❖ short on few emotional breaks
- ❖ members of groups with like interests, for example gangs without fear
- ❖ driven to exert power with violence
- ❖ often TV, video or computer over users, with a preference for violence.

Similar results have been identified in adult murderers, especially the being ignored as children, lack of play and an absence of positive involvement or participation in family life.

Professor Fiona Stanley of the Telethon Institute for Child Research in Perth Western Australia has been very concerned about the health of Australian children for quite some time. She has co-authored a book called "Children of the Lucky Country: How Australian society has turned its back on children and why children matter." These same concerns apply to all countries in the Western world. The paradox she explores is why has the economic progress and prosperity in recent times not been translated into better health and well being for our children? It seems social inequalities are widening,

"people in more disadvantaged circumstances have more problems, are less healthy and have fewer opportunities to succeed than those in advantaged circumstances."
(2005, p 5)

Another paradox is that we now know more than ever before about the importance of early brain development and early child development and yet even with this knowledge "we are failing to put this knowledge into action." (2005 p5) This book is my humble contribution to helping build the preventative wave of childhood protection, improved parenting and schooling for children under seven years of age so that we can make things better for everyone's children not just the advantaged ones.

A summary of some of the knowledge that we have about early brain development and growth is as follows:

Key positive attributes for early brain development

1. Bonding and attachment with a consistent, nurturing care provider, especially for the first five years of life
2. A caring and supportive environment that maximises love and limits and minimizes harmful stressors
3. Whole body integration through movement and play as the primary modes of learning
4. Nurturing and encouragement of the imagination
5. Attending to emotional development as a key focus to build healthy independence, social competency and higher intelligence
6. A comprehensive use of the arts and music, central to the learning process, especially story telling, singing, painting, drawing, dancing and movement to music
7. Encouraging lightness and laughter in learning and life - allowing children to be children!

8. Time for silence and stillness, with pauses in children's lives so their brains can effectively process rapid new learning and integrate meaning for themselves
9. Involvement in routine authentic tasks to encourage problem solving, critical thinking, creativity and development of meaning
10. A sense of connectedness - personally, interpersonally, globally and with something beyond the self
11. Opportunities for self transcendence

Emotional illiteracy and social incompetence starts early in life. Indeed there is a high incidence of transference of low patterns of coping and resilience that is quite easy to discern by three or four years of age. When these patterns continue long term the damaging effects can be very debilitating in later childhood, adolescence and adulthood.

A build up of unresolved emotional wounding over a long period of time can also contribute to emotional overwhelm, mental illness and suicide. An accumulation of unresolved emotional pain distorts a person's view of reality. Once again, the final straw may be small and unexpected but at other times a young person may make a carefully rationalised decision. Either way, low personal regard, a deep sense of disconnection from a group or community and sometimes a need to take revenge are evident. The resulting tragedy impacts far wider than on the families and communities immediately involved.

It is incredibly challenging as a parent to know that the child you love has chosen to take their own life. In my work in the funeral industry I was present at many suicide funerals. They were always well attended by the family and friends who obviously loved the deceased person. How can one so loved feel so unloved, alone and of such little value that they end their own lives? I believe part of the resolution lies in building emotional intelligence and finding ways and means to be stronger emotionally, socially and spiritually.

Families, schools and communities need to learn how to nurture kids' hearts and souls as well as their minds and bodies. So many parents nag their adolescents about little things – like tidying their room, cleaning their teeth and doing their homework. Is there any wonder that many 'switch off' from their parents, sometimes before the teen years, and do not even consider sharing their fears and feelings with them? One of the main reasons that kids do not warn parents that they are feeling suicidal is because they don't think they will be understood and they believe they will just get another lecture. They also don't want to let their parents down again. Often they feel they are a disappointment to their parents. Constant nagging has reinforced these perceptions even if they are totally wrong.

A beautiful model to explore that may help us unravel the confusion for parents is the following by Vickie Falcone, from her delightful book "Buddha Never Raised Kids and Jesus Didn't Drive Carpool: Seven Principles for Parenting With Soul".

"The Seven Principles "

1. Connect: With your source, yourself, and your child. This is the heart of parenting with soul.
2. Awaken Your Intuition: Learn to hear your soul's messages so you're guided to the right action.
3. Become a Conscious Creator: Master the Law of Attraction to manifest the parenting results you want.
4. Live in Integrity: Parent on higher ground when you live in impeccable honesty and keep your commitments.
5. Transform Your Life with Gratitude: Make gratitude second nature and transform your life.
6. Create Abundance: Model for our children that life is rich and there is enough.
7. Infuse Your Life with Peace: Joyfully accept life on life's terms to create more peace at home and in the world.

From Vickie's web site www.parentingwithsoul.com

These principles will work for all children – the gifted, the challenged, autistic, the hyperactive, the ADD, the depressed, the angry, the Indigos and the Crystal children. They are a holistic template that will help nurture the "whole child."

Nurturing kids' hearts and souls is the most effective way of helping build a healthy self esteem and self concept, and this begins early in life. Indeed, it is believed that most negative core beliefs are in place before the age of seven. These distorted beliefs then influence their behaviours and choices. An example to demonstrate this is the common core belief that 'I was not wanted when I was born'. This can become part of the belief structure of many unplanned children and accompanied by, if I was not wanted then I am not loved or appreciated. As the child grows older they unconsciously seek validation of their own belief system; any incident that occurs to make them feel unloved, unimportant and unvalued is seen as proof that their deeply held beliefs are indeed true. Many childhood core beliefs are based on distortions of the truth and are not based on the truth, just the child's perceptions of the truth. Children from 'normal', stable, loving families can still suffer from low self esteem and self destructive patterns of behaviour.

To complicate the picture further, the unconscious mind appears to be able to hold onto perceptions from as early as conception. Children conceived as a result of unloving or uncaring unions can develop beliefs about love and self value that are quite negative. These core beliefs form without rhyme and reason. Studies on the formation of healthy, resilient life skills suggests that kids from highly dysfunctional families can develop positive behaviours providing they have caring, supportive relationships in their lives. They can develop positive and realistic expectations and create opportunities to be involved in their families or their schools. A sense of humour is also an essential part of a resilient individual. Protective factors need to be demonstrated and encouraged in families, schools and communities. Fortunately, schools are recognizing that programs that build life skills for children have a valuable part to play within our education systems.

Loneliness and feeling disconnected from others are epidemic in the Western world right now, and this is not just in our youth. I meet people, even those in long-term relationships, who feel exactly this way. We need to educate and encourage our children and teenagers to build firm friendships and to care and support each other.

Maybe we need to go back to some of the basics of parenting, like creating lots of time to read to our children in comfy places up close. This is an excellent way of building connectedness and emotional literacy!

"A World to Read"

We are needing a world of reading.

Help us get a wondrous start

Feed our minds, our souls, our hearts

Fill us with language as we mature

Read to us much much more

We are needing a world of reading.

Give us something we can never lose

Something money can't buy that we'll always use

Thoughts to excite our imagination

Books to inspire us – the next generation

We are needing a world of reading.

Bring the Universe to our door

Teach us to open it and explore

If the whole world is a stage

Show us how to turn each page

We are needing a world of reading.

Lindamichellebaron The Sun is on, p92 (2002)

Low emotional competency impacts on so many levels and this will be explored in the chapter on emotional; intelligence. To help rebuild a low concept of self and poor personal regard it is important to work on both emotional wounding and our belief systems. Emotional diffusing is helpful to rebalance emotional stability and to release unprocessed emotions. [This will also be covered in greater depth later in the book in the chapter on 'Helping KIDS TO HEAL] Simply talking about emotional pain rarely removes it from consciousness or reduces the tension it causes in the body. An individual will store emotional pain in some part of the body. It is commonly accepted today that unresolved emotional distress can be linked to later health problems, especially emotional overwhelm, anxiety and depression.

How do we help our children to transform negative and untruthful core beliefs from the unconscious mind? With a burst of research over the last ten years, much more is now known about how the brain processes emotions and the links created between the conceptual level of the mind and actual behaviour. What this essentially means is that we can only behave in accordance with our core belief systems. Take, for example, a child who struggles with reading in year one at school. This child may believe that they are dumb and stupid. Given that readiness to read 'comes on line' any time between four and fourteen, this child's belief system unjustly inhibits him or her from learning to read. Children will set up a self-fulfilling prophecy towards their schooling and all learning. To transform negative self concepts is essential in improving many child behaviours. John Joseph from Focus Education believes that schools waste vital time and energy implementing behaviour management programs because while the core concept is in place it is impossible for students to behave differently. As a way of helping students change their core concepts I use visualization. I have witnessed excellent results from the frequent use of creative visualization. A School Mastery CD, which has three tracks to improve self concepts as well as concepts around reading and school performance. Both kinesiology and Neuro-Linguistic Programming (NLP) have many excellent techniques that can facilitate working with self concepts.

Implanting positive beliefs into the mind, on all levels, is part of a second stage of building up low esteem and changing beliefs that have been anchored as perceptions of incompetency, inadequacy and unacceptability. Many people cannot say 'I love and accept myself exactly as I am right now' and 'I am lovable and capable'. These beliefs do not exist in the psyche of many kids, adolescents or adults who have not used their experiences to grow positively. The ego mind may state that it believes these things but the body does not hold that truth authentically. This is why so many people sabotage themselves when they are presented with experiences of unconditional love and profound happiness. Their core belief system does not support those gifts. (Kinesiology is a great way to determine our core truths with muscle testing. Children are fascinated with how accurate this form of analysis can be.) We act in response to our belief system, both conscious and unconscious. This means that no amount of talking, coaching or lecturing can change a person's core belief system for them, they have to do it themselves. If we believe in conditional love, then receiving unconditional love will cause structural tension in our minds. You have all heard of people who have ended relationships because someone was too good for them. Other than working directly with transforming the unconscious mind, the only way to change the negative core concepts for a child or individual is for them to achieve success or mastery over something. Examples may simply be for the reluctant reader to suddenly find they can read; a weak maths student to be able to master a task or maybe a noisy child to find they can be quiet.

A common negative concept in children is 'no-one likes me' and 'I have no friends'. My way of dealing with this with young children has been to help create an imaginary experience for children where they get to school in the morning and are greeted by kids they like. They visualize this in their minds and then I get them to talk about how they felt so that the experience is linked in on an emotional level. I also spend time sharing 'how to be a good friend' because sometimes they have gaps in their emotional competencies about how to be this. By using mental imagery, the new perception about how it feels to be a good friend and how one behaves equips a child with important tools for change. I have also discovered that young children have much more fertile imaginations than teenagers and change comes quickly.

The third level to address when healing a low concept of self and the accompanying low self esteem is at the soul or spirit level. The map of our personality, below, shows where the human spirit may exist within a person's personality characteristics.

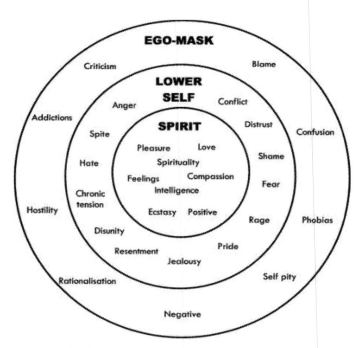

The human spirit is difficult to describe or quantify and yet when it is flowing and healthy a person is happy and enthusiastic about life. Some people with serious disabilities and physical challenges can experience much happiness and achieve stunning successes in their lives. Even within my experiences associated with death and dying, especially in palliative care, I witness events that are inexplicable from a logical and intellectual level and yet they are inspiring and magical to those who are present or who share the experience. This is explored in depth in the chapter on Spiritual Intelligence.

Our children and our youth have enormous thirst and hunger for the domain of the human spirit at present. To be inspired, moved, or to transcend the mundane level of ordinary living and find one's life purpose, to pursue unrealised dreams, and find a sense of inner being. The higher sense wants to be empowered and made stronger or just 'opened' up. Genuine healthy self esteem comes from connection to a benevolent power, something greater than us. It may be the love and joy at the birth of a newborn baby, the awe of seeing a whale, enjoying a moment of deep honesty and intimacy with another person or a moment of absolute stillness in our normally chaotic world. It is a moment when our mind, body, heart and soul come together at a place of unity – each silently aware of the other. It is the missing link in many people's lives. Fewer people now find this connection in traditional churches. That is why it is so important to reconnect our kids to spirit in ways that are healthy and acceptable to mainstream people. One of the simplest ways is through a deep appreciation of the natural world, through time spent in natural surroundings and in caring for nature's creatures. Three incredibly wonderful picture books can help build this connection and they work for all ages. These are: Remember, and Dear Mother of Earth by Schim Schimmel and The Spark in the Dark by Richard Tichnor and Jenny Smith.

Story telling, singing, music, laughter and gentle touch are powerful ways of building a sense of the human spirit. This is why I have created guided relaxation CDs for adolescents to help train their busy minds to become quieter so that they can gain a sense of their inner self and how to find it. This doorway can be re-found more easily once discovered and opened for the first time. This is so important.

Thought is creative. Everyone effectively guides the direction of their lives by their own thoughts. This is essential knowledge for all children and young adults. Much more than the power of positive thought is involved although the power of intention is a key feature in the lives of all successful people. If people simply stop dreaming they can find themselves stuck in repeating patterns of disappointment or personal suffering. I cannot stress how important the awareness of this is in terms of helping children, teenagers and adults transform their lives in a positive way.

Healthy self esteem and high self value come about through the doorway of self love and self appreciation; they influence all the relationships we form in life. Young people find this wonderful gift for themselves but you can encourage them to give this gift to themselves by:

❖ modelling unconditional love and care

❖ allowing children space to be

❖ being truthful and honest

❖ creating a safe place for them to share their emotions

❖ being a positive dreamer and goal setter yourself

❖ being real, not perfect or a know-it-all

❖ being joyful and laughing often

❖ having clear, firm boundaries

❖ modelling personal health and wellbeing

❖ being connected to your own spirit

❖ having relationships that you value and nurture

The way to create healthy, happy children is for you to nurture them holistically, their minds, bodies, hearts and souls. Allow them to feel connected and valued in their families, friendships, schools, communities and in our natural wide world. Allow them to experience REAL life, to fall over, make mistakes, and get hurt. In this way they find that life goes on. They will recover, though some times quicker than others. A recent article in The West Australian newspaper (Oct 22nd 2005, p 62.) showed that kids are likely to rate a hug from Mum as of higher importance than the latest X-Box game. Special education and behaviour management lecturer Jonathon Sargeant from New England University found in his PhD study "cuddles, affection and happy parents" were high on the list of what pleased children the most.

Reflect on this:

ALL THE KIDS WHO SURVIVED the 1930's 40's, 50's, 60's and 70's !!

First, we survived being born to mothers who smoked and/or drank while they carried us.

They took aspirin, ate blue cheese dressing, tuna from a can, and didn't get tested for diabetes.

Then after that trauma, our baby cribs were covered with bright coloured lead-based paints.

We had no childproof lids on medicine bottles, doors or cabinets and when we rode our bikes, we had no helmets, not to mention, the risks we took hitchhiking.

As children, we would ride in cars with no seat belts or air bags.

We drank water from the garden hose and NOT from a bottle.

We shared one soft drink with four friends, from one bottle and NO ONE actually died from this.

We ate white bread and real butter, but we weren't overweight because WE WERE ALWAYS OUTSIDE PLAYING!

We would leave home in the morning and play all day, as long as we were back when the streetlights came on.

No one was able to reach us all day. And we were O.K.

We would spend hours building our go-carts out of scraps and then ride down the hill, only to find out we forgot the brakes. After running into the bushes a few times, we learned to solve the problem.

We did not have Playstations, Nintendo's, X-boxes, no video games at all, no 99 channels on cable, no video tape movies, no surround sound, no mobile phones, no ipods, no personal computers, no Internet or Internet chat rooms.........

WE HAD FRIENDS and we went outside and found them!
We fell out of trees, got cut, broke bones and teeth and there were no lawsuits from these accidents.
We ate worms and mud pies made from dirt, and the worms did not live in us forever.
We were given BB guns for our 10th birthdays, made up games with sticks and tennis balls and although we were told it would happen, we did not put out very many eyes.
We rode bikes or walked to a friend's house and knocked on the door or rang the bell, or just walked in and talked to them!
The idea of a parent bailing us out if we broke the law was unheard of. They actually sided with the law!
This generation has produced some of the best risk-takers, problem solvers and inventors ever!
The past 50 years have been an explosion of innovation and new ideas.
We had freedom, failure, success and responsibility, and we learned HOW TO DEAL WITH IT ALL!"
  (Source world wide web.)

Keep healthy balances between the needs of the physical and intellectual self while nurturing emotional and spiritual needs. The good news is that children have a sense of 'knowing' early in life. Rather than feel you have to teach them how to be happy and authentic, have the wisdom to know that your role is to help them to remember the unique wisdom they themselves brought with them and which is within their nature. While they may have a spiritual or God-like knowingness from birth their emotional intelligence has to grow little by little, experience by experience.

The amazing mystery of parenting is that as you grow in emotional wisdom, so does your child. As you heal some unhealed aspect of yourself, you separate it from your child's path. As you learn to forgive and actually forgive someone you have withheld love and acceptance from for quite some time, you show your child how to do the same. As you learn to love others unconditionally you receive this amazing gift from your children – no matter how old they are! As you learn to laugh at your flaws and imperfections, you show your child the strength of this gift of resilience.

It is now easy to see that the most effective parenting advice you can ever receive is to invest in your own personal healing. Unashamedly, face the things you dislike about yourself in whatever way works for you. At the same time, know that reading self-help books may give you awareness but not necessarily healing. Also avoid following a "guru" who supposedly has all the answers. There is never just one path that will bring you to a place of healing or wholeness. There are many possibilities and doorways and the best growth occurs when you are in relationships with people. Finding the core of goodness within you, or coming home to your own heart, is recommended in whatever healing journey you follow. Also accepting total responsibility for your share in any problem or conflict is also the sign of an emotionally and spiritually mature person.

My experience is that obtaining some perspective from an objective source is helpful, especially when it allows you to identify and diffuse old, blocked or stuck emotion. If you hold the image of dragging around suitcases of belongings from the past, wherever you go, you will better understand the need to cut yourself free. This emotional clearing work is essential for our true health and wellbeing on all levels. The best time to start is NOW.

"If you have the choice to be right or kind, always choose to be kind."

Source Unknown

Key Points

- ❖ Extreme violence is the result of emotional illiteracy and social ineptitude
- ❖ Suicide can be the result of unresolved deep emotional wounding
- ❖ Nurturing kids' hearts and souls is the most effective way of helping our children build a healthy self esteem and self concept
- ❖ Most negative core concepts are in place by seven years of age
- ❖ Children from highly dysfunctional families CAN develop positive self concepts and behaviours
- ❖ Loneliness and feeling disconnected from others are epidemic in the Western world
- ❖ Transforming negative belief systems is essential for personal healing
- ❖ The human spirit is a powerful part of every individual and needs to be nurtured
- ❖ Self love and appreciation are the doorways to healthy self esteem and a positive self concept
- ❖ Emotional clearing work is essential for true health and wellbeing on all levels.
- ❖ Emotional competency and wellbeing flows from parent to child
- ❖ The best time to start healing the past is NOW
- ❖ The best person to start with is YOURSELF

Chapter 3

Emotional Intelligence Unplugged

"Academic intelligence has little to do with emotional life. The brightest among us can flounder on the shoals of unbridled passions and unruly impulses: people with high IQs can be stunningly poor pilots of their private lives."

Daniel Goleman. Emotional Intelligence

Daniel Goleman's book Emotional Intelligence was an important milestone for me. Finally, a well recognized and respected expert was exploring the emotional domain of us mere mortals. His book is exceptional and the knowledge he brings into prominence has changed many things, the direction of people's thinking, education and consciousness. The actual term emotional intelligence was probably first coined by Howard Gardner in his book Frames of Mind, in 1993.

So what are the key characteristics of emotional intelligence?

Emotional Intelligence

- ❖ Knowing your emotions and feeling states
- ❖ Managing your emotions
- ❖ Motivating yourself
- ❖ Ability to accurately empathise with others
- ❖ Handling relationships
- ❖ Ability to not be swamped by your emotions

- ❖ Belief in your ability to cope
- ❖ Persistence in the face of frustration
- ❖ Impulse control
- ❖ Delayed gratification
- ❖ Hopefulness

These are the characteristics of healthy emotional intelligence. A person with emotional competency would have patience in queues, resolve conflict without verbal or physical abuse, overcome set backs quicker than others and enjoy being themselves most of the time. There is no clear outward way that we can test emotional competence, it can only be gauged by making a judgement around how a person is behaving or interacts with others. Emotions can make life really interesting for all of us! Here are some core concepts of emotions that I have discovered.

Core concepts about emotions

1) All feelings are OK

2) It is important to identify difficult feelings, that is those that get us into trouble

3) We have choices about our feelings

4) We cannot change other people's feelings

5) Emotions are contagious

6) When we have no outlets or choices for feelings our bodies can become sick

7) We can learn to become more assertive in identifying and expressing our needs

8) Emotional states can be changed, by choice

9) Emotional overwhelm occurs when concerns are unresolved

10) Defences are:

a)   feelings that are covered over by other feelings

b)   feeling one thing and showing another so that our inner and outer expressions do not match

c)   feelings that we hide from ourselves and others

d)   walls or barriers we construct that keep others out;

e)   we all have defences.

11) Emotional honesty combined with compassion is good for our emotional, physical, spiritual and social health

Each individual has their own unique level of maturity in the various areas described as emotional intelligence. Young children, and indeed adolescents, can have complete gaps, such as an inability to control impulses or to empathise. In today's world we witness a large degree of emotional instability and illiteracy, especially around anger. We must appreciate that brain development takes time and the last part of the brain to develop and mature is the pre-frontal where emotional reasoning and processing occurs.

That is why children often repeat behaviour that causes pain AFTER they had had it explained to them why it may be unacceptable. They lack the processing and mental wiring that makes new learning become unconscious or automatic. The same goes for boys and cleanliness, or manners or risk taking behaviour. They do not consciously decide to be wilful, disobedient and disrespectful – it just happens sometimes because the brain development has not occurred. Adolescence is the last stage of development before full development of the pre frontal brain and this is something that comes with physical and personal maturation. The templates for positive emotional and social maturity still have to be laid down in those early years – or the pre frontal will be stunted in it's final growth. This is one of the reasons why we will always lose some of our adolescents to inexperience and impulsive decision making. It has always been the case and sadly, inexperience and immaturity will always be a part of the journey into adulthood.

Why are the early years of development so important and so critical? Emotional intelligence underpins everything we do, personally, in relationships and at school or work. In recent years, researchers have discovered the enormous importance of events in the early years of life and the role they play in the shaping of emotional intelligence.

"Adequate nurturing and the absence of intense early stress permits our brains to develop in a manner that is less aggressive and more emotionally stable, social and empathetic."

Martin Teicher, The Neurobiology of Child Abuse, Scientific American, March 2002, p75.

Babies and children are continuously interpreting others and the world around them, by how they see their experiences. The absence of nurturing when young creates core concepts that direct behaviours later in life, usually unconsciously. I have met many very anxious and stressed teenagers who suffer from panic attacks and whose mothers were told to let them cry at night; they practised the then recommended controlled crying method for improving sleep. This is an example of what happens when the need for nurturing and reassurance is ignored. The baby encodes a pattern of fear around being alone, separated or abandoned, which can play out through the rest of their lives.

Joseph Chilton Pearce believes that,

"the growth of the prefrontals [part of the brain] is determined by mother-infant interactions in the first eighteen months or so after birth and the prefrontals are critical to all higher intelligence and to transcendence itself."

(The Biology of Transcendence, 2002, p134).

Fortunately, the brain has a plasticity that allows growth to occur at any time of life, if stimulated and in a stress-free environment. Can you now see how important nanny training and early childcare training are? It is important that this essential information is clearly understood by caregivers of children less than two years of age. Western society can only benefit by taking full note of the results of brain development research and actively supporting mothers (and fathers) to stay home until their babies are at least three years of age, preferably five or six. Pearce is also very concerned that:

"The child is impelled by millions of years of genetic encoding to interact on a full sensory level with the events of the living world, through which he builds his structures of world knowledge."

(Pearce p135).

We have created worlds that do not support this level of exploration by our toddlers. Instead, every few minutes toddlers are given prohibitions like 'No' or 'Don't Touch', which is the exact opposite to what the developing child needs to allow the higher brain to grow optimally. We have a culture in the Western world where:

"keeping the natural world out of the reach of children seems to be our national passion. In fact greater numbers of children are brought up in the artificial world of cement, asphalt, plastics and the virtual reality of television while fewer each year experience a world of nature and the unfolding of organic life."

(Pearce, p137).

I totally salute this view and urge parents, grandparents and carers to allow children to explore the natural world with the vim and vigour that is encoded in their genes. One researcher wrote "parents are wasting money on expensive educational toys for children when the humble shoebox, saucepan or even pieces of fruit can be used during playtime." Associate Professor Margaret Sims from Edith Cowan University explained further,

"the idea of play was for children to explore and experiment with their surroundings so they could see how things worked and to observe cause and effect relationships in the world."

(West Aust, p62, 22-10-2005)

The natural world is full of interesting things for children to explore and they do not need bells and whistles to entertain themselves! It is also important that babies and toddlers explore and learn around the family environment as it builds their sense of belonging. The following is a reading often used in baby naming ceremonies - it unashamedly celebrates little children.

"The idea of life is the spirit of a little child. We glorify adulthood and wisdom and worldly knowledge, but to see life through the eyes of a child is truly to see the beauty of the world. To a child a blade of grass is a miracle, a flower a blaze of light and colour, each day is a new opportunity to learn, grow and discover. As against our natural judgement we must again become tender and full of wonder and unspoiled by the hard scepticism on which we so often pride ourselves. We must look into the heart of a child and set aside the petty grievances and selfish thoughts, which are all a part of our lives.

Children are sent into the world not only to replenish it, but also to serve as sacred reminders of something infinitely precious which we are always in danger of losing. Today we look at children and rejoice in the miracle of their lives and love their potential for growth and the inexpressibly sweet gift of their existence in our lives."

Author unknown

I had the experience once of one of my boys, at toddler stage, exploring the back yard while I was hanging out washing. When I found him he was pretty dirty and was chewing on something dry and hard. To my horror I found it was a dry piece of kangaroo poo – he had just found out that it hadn't tasted so good and thrown it away and was promptly crawling off to explore the next treasure he could find! The thing I remember the most was the shining brightness of his eyes as he explored the world with great gusto and freedom and oblivious to harm.

Another precious moment occurred when I had to run inside to answer the phone and left my toddler sitting on the lawn. I had been watering and when I came back this little lad was exploring the running hose. The look of shock when he directed the hose onto his face was priceless – the water coming out of it was cold! He held a fascination with water from that moment on and started swimming classes as a four-year old because he spent all the time in the bath completely under water. He became a strong swimmer and then a surfer with a deep love of the ocean.

Early emotional competencies are learned by children through their relationships with key caregivers. This happens in the first years of their lives.

Anne Manne in her book "Motherhood" explores deeply the early years of child care and how they impact on our children's development emotionally, mentally and socially. A quote from the "Early Years Report : Reversing the Real Brain Drain" goes like this ...

> "Brain development is especially rapid and extensive in the first year of life more than was previously realised and suspected...and is much more vulnerable to environmental influence than we ever suspected...this influence is long lasting..." That means that if there has been extreme neglect through the critical periods – a child who is rarely touched or talked to or soothed – it may be difficult to make up the effects of severe deprivation later on."

(Manne (2005) p135

Researchers are able to determine the stress levels in young children by measuring cortisol levels in their saliva and they are now able to determine the stress level of a child in certain environments.

> " this clear new evidence concerning the significant neurobiological changes to the underlying structure and chemistry of the brain as a result of early deprivation, neglect

and/or abuse has begun to transform our thinking when dealing with delinquency, violence and criminal behaviour. To begin expensive reparative work by the time children have reached adolescence may well be shutting the stable door after the horse has bolted. Prevention is better than cure."

(Manne p 235)

This new knowledge means that we need to be mindful of the early years without becoming despairing of the prospects of children raised in challenging deprived environments. It does make us more aware of the need to offer the best support possible for families in their communities in the early years. Social isolation can have disastrous effects on families in crisis. The Western world has recognised this area of concern and many have government funding to run programs such as "Smart Start" as is run in Australia. This innovative e program has created a model where communities can get funding to run free programs for parents of children under four years of age so that young children can benefit from having parents aware of the critical early needs of children.

Before moving on to further explore the growth of emotional intelligence in the early years it is important to share some other of Anne Manne's findings in her controversial book. May we begin with the fundamental statement 'the drive of the human infant is towards connectedness, towards forming relationships with other human partners." (p137) Babies and infants that have a strong sense of connectedness also have a sense of safety. The latest researchers in the field of early childhood development have been exploring "the secure base". This explored the pattern of young infants and babies when they noticed that secure babies with a healthy sense of attachment to their mothers were able to explore freely keeping an eye on their mother and yet more focused on their environment. In experiments done with mothers and their babies who would leave their babies for a short time and return the researchers found there were different patterns of response from the babies on their mothers return. Some babies (who seemed to feel secure) would seek their mothers out immediately and then return to playing, others (less secure) would express great distress and anger, and were also unable to feel comforted on the mother's return or they would pull away and be indifferent to their mother's return. The researcher Mary Ainsworth concluded that it was the

"**behaviour on reunion- whether or not the babies asked for comfort and reassurance and how they did it – that was the most important indicator of inner emotional security, not the inevitable separation protest itself.**"

(p 141, Manne, 2005)

This research together with many others have demonstrated the enormous importance to a child's emotional, mental and social development of positive attachment to a primary carer, preferably a caring mother. Babies who have this sense of security from early on become more flexible, curious and socially competent. In the US, a new condition has been identified in children under five. It is called 'tactile defensiveness' and is prevalent in children who have had little opportunity to play with other children and spend their beginning years in front of TVs. These children have a complete inability to mix with other children. Social workers and others then have to work with them to improve their emotional and social skills.

There is more research that supports the idea that we must avoid hurrying early independence in our infants – especially if it is for the convenience of the parents. The clingy insecure baby needs to be reassured for as long as it takes to grow into a place of new emotional strength. Those toddlers whose dependency needs as a baby were accepted and responded to promptly and sensitively later became the most independent children in preschool and school later.

"**Those preschoolers whose dependency needs were rebuffed or rejected were more dependent seeking out the teacher more often than the securely attached children. That they were frequently sullen or oppositional and not inclined to seek** help when injured or disappointed however, spoke poignantly of their avoidant patterns."

(Manne, p144, 2005)

This impacts on the deep levels of unconscious beliefs that have already explored. A baby whose needs are rejected will feel unloved, and runs the risk of creating beliefs that they are unlovable, not enough, unwanted and they will expect further rejection in their lives. Even children with healthy attachment can still create these beliefs. However the repeated early rejections according to Daniel Stern create RIG's or Repeated Interactions which are Generalised.

"What began as a pattern of interaction in relationships becomes generalised into expectations of the world, coded unconsciously, part of the structure of the mind. It becomes a kind of internal map of the self, of the other, of self with other."

(Motherhood 2005, p147.)

Given that secure, loving attachment of our babies is essential for the healthy emotional, mental and social growth of them later in life what is the current situation in Western countries about early childcare. In a perfect world all mothers and fathers should be able to choose that which is best for the baby. We do not live in a perfect world. The key focus is connectedness and presence. Babies who have someone who is able to offer these things consistently in a safe environment will be creating the optimal conditions for healthy growth and development. This may sound simple –it is not. Jenny Roberts in her ground breaking book "Freeing Noah" discovered that by being calm, fully present and "in tune" with their child, a parent can create powerful change, even with autistic children.

"I showed the mother that if she was calm and had no agenda, with no emotion or attachment to need to control him, things would change. Things did change, very quickly."

(2005, p114)

Jenny also believes that parents are at a loss when becoming a parent and they

> "get frightened, reacting rather than relating. Instead they assume the worst and seek outsiders to give them advice. They think that searching for answers will help, but knowledge does not give you what your child needs.... understanding about the relationship is what is needed and knowing how to create the space for children to learn themselves."

(Roberts, p129)

Jenny believes that "pockets of silence are essential to be able to tune into our children. This helps parents "be in the moment" and this creates the same sense of calmness within children.

This same view of focusing or tuning in to the needs of our babies and toddlers is also reflected in other more research based literature. As Daniel Stern explored in his wonderful book "The Interpersonal World of the Infant" a baby may learn that it's safe to have her needs met including her emotional needs and that sense of "secure attunement" allows her to grow naturally. This is instead of being pressured by frantic parents waving placards, teaching writing and reading before readiness has developed in some strange form of parent Olympics where young toddlers are unwitting victims of some misguided notion that acceleration will create a better "winner." Indeed a parent who has the secure and aware relationship with their toddler will also recognise the need of their toddler to have "leave alone" time for them to grow in their independent search of the world. The notion that "fast is good" and that "more is better" are adult experiences of the world – and not babies or toddlers. Please resist the urge to join the competitive ranks of many of today's modern parents. I am still pretty staggered that three of my boys who have left school - still could not tie their shoes laces on entry into year one and who weren't too good at writing their names are at university. They had lots of freedom outside because it had been normal for me as a child, and I coped with the chaos of four sons better with a lot of time outside or at the park or the beach. I do remember giving up many social functions and occasions when they were babies to keep our connection as calm and relaxed as possible. Accidentally I may have created the conditions that Daniel Stern has written. In today's world it can be about choice rather than accident.

Back to the current thinking on child care - there are a few findings that support my experiences both as a counsellor and a teacher. Being aware of the optimal conditions for the healthy early development of our children gives us all a better place to make choices. There is no such thing as a perfect parent or perfect child and decisions are made from so many perspectives given changing circumstances. This book has a priority about nurturing kids' hearts and souls not filling bank accounts or creating brain surgeons or winning baby competitions. To me this means raising children who are able to manage their lives positively, create loving sustaining relationships that strengthen families and communities and in some way contribute to the world being a better place, using their unique gifts and talents.

Recommendations for Early Childcare

❖ Become informed about babyhood and early childhood before becoming pregnant

❖ Take care of your physical and emotional needs during pregnancy

❖ Create as much time as possible to mothering and caring for your new born

❖ Create a supportive network before baby arrives

❖ Develop secure "attunement" with your baby

❖ Avoid childcare outside the home for as long as possible

❖ Toddlers under two may not be able to socialise easily so be aware of this developmental delay

❖ Avoid using TV as a babysitter

❖ Avoid too many toys

- Avoid too much talking and coaching

- Less time infants spent in day care the better

- Long term effects of extensive childcare more than 30 hours were week can be more problem behaviour especially anxiety, aggression and oppositional behaviour

- Committed parents sharing childcare of young in their own home is preferable to outside childcare of babies and toddlers under two years of age

- Carers of children need to be chosen on the grounds of their capacity for loving care – safe gentle touch, soothing words, capacity to reassure and time to do so

- Become informed about the key issues in outside childcare. Enquire about staff ratios to children, how they manage challenging behaviour, fussy eaters and anxious children. Check on staff turn over.

- Family based childcare is better than en masse if the above concerns are explored. Familiar place and consistent carer build security for toddlers.

- Trained nannies in the home who meet the above concerns and who become a part of the family net work offer a positive alternative to outside childcare.

    Remember two of the key characteristics of teenage murderers in the US were "ignored as children, deprived of play activity in early childhood."

Until we are able to offer smaller better trained childcare centres who are able to offer smaller ratios of children to carers I will continue to have serious concerned about the long term effects of large day care centres. Many staff are quite young and have never been a mother and are often left in charge of up to five babies at once. Staff turnover is high and they are simply not paid enough to show the value their work has on the future lives of the children in their care. Anne Manne expressed her deep concerns about the "McDonaldisation of child care" in her book where mass institutionalised childcare is growing in Australia at a frightening rate. It has become the new norm. When the federal government in Australia also embraces childcare to keep the Australian economy booming one wonders about where this pressure to institutionalise children as commodities will end. When will the powers that be note that our adolescents are more troubled than ever before and our psych wards are overloaded by children and teenagers with deep emotional and mental problems? When will they acknowledge that economic wealth and prosperity comes at a huge price and that the declining social culture could actually be the result of the drive to have the best surplus or the best economic growth possible. As Joseph Moore writes "on all accounts soul is absent." The emotional and social immaturity and illiteracy will continue to grow and we may very well end up living in homes with bars, too scared to leave venture out frightened of the violence nature of most of today's youth, especially urban youth. It is already happening in some suburbs with uncontrollable teenagers holding decent people to ransom. Our public transport systems are experiencing escalating violence and aggression is present in every area where people gather from classrooms to function centres. The emotional and social health of tomorrow's parents is in our hands now.

Many very young children today experience huge discomfort in the face of failure or less-than-perfect performance. This can be the result of the well meaning pressure of parents to get their children ahead. This is an area of concern, even in early childhood. Preschool teachers have shared with me their challenges with the levels of frustration and anger when blocks won't sit correctly or paintings look too amateurish. Some children will only have one attempt at a task and if unsuccessful refuse to attempt the task again. Primary school teachers are having similar experiences, with increasing frequency as time goes on.

I remember a year-one boy who refused to write. His explanation to me was that when he wrote on paper he could not reproduce what he saw in his head, and it was all too slow. He was very interested in anatomy books, could say all sorts of long names and knew what they were. His very powerful thought patterns demanded an unrealistic expectation of competency in his efforts. This is a clear example of how intellectual intelligence without accompanying emotional development can create serious conflict and confusion.

One of my sons experienced a similar level of frustration at the same age. His impatience with things that took time, like Lego, could be likened to igniting a small volcano. Once he punched his fist through a nearby window when the model he was building did not turn out how he wanted it to. His personality was very strong and he was highly focused. To deal with his personality, I ensured we had lots of play time in parks, at beaches or outside as his frustration was always worse when he was not physically active. This same little lad used to bring his pencils home in year one to sharpen them, as he did not want to waste time in class doing this, in year 1! Fortunately he took up competitive swimming at around eight years of age and, with the regular strenuous training program, his 'agro tank' was kept at a low level. His strong personality still sees him through life and physical exercise remains a useful life tool for him, keeping his frustration at a manageable level. When he gets really annoyed he expresses his annoyance loudly and clearly and then it is over. Exercise also provides a way for him to fill his 'happy cup'.

An ability to be emotionally honest about our feelings, particularly our negative feelings, is a sign of healthy emotional competence. Those who always bury their anger or frustration are likely to feel more stressed and anxious. Indeed, buried anger and rage are possible causes of depression, which I have seen time after time as a counsellor.

Brain research identifies a period of time in a child's development where if they miss out on gentle, loving and stimulating relationships, as with parents or pets, they do not develop an ability to be caring or empathetic. Many children are raised with both parents working and a lack of fulfilling relationships in their lives is more and more likely in our present world. This issue of time, the quality of that time spent with their children and its significance. Many parents are unaware of the importance of this stage of development. In the first two years of a child's life the reptilian brain develops and a baby learns the basics of trust, bonding, sensori-motor skills and basic survival. Some describe it as the time when 'goodness orientation' is formed in the brain. The capacity for goodness is the ability to be aware of making choices for good rather than for evil, and for positive rather than negative experiences. This thinking fits in with the model of emotional illiteracy and where those perpetrators of mass murder had little opportunity to play or have positive connections with family as young children. Goodness orientation is one of the main motives behind 'attachment parenting', where parents are encouraged to be as physically close and tender as possible in the early years of a baby's life. My experience as a breastfeeding mother certainly supports this and I have fond memories of the close intimacy of looking into the wide open eyes of my baby as he fed at my breast.

> "The parts of the brain concerned with regulations of emotion and deeply held attitudes to human relations are particularly dependent on human contact in order to develop. A mother's joyful interactions with her baby actually provide an essential building block to these areas of the brain."

> Robin Grille, Parenting for a Peaceful World 2005, p237.

Close interactions with an infant include tender touch, sustained loving gaze, smiling, singing and rhythmic soothing and rocking. They are essential for healthy emotional development (See S Greenspan. Building Healthy Minds 1999).

The same depth of intimacy can be achieved with bottle-fed babies using continued gentle stroking and close physical contact, especially when it involves direct skin contact and close, loving eye connection. Researchers have shown that babies can tell the difference between a dispassionate look and a genuinely passionate look! The same goes for genuine smiles. Knowing this, we can be mindful that we are looking and smiling lovingly at as many babies as possible, to help improve the emotional wellbeing of the future world. Indeed, to know that connectedness and bonding can shape the level of empathy and kindness a child is capable of in their adult years is illuminating. The absence of such bonding and physical tenderness may have life-long effects.

> "When an infant receives too little direct loving contact, this causes the area of his brain that regulates emotion, self image and beliefs about relationship to become atrophied, with serious, long-lasting – often permanent – consequences for behaviour. Touch deprivation releases steroids that damage the hippocampus leading to cognitive and behavioural problems later in life."

Robin Grille, Parenting for a Peaceful World 2005, p232.

Keeping pets is another definite way of adding to loving committed care and nurturance early in a child's life and to build early emotional growth. Learning to be gentle with a kitten, puppy or guinea pig provides a child with early training in intimacy. My hat goes off to the many preschool teachers who have pet days or who hatch a batch of chickens or ducklings in their preschools. This has long-term emotional benefits for the children. It can help create tenderness in a young boy, and an appreciative wife will benefit from this one day; or you may give the gift of tenderness to a child who has never experienced it before. Thank you.

Children with pets have a tendency to be more empathetic and thoughtful of others. This is not just because pets exist in the home, it is because they are shown how to care for their pets. To experience the death of a goldfish is also a tough and effective way to learn what happens if a pet is not fed. Encouraging children to feed and exercise pets is a great way to develop a sense of shared responsibility; a happy dog or cat can make anyone feel appreciated!

Pets do die, especially if they are guinea pigs, goldfish or mice. This is a wonderful opportunity to share with young children the journey of life and death and the grieving process. Yes, it is painful and the whole family may be upset and experience all of the emotions around loss and change. It provides an opportunity to learn that the pain does go away and that they can continue to love Bobsy or Nemo; and they do not come back. Children learn why a funeral is important and that it is OK to cry. This is essential life training - for the time when some person they love dies, as they will one day.

My sons are pretty used to managing the loss of loved ones. We had two old well-loved dogs, Basil and Sam, who died within a few months of each other. A new puppy Jack Russell was run over only a few months later. When my Dad died the same year my boys wept openly. They quite comfortably spent time with their beloved Pop as he was put to rest. They chose a special 'thing' to include in the coffin and each, in their own ways, said their goodbyes. The funeral was a fitting, ritualistic goodbye and, more importantly, a celebration of a wonderful life. To see the boys sobbing as they helped with placing petal baskets around the grave has left me with a beautiful memory. At the gathering afterwards we shared stories and much laughter, just as Pop would have wanted. It is important to prepare our children for the reality of death as early in life and as naturally as possible.

Finally, pets also create conversation and stories that help build a positive family history. We have many stories that we still share about our pets. They instantly remind us of happy times.

Our family dog Jess is a hyperactive fox terrier. When the boys come home from university she does amazing laps around the garden or inside the house. Her complete excitement at their return is a sheer delight to see. When the boys take care of her during the times I am travelling she is always happy to see them return at night. Coming home to an empty house is never pleasant and a welcoming pet can make a lousy day seem OK. On our last trip away she had been allowed to sleep on a blanket in the oldest boy's bedroom; this is my tough career-focused son who usually complains about her! Pets open our hearts to tenderness and kindness. Among our family photos many include family pets and animal friends. These pets not only become part of the family, they are key teachers in the areas of care, kindness and unconditional love. No wonder animals are brought into aged care facilities and hospitals, to help people smile and feel happy. Never underestimate the emotional intelligence that can be created and developed through sharing the world of animals.

Following the period of reptilian brain growth, the next stage of development is of the limbic cortex. This stage of growth spans four years, roughly between two and six years of age. During this time the brain grows very rapidly and forms much of the early emotional pathways. This is why stress-free environments with clear, firm boundaries are so important for young children. They feel safe with set routines and predictable patterns of behaviour, which allows their imagination to grow and their capacity to play creatively expand. Indeed, some researchers argue that the neuro-pathways for all multiple intelligences are laid down during these critical years. That is why it is essential that young children are immersed in real experiences and much creative play.

"Many children played and learned in the streets, woods and fields without the looming presence of adults and albeit well meaning coaches. Their experiences were real, varied and enormously engaging. These hands on or concrete experiences with the real world prepared the brain for learning. What may have seemed to be unstructured play had a very serious purpose. It allowed children to discover the underlying rules and patterns that organize and make sense of the world. It may have set up a filing system for the storage and retrieval of information. Many of today's children are starved of real life experiences."

Terrence Parry and Gayle Gregory, Designing Brain Compatible Learning, pp30-1.

Play has the added advantage of giving children the opportunity to learn how to wait, share, take turns and to work alongside one another. Non-directed play is also essential for a healthy imagination. A healthy imagination is an excellent antidote to pessimism, negative thought patterns and unhappiness. Tim Burns, an education consultant from the US, outlines the key elements of healthy play:

- ❖ a great love of the experience, in and of itself
- ❖ absolutely no fear of censor
- ❖ a complete sense of entertainment and flow
- ❖ absorbed play, as a natural transcendent experience
- ❖ imagination and creativity.

My sons attended a Christian primary school. I wanted to ensure that I was supported in the development of healthy values and in providing an opening to a spiritual understanding of faith. It was an excellent primary school and one of the best things about it was the 'bush area'. This was exactly as it sounds – an area of bush where students from grades three to seven could play during recess and lunch time. The boys still talk about the fun they had in that bush area and the games they played that could last for weeks. They made castles, forts and cubbies, a perfect example of the power of play in the company of others during the early years of childhood.

"Students who feel deeply connected don't need danger to feel fully alive. They don't need guns to feel powerful. They don't want to hurt others or themselves. Out of connection grows compassion and passion -- passion for people, for students' goals and dreams, for life itself."

Rachael Kessler, The Soul of Education.

Nowadays our children spend more and more time inside or they are kept confined in small back yards. We have the perception of an increased threat of danger in the environment around them. In this we are contributing to a decline in their mental and emotional worlds. Children need to learn how to walk to school, play safely in the local park, get their bottoms off couches and be active and involved in having a childhood! As we 'wrap them in cotton wool' we do them a great disservice. If there is ever a time that we enjoy getting wet, being covered in mud, stuck up a tree or falling in a duck pond it is when we are children. Through these experiences children learn how it feels; you cannot learn this by reading about it or watching it! Once experienced, you can decide if you want to repeat the experience! I have fond memories of swimming with lots of kids of various ages in a farm dam. I remember almost drowning once when I became tangled in duck weed. Fortunately for me a fifteen-year old friend of my older brother spotted me and pulled me out! I have had a healthy respect of water ever since. I am pretty sure that my parents never heard of this near disaster. It was a learning experience and yes, sometimes such experiences can be fatal. Life is like that.

For me, it is healthier in the long-term development of our children that they learn for themselves that life has risky experiences and that they are responsible for 'rowing their own boat'. Parents are now constantly in touch with their children by mobile phone. I think we are disempowering our kids and preventing them from growing in self awareness, reliance and responsibility. When they are twenty they may still be calling home, to ask how to cook, to fix a damaged tap or a fuse! One of my toughest lessons as a Mum was to stop running lunches to school when my boys forgot them. 'Tough love' is tough for both parties and yet it is an effective way to allow our children to grow both emotionally and socially and to accept responsibility for their own actions and choices. This will give them "self-efficacy" or a confidence in being able to cope with life's challenges. This ability will give them a sense of control over one's life. Nathaniel Branden author of "The Seven Pillars of Self Esteem" believes this has to be a key quality for authentic self esteem. Children can only learn this by having the opportunity to make choices and have input into the experiences that occur. How often do we get children to put jackets on because it is cold and the child is actually quite warm because they have been running around? The "just in case" reasoning of parents can invalidate a child's emerging decision making. We need to let them practise and also see the consequences of their actions.

Patrice Thomas in her lovely book The Magic of Relaxation agrees with the need to allow children to grow in their ability to do things for themselves.

> "Our children have become the unintended victims of constantly being hurried. We often complete tasks for children (for example tie their laces, clean up their belongings and complete chores for them) because it seems simple and quick for us. By doing this we are robbing our children of precious practice in learning

> life skills and self esteem. In addition we are sending the unintentional message of disapproval to them (you take too long to set the table, you don't fold your clothes correctly...). We all need to learn to be more patient and consistent with our children giving them the gift of our time and our belief in their abilities. Hurried parents and teachers produce harried children. Children are often left feeling inadequate, helpless and despondent."

Patrice Thomas, The Magic of Relaxation 2002, p2.

Research on families has identified the following characteristics as the strengths of those Australian families who cope well with life's challenges:

- ❖ Communication
- ❖ Togetherness
- ❖ Sharing activities
- ❖ Affection
- ❖ Support
- ❖ Acceptance
- ❖ Commitment
- ❖ Resilience

Geggie, DeFrain, Hitchcock and Silberberg Family Action Centre, University of Newcastle, 2000.

Each of these strengths depends on emotional intelligence and competencies. The ability of a family to have a genuine sense of connectedness is determined by the emotional maturity and stability of its members. When children are young, the emotional health and wellbeing of their parents is a key determining influence on the rest of the family. Where there is emotional illiteracy or immaturity, shouting, abuse, stress and family violence are more likely to occur.

A lack of a sense of safety impedes children's development on many levels. When they start school, the need to survive will preoccupy the brain and impair their upper cognitive functioning. A shift in home, family death or serious illness can cause deep emotional stress and, without support, can also cause the brain to be impaired in its ability to learn. Remove or reduce the threat and the brain can return to normal functioning.

❖ Early care and nurturing have a decisive and long-lasting impact on how people develop, their ability to learn and their capacity to regulate emotions.

❖ Human development hinges on the interplay between nature and nurture.• The human brain has a remarkable capacity to change but timing is crucial.

❖ The brain's plasticity also means that there are times when negative experiences or the absence of appropriate stimulation are more likely to have serious and sustained effects.

❖ The major risks to early brain development include exposure to abuse or neglect, maternal depression, parental substance abuse, poor nutrition and poverty.

Professor Fiona Stanley. Brain development in early childhood. Checking the Pulse Education Conference, Perth 2004.

Clearly, the emotional development of a child is influenced by their carers and the environment that surrounds them in their first years of life. Brain development and emotional growth are completely interwoven and symbiotic. This is why the first years of a child's life are so important for his or her future growth and development.

Healthy mothering provides the best environment for babies and toddlers to grow. What is that? These are some key elements of healthy mothering:

- ❖ Commitment from birth to create the best maternal health possible for the baby

- ❖ Strong bonding and attachment in first two years from at least one parent, preferably two

- ❖ A supportive network that acts as family and who can be non-familial

- ❖ Freedom and spaces of quietness for baby and toddler to self explore

- ❖ Avoidance of TV, too many commercial toys

- ❖ Avoidance of over-stimulation and pressure to "push" normal child development Honouring individual growth of each child and being mindful of "readiness."Knowing that it is physically impossible for a man to give birth, much of the healthy mothering from conception and in the first months is a woman's responsibility. After that healthy mothering can be provided by fathers, grandparents or carefully chosen carers who live in the home. In a perfect world it is best if healthy mothering is the responsibility of either the mother or the father of the child.

Knowing how important stability and routine is in a child's life, it is easy to understand why many children whose lives are in turmoil are emotionally unstable at school. Where there is childhood stress emotional immaturity or illiteracy will often be present as well. Teachers in the Western world are struggling with 'unreachable, unteachable students'; an enormous amount of time is wasted on behaviour management. A focus on building basic emotional competencies in the kindergarten and preschool environment, in the formative years, is an important part of education. More unstructured play, games that build cooperative skills, more time for quietness and stillness, and more arts and activities that safely diffuse stored emotional energy are all important. The other essential in these early years is the presence of loving, nurturing adults who model kindness, empathy and tenderness.

When a program that embraces building emotional and social skills is joined with a healthy nutrition program, in a richly imaginative environment, young children can develop rapidly and happily. The Kinda Yoga program was created by a dedicated preschool teacher, also a yoga teacher, and is a great example of activities that enhance a young child's emotional, mental and physical health. In the type of environment that Leonie McLachlan has created, children spontaneously do yoga poses out in the playground and chicks or ducklings hatch each year, much to the total delight of the children. I thank dedicated preschool teachers like Leonie who teach from the heart as well as the head and allow children exquisite moments of discovery.

"Emotions are aroused in response to any event that is perceived as important. Emotions strongly influence attention and memory."

Tim Burns USA

Our memories of music and smell can bypass the cognitive parts of our brains so that hearing the music again or re-experiencing a smell can bring up instant emotions from the past. National anthems can be emotionally powerful for adults, especially around days of national pride. I often end up in tears hearing the Australian anthem when it is played at an Olympic Games as I am accessing the memory of a previous powerful moment of national pride. The smell of biscuits baking has a warm fuzzy effect on many of us also, because of memories from our past and a triggering of a state of anticipation. This is why real estate agents encourage people to have coffee brewing when their home is open for inspection. The coffee can unconsciously evoke a positive feeling of enjoyment and pleasure. However, if previous experiences were not positive then the opposite is the case and we feel emotionally uncomfortable.

Creating moments of joy and delight with music and smell is really important for young children. By playing and singing happy songs and tunes we fix them firmly into a child's mind. Songs that are well known or repeated often, like at night, evoke a familiar response. I used to sing, not very well, a lullaby to the boys when they were babies. I noticed that when they became toddlers I was less and less likely to do so. As a new baby came along the toddler then heard the lullaby again and was still soothed by it. When the boys were ill with a fever I would hum the lullaby or sing it to them and it really helped them to settle. Recent research on the power of lullabies confirms that they soothe upset babies; apparently the number one lullaby is Twinkle Twinkle Little Star. Relaxation CDs with music and calming voices have the same effect and evoke feelings of safety and calmness. This is why it is so important to surround your child's life with music, to calm, play and have fun to.

Similarly with smell, the smell of vanilla always makes me feel good even though I cannot remember the original experience that evokes that response. I feel the same with roses, English lilac, lavender, many wild flowers and chocolate. This instant feel good experience changes my emotional state very easily. I encourage you to fill young children's lives with positive experiences around smell and sound so that you give them an easy way to transform a negative mood, now and later in life. It is helpful to build these unconscious positive connections while children are young. What happens when you smell chocolate or fresh strawberries? What happens when you play a favourite song? If you are interested in reading more about changing emotional states, read William Bloom's The Endorphin Effect.

What else can we do for young children that builds their emotional intelligence?

Activities that encourage emotional intelligence

❖ Sharing in pairs – using conversation to build connectedness

❖ Role play and drama – pretending and imagining

❖ Reflection time - pondering

❖ Inspirational songs and movies - shared together

❖ Journal and poetry writing – creative pursuits

❖ Drawing and creative arts – more creative pursuits

❖ Circle talks - learning to listen and share

❖ Creative imagery - using visualization

❖ Dancing and singing - movement to music and having fun

❖ Laughter - developing a sense of humour

❖ Feedback times – that allow honest feelings to be expressed

❖ Storytelling - a skill to develop

❖ Freedom to take risks, and learn

❖ Creating choices, with possible consequences – new and extended patterns

❖ Play - as spontaneous and unstructured as possible

❖ Creative problem solving - allowing children to develop the solutions

❖ Regular quiet solo time - allowing gaps in busy lives

❖ Random acts of kindness - letting children experience providing them

❖ Care, concern and connectedness - modelled every day

❖ Emotionally honest communication - don't fake it

❖ Safe touch - allowing genuine intimacy

❖ Listening attentively and empathetically

❖ Practicing the power of prayer

❖ Encouraging dreaming and highest vision

❖ Modelling life-enhancing language

The Wiggles are Australian children's entertainers who have taken the world by storm. They were not around when my boys grew up and I am looking forward to connecting to them when my grandchildren arrive. Their ability to embrace many of the ways of building emotional intelligence supports their success. They model great manners, positive language, sing happy songs, role play and have lots of fun. One of the other things they do is empower children. Kathleen Warren is the group's former teacher from Macquarie University and she believes that by inviting children to wake up Fatt when he nods off on stage they are allowing "children to build confidence in themselves as human beings and to have some say in their lives" (The West Magazine, June 25th 2005). The Wiggles have a very high code of performance, both on stage and off stage, because they know that parents have trust that they will act with integrity and true character.

I often notice parent's confusion around how to behave in front of children when a death of a loved one occurs. In many ways both the Australian and UK cultures hold a perception that grief is best held in or hidden from view. I believe this is a pattern from the war years when death was more common – few were able to grieve openly and people were encouraged to bury their loved ones and get straight back to living. European cultures still grieve in a more healthy way. The family and friends gather and openly grieve for days after a funeral with healthy wailing and crying. Children are a part of this journey of coming to terms with the loss of a loved one.

I once had a ten-year old say to me, "Maggie I don't think Mummy loved Nan." When I asked her why she replied, "I never saw her cry, not once, when Nan died."

Hiding our feelings teaches our children to do the same. When we hide our emotions we create an armour around our hearts that impedes our capacity to feel loving.

The need for emotional honesty with our children is enormous. Many of us are unaware of bottling emotions yet think we are acting in a loving way towards our children. We may be withholding anger and frustration towards someone in our work place or elsewhere and in the process make it difficult to be open hearted at home. Intimacy is a fragile thing. Without emotional honesty it simply disappears. Being open to love means that we allow others to embrace our innermost being, our vulnerable and most sensitive emotional being and in the process know that we can still be loved. If there is an unexpected serious threat to a person we love, like an accident, an illness or even a death, the walls of protection may come down. We can be more likely to be openly loving and emotionally honest in times of crisis. This was one of the main reasons why I loved working in palliative care and around the funeral industry, because it was full of really honest expressions of love. So much hugging, caring and telling people that they were loved took place. I could come home from a funeral uplifted by the power of love, and then I proceeded to spread the same love around my home. If only we could be open and loving often rather than just when there is a moment of threat or a crisis in the home!

Emotional honesty with our children is healthy yet I urge you to be mindful of using your children as your venting posts or confidants. This is something different and is incredibly overwhelming, confusing and upsetting for children. It is best avoided. I have seen some incredibly unhealthy enmeshing over the years where children and teenagers have been used as friends or counsellors in the place of their parents seeking adult support systems. An instance is when relationships break up and parents use their children as emotional pawns. Keep the adult emotional dramas and hurts between the two adults concerned and do not fight in front of your children. This distresses the children so much. They love both of their parents and suffer when they witness verbal or physical fighting between them. If you are able to put aside your emotional suffering and honour your role as co-parents your children will be happier and recover from the 'death of their family' with fewer scars. Objectivity is really difficult during these times and I urge you to engage a neutral mediator as soon as possible during a relationship breakdown.

A child can feel unloved by a parent who really loves them a lot! This is an interesting phenomenon that I have noticed again and again over my years as a counsellor. The parent thinks it is obvious how much they love their child because of all the things they do for them and because they know how they feel about their child. Children can feel gratitude for what is done for them but still feel unloved!

How do you ensure that your child feels loved?

Firstly, remember that every child is unique and different. What works for one child may not work for another. Secondly, the metaphor of a 'love cup' is really helpful to remember; if your child's love cup is full they feel loved. If not, they may feel disconnected, unloved and un-special. Hug them! Unfortunately, I cannot remember being held tenderly by my mother when I was young. I am a highly kinaesthetic person so this was a serious deprivation in my life. If I had been more dependent on vision or sound as my first sense it may have been less of a problem for me. Physical touch and intimacy is really important for my wellbeing and I am blessed to be surrounded by an abundance of it in my life now.

An excellent book that explains how to fill your child's love cup is The Five Love Languages of Children by Gary Chapman and Ross Campbell. There are five ways that we fill our children's love cup.

1. **Physical touch** – children and teenagers who really love physical touch will often touch you, sometimes in an annoying way! This is why some boys love to fight or wrestle with their Dad, it is an intimate safe touch that fills their love cup. Teenagers who needed touch to feel loved as a child STILL need it, ask them what works best for them.

2. **Words of affirmation** – hearing words of love, encouragement, guidance and appreciation works for some

children. They are sensitive to tone and criticism, often very sensitive. They need to hear 'I love you' often!

3. **Quality time** – if this is the primary way your child feels loved they may sometimes drive you nuts with wanting your full attention. They value real eye contact, one on one time, real conversations, sharing feelings and bedtime rituals.

4. **Gifts** – these children are very attached to the gifts you have bought them over the years and rather than be concerned with cost, size or shape, they are more tuned into the thought you put into purchasing the gift. Be very careful about buying meaningful gifts and of bribery and manipulation as your child will know the difference!

5. **Acts of service** – these children respond to acts of service and notice and mention when you cook their favourite meal, come to watch them play sport or make their school lunch in good time. The main motivation must be love, not manipulation or to get something. Also be mindful of making requests and not commands.

I recommend that you read the Five Love Languages of Children, explore with your child their preferred love language and see how you can build on their feelings of being loved.

Families can also use the love cup metaphor. Ask your children what makes them feel happy, calm and really valued. What family rituals support this state of wellbeing? As a teacher I learned about the importance of happy family memories by asking my students to create a time line of their lives so far. What staggered me was that most of the significant moments on their time lines were painful or unpleasant times. It was much harder for them to remember the good things, and this tendency was expressed over and over again. My suggestion to parents is to consciously build in special moments and family rituals that are more likely to be remembered because of their repetition. Really celebrate birthdays and end of school terms, Easter holidays and 'rites of passage' in a child's life. This helps to anchor the good memories and hopefully your children will more easily bring patterns of positive living into their own families when they become parents.

Knowing what can transform an emotional state from one of disappointment, sadness or stress to something more positive is an incredibly important resilience tool for life. Helping your children work this out is helping them for life! My own boys know that physical pursuits, whether it is golf, surfing or kicking a footy in the park, help them manage stressful times such as around exam time. For me, taking myself on my favourite walk, playing certain CDs or having a bubble bath works wonders. No matter what time of day or night it is my happy cup is filled. I also love to read and prefer the escapism in reading to a glass or two of red wine! Usually the quick fixes to resolve unpleasant emotional states involve things that are toxic to our bodies and they seldom have as lasting effects. Whether it is smoking, alcohol or a packet of Tim Tams, know that your body will pay a price of some kind.

Our emotional wellbeing can be improved at any point in our lives by working with someone who is a professional psychotherapist or a life coach. I spent around ten years of my life transforming my childhood wounds, irrational fears and insecurities by going to workshops, seminars, doing body work, and undergoing counselling and self-awareness work. The best thing to come out of all of this was the knowledge that I like myself, with all my imperfections, and I am able to give and receive love generously. Self love, acceptance and appreciation, and a desire to help others to experience the same are probably the best signs of emotional intelligence that I have identified. Many of us love from our head and are completely unaware that our hearts are closed, numbed or armoured.

The best way to help a child build a healthy emotional intelligence is for us, as the primary carers, to work on our own capacity to love and feel safe about being our own authentic self. Life experiences will create plenty of opportunities for you to grow emotionally, mentally and socially. Enjoy the ride and try to keep your heart open especially to the children of the world.

Map of Emotional Intelligence

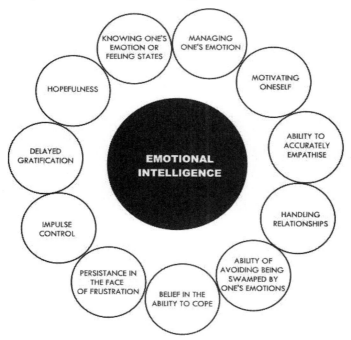

Key Points

- ❖ Emotional intelligence underpins everything we do - personally, in our relationships and at school or work.

- ❖ Nurturing and loving care creates emotional competencies later in life

- ❖ Early emotional experiences determine coping mechanisms for later life

- ❖ Be mindful of who cares for your baby or toddler

- ❖ Create secure attunement with your child

- ❖ The first two years of life are critical in the development of healthy emotional intelligence

- ❖ Avoid the pressure to accelerate your child

- ❖ Emotional honesty is a key characteristic of emotional intelligence

- ❖ Tender touch, a sustained loving gaze or smile, and rhythmic soothing of an infant build emotional intelligence

- ❖ Pets can help build emotional intelligence

- ❖ The presence of loving, nurturing adults who model kindness, empathy and tenderness is essential for emotional intelligence

- ❖ Be emotionally real around our children

- ❖ Learn what fills a child's love cup

- ❖ Learn healthy ways to change emotional states

- ❖ Emotional intelligence can be improved at any point of our lives with professional help

- ❖ A healthy emotional intelligence involves self love, acceptance and appreciation

Chapter 4

Emotional Distress, Overwhelm and Wounding in Children

If I Had My Child to Raise Over Again

If I had my child to raise again
I'd finger paint more, and point the finger less
I'd do less correcting, and more connecting,
I'd take my eyes off my watch, and watch with my eyes,
I would care to know less, and know to care more,
I'd take more hikes, and fly more kites,
I'd stop playing serious and seriously play,
I'd run through more fields, and gaze at more stars,
I'd do more hugging and less tugging,
I would be firm less often, and affirm much more,
I'd build self esteem first and the house later,
I'd teach less about the love of power
And more about the power of love.

from the book "100 Ways to Build Self-Esteem and Teach Values" 1994, 2003 by Diana Loomans. Reprinted with permission of HJ Kramer/New World Library, Novato, CA, USA.(www.newworldlibrary.com)

All children receive some degree of emotional damage during childhood. It is impossible to meet every need of a baby, toddler or child and to never cause pain. In this chapter we explore how babies and children interpret behaviours and experiences; how this helps to shape their personalities; and how to tell if a child is emotionally or mentally struggling. I am not writing from child psychology theory as there are thousands of text books to be read on emotional wounding from that perspective. My interpretation is one gleaned from observing children and teenagers as students at school, community participants, and clients in my work. These views are also based on what is happening now rather than from theory that emerged in previous centuries. The older models of interpreting human behaviour are sometimes no longer valid in today's fast-paced rapidly changing world. The unique nature of our world and how we live, what influences us and changes to thinking all affect child psychology. During my early studies of psychology we were given a mouse to study. When mine refused to modify its behaviour and died I thought it was a sign that traditional behaviour modification did not sit well with me. I was right. Now I have come to a holistic and simplistic view of what damages our children's minds, hearts and souls and that is what I am exploring in this chapter.

As I was finalising this book the following email came to me out of the blue. It is from a student I once taught over twenty six years ago. Its arrival into my inbox at the time it arrived is an example of perfect synchronicity. In her words Robyn writes of the wounding and damage that she experienced while at school and the result it has had on her life since school.

> Hiya
> You might not remember me, but I certainly remember you. I was a student of yours at Mirrabooka High in 1979.
>
> I have for many years, wanted to thank you for making my final few months of high school bearable. I don't know what would have become of me if you hadn't stuck up for me one day in class. I was the one who used to have a chorus of barking dogs whenever I entered the room, was constantly teased, and basically, had my self esteem crushed at quite an early age.
>
> I endured years of bullying from those in my school, and in my class especially. I still remember their names, all

of them, and to this day am still haunted by the years of humiliation.

As a result, I have not managed to develop many friendships, been quite a shy person, dislike social activity, and have ended up pretty much a prisoner to my own fears of being embarrassed and humiliated.

I was diagnosed as social phobic at 19 after spending three months in prison for bouncing cheques (my own) and well, now 40 has arrived, and it finds me still unmarried, still a social cripple, and living a life which is far from exciting.

I am writing a book on my life, mainly for my family as I have felt they never really understood what went on in my world through my eyes.

This is how I found you on the web, looking for pics and seeing where other people I knew when I was younger, have ended up.

Seems you have been very successful in your career, and I wanted to let you know how much I appreciated what you did for me all those years ago. It was probably something quite insignificant to you in the scheme of things, but to me, it was like a life raft.

I think I probably would have taken my life at the tender age of 15 if it hadn't been for you Maggie.

I've wanted to thank you for many, many years, and now I have.

Thankyou!!

Robyn C November 27th 2005

The long term effects of bullying and teasing can be easily seen from Robyn's email.

There is no such thing as either a perfect child or a perfect parent. In today's consumer-driven world many parents zealously strive to have a well behaved, well dressed, courteous, considerate intelligent child who behaves perfectly and respectfully at all times. This is largely based on a competitive world that is absorbed in illusionary judgement. This drive can curtail the growth of unique human nature. By nature children are meant to be unpredictable, exuberant and noisy at times.

Children are often seen as a commodity that 'needs to look a certain way' in order to meet a parent's view of the good child. This is more often about how good the child makes the parent look and feel than on any responsibility for how the child is being raised. Highly spirited children who have strong personalities are difficult to control and can wreak havoc in families where the image of the parents is more important than authentic love, guidance and nurturing of children.

Yet we all do the best we can for our children given what we know at any point in time and the skills that we have at that time. Even the best trained child psychologist or paediatrician has moments when he or she is unkind, impatient or irrationally angry toward their children. That is life.

Before I begin the exploration of emotional wounding in children under seven may I emphasize the importance of restful, regular sleep from birth. The body needs sleep to rejuvenate and renew cells, to rest the physical body and to allow the brain to process and store new learning. It is one of the things that have changed is the lose boundaries around young children's bed times. Many children I see who are experiencing inappropriate erratic behaviour in our homes and classrooms are up until well past 10 pm at night! Sleep deprivation needs to be attended to before anything else other than diet. A child who is "wound up" at 9.30 pm may look like they don't need as much sleep, however being wound up is often a sign of sleep deprivation! Children need to be shown early in life how to relax themselves and self soothe. Our children's world is over stimulated and this is also impeding their ability to switch off and drift off to sleep. If you are pulling your hair out and want some sleep in your own bed with just your partner, get some help! A simple relaxation CD that includes relaxing stretches, breathing and an imaginary journey works a treat for everyone. A wonderful resource other than my own Just for Kidz pack is the Floppy Sleep Game Book by Patti Teal. (See children's resources at the back of the book.) Patti has worked with all kinds of challenging sleepless children and her book has an excellent in-depth exploration of the causes of sleeplessness in children and how to turn it around. Please start with improving the sleep patterns of your children before you do anything else. Your hyperactive volatile child may very well be sleep deprived.

In early childhood some experiences seem unimportant and yet can be life changing while others may seem very confronting and frightening and yet make little difference to a child. We can never know what happens within a child's mind and heart, we can only guess. Some people have created for themselves lives of enormous worth and value BECAUSE of the unique wounding they experienced during childhood. That is, it may not be the wounding that is the problem, it may be the healing of the wounding when it impedes our lives and forms the greater challenge.

One of the things that brain research has shown is that the brain will focus on surviving as its first priority – this is a brain stem activity. So whether a child is being abused or is processing the death of a close loved one, the brain will make sure the child survives. This focus will mean that the brain is greatly impeded in its ability to perform upper cognitive functions like problem solving or being creative. This is why many children living with serious stress in their lives have times when their schooling is negatively influenced. Many people have shared this to be true around the time a parent died suddenly. Once the threat has been removed or a grief resolved to a healthy degree, the person remembers getting "smarter."

Recent research supports the concept of foetal awareness, which occurs when a foetus is responsive to his or her mother's changing emotional states passed hormonally through the placenta. Indeed, through the work of L De Mause (2002) it has been shown that "behavioural problems in later life are linked to stressful experiences in the womb". This is also supported by the work of S Gerhardt (2004) in his book Why Love Matters – How Affection Shapes a Baby's Brain. Stressful and traumatic experiences in the womb, through birth and in the early months of life are registered in the brain as 'emotional memory' and help to shape the forming psyche and personality of a child.

As a transpersonal counsellor I have been able to trace many patterns of behaviour and belief systems back to very early times in life. It is sad to discover that a child's deep despair or incapacity to feel comfortable with laughter and fun could be linked to painful memories within the womb or to the birthing experience. An emotional scar can occur with children who are born after their mother has previously miscarried or lost a baby. The unresolved grief, sadness and fear that the mother still feels can be accepted by the new baby so that their capacity to be joyful and happy is irrationally impeded. Sometimes the baby interprets that this sadness is because of them, and this can be enormously damaging to an emerging psyche. Knowing that you were unwanted, unexpected or unwelcome is another deep emotional wound that some individuals carry from pre-birth. I have experienced this and have had to struggle with a low self esteem and poor sense of self worth for many years of my life.

"Behavioural disturbances as serious as delinquency, schizophrenia, ADHD, depression and substance abuse have been associated with highly stressful experiences in the womb; such as severe marital discord, or maternal hostility or rejection towards the foetus."

Robin Grill. Parenting for a Peaceful World, p 278.

Another pattern that emerges is awareness that life is not safe. This can occur when a baby hears verbal abuse or senses physical abuse of its mother. The child may become fearful, needy and open to being a victim. It is common in children who are bed wetters and anxious sleepers. Other affected children take on the role of the bully to ensure they do not feel vulnerable and undefended.

An interesting pre-birth pattern I was led to discover involved a beautiful teenager who was self harming, mainly by stabbing her thighs. We discovered that a family member had molested her at around the age of seven. Following treatment she still experienced a desire to self harm. When we explored deeper it became apparent that she had been a very well-planned event in her family's life. Her dad had undergone a vasectomy reversal and both parents eagerly awaited another child in their family. They sang to her and spoke to her throughout the pregnancy, which created an amazing world of love, joy and eager anticipation in the womb; the little baby did not want to leave. She was late and resisted birthing (I had an intuitive sense of this baby pushing with both legs against her mother's pelvis saying "Leave me in here!"). As a consequence life was a disappointment. The girl has since stopped self harming but still has difficulty surrendering to joy and happiness. She does well in her academic and sporting life but is easily wounded by others and keeps getting disappointed by life. Relationships are also a challenge because she still feels, unconsciously, that her parents betrayed her by bringing her into this world rather than leaving her in her heaven. The shaping of a baby's emotional and psychological world is complex and even the most loving parents can inadvertently create wounding.

John C Pierrakos was the co-founder of the Institute of Bioenergetic Analysis (with Alexander Lowen) and then the Core Energetics Institute. He described these early woundings as 'sources of dysfunction'. He explored the role of the conscious and the unconscious mind in our lives.

"The involuntary sector comprises the unconscious processes; our innate impetuses and our unconscious energy

formations, plus the buried experience of our unremembered past."

John C Pierrakos. Core Energetics 1990, p87.

Dr Pierrakos also explored how the physical body and the energy flow within the body can mirror emotional wounding from childhood. For example, men who as boys were unable to express anger in a healthy way often bury it within their bodies. When they are unable to create a balance between their receptive (female) and assertive (male) principles they may become aggressive and brutal. Unfortunately many men equate these same characteristics with manhood and seldom do anything to heal the imbalance. Later in life they may become violent in their family relationships or create a distortion in their sexual world; they may have a deep need for hard core pornography or become a 'pub brawler'. Some continue to hold anger within their bodies and end up with cardiovascular disease. These men can cause deep damage to their sons, especially those sons who have a good balance between the receptive and assertive parts of their beings, when they shame and tease them for being weak or a 'woose(y)'. I am aware of several teenage boys who were suicidal and who had experienced this response from their fathers – of being teased and shamed for being gentle and kind. Such talk becomes damaging to a boy's ability to claim his own power and causes a struggle during manhood, often because the boys do not want to be a man if it means they have to behave like their dad.

"During infancy and childhood, each human being seizes upon strategies to fend off pain and suffering and to exert its own will. All of these strategies however are counterproductive because they fragment the unitary flow of energy within the human organism."

John C Pierrakos. Core Energetics 1990, p93.

Essentially we all create dysfunctional patterns of behaviour that we use to help us survive this thing called life. Pierrakos believes that these defences form three different ways of denial:

❖ self will

❖ pride

❖ fear

Healing psychotherapies explore these three core areas and investigate how humans create illusionary ways of existing that are actually dysfunctional. Indeed, if we follow the assertions of the excellent child therapist Aletha Solter we come to a similar place of agreement as to the origins of wounding and subsequent inappropriate behaviours of children. Dr Solter believes that the three reasons for inappropriate behaviour in children are as follows.

1. The child is experiencing a need, where unrecognised and unmet needs can cause children to act 'badly'. Needs may be around food, sleep, thirst, touch, affection, recognition or acceptance. An unmet need is often linked to a perception of a lack of love.

2. The child has insufficient information to make a   better decision, being mindful of misinformation or misinterpretation. Always remember that children are interpreting the world through their own eyes, not an adult's.

3. The child is harbouring painful, pent-up feelings that need to be expressed in a harmless way. This is what we call emotional discharge or diffusing.

Aletha Solter

Inappropriate behaviour around needs occurs with what many parents describe as attention-seeking behaviour. By describing it in this way we are actually negating a way of expressing a very genuine need for a child. Attachment parenting, especially under two, helps to overcome many of these needs. The child is close to you and their needs for physical touch and comfort are met spontaneously. Thirst and hunger create discomfort for children and babies and we often underestimate the distortion that can be created in a baby's mind when resolution to that simple need is withheld. The yearning for comfort and safe physical touch is one that modern parenting and child care struggles to meet. With the increase in number of working mothers and use of child care outside of the home there is little time and emphasis on quiet safe touch. A baby or child may translate this as "I am unlovable" or "I am unloved". The rapid pace of living also creates less time for snuggle time in bed with mum or dad or hugs that are not rushed.

Dr Louise Porter in her book "Children are People Too: A parent's guide to young children's behaviour" expressed similar views around children's needs. She noticed the following four triggers in young children.

> 1.   Children are naturally exuberant and excitable and can crash into each other and hurt each other – often they feel a need to retaliate.
>
> 2.   Children learn through exploration both physically and socially and some of their actions like throwing food on the floor is a result of this rather than a deliberate act of defiance.
>
> 3.   Children under three may not know any better – yet. They are still learning.
>
> 4.   Sometimes children loose control of themselves – just like some adults can do! Yes they know what they should do but they loose control – like a person on a diet who can't resist a bucket of hot chips! (p 8, Porter)

Dr Porter has a similar viewpoint to raising children as Jenny Roberts the autistic specialist. She believes that neither parents nor children are bad or wrong – it is more the dance that's not working, not the dancers. Why? It is partly the reality that old parenting paradigms no longer work. The use of power to control no longer works. That was the model of last century. Children will resist and rebel against attempts to control them, and the natural tendency of children to learn, explore and discover how things work unsupervised is taken from them. Toddlers and young children year to feel connected and loved and they learn every day how life works and behavioural mistakes are inevitable. Indeed this is the best way for the brain to grow and develop. Obviously parents need to hold firm boundaries especially around sleep, aggression towards others, personal safety and protective behaviours.

"The alternate approach to disciplining children is based on guiding or teaching them to act thoughtfully, rather than rewarding or punishing their undesired behaviour." (P5, Porter)

One of the best things you can do to reassure your children of your love and connection to them is to develop the art of being present, really present, when you are with them. Clear from your mind all the other things you could be doing, should be doing and ought to be doing - Give a child some complete concentrated quality time and listen. Many parents tell me that even though they work they have great quality time in their family. Hopefully this means they are fully present to their child everyday because that is what quality time means.

Maybe it is worth trying the following.

Being heard

❖ Let me put this down so I can give you my full attention.........

❖ Wait a second while I turn off the TV, radio, computer, so I can really hear you...

❖ Let's have some time together, now.........

❖ What would you like to do when we have our time together tomorrow afternoon?.........

❖ So what you mean is ....

❖ Tell me more about this.........

❖ In other words.........

❖ Let me see if I understand you so far.........

❖ That must have been.........for you.........

❖ Are you open to some feedback from me?.........

Remember to keep mouth closed and ears, eyes and heart open – fully present - bring in your sense of humour.

The second of Aletha Solter's concerns around inappropriate behaviour is the notion that children do not have enough information to make any other choice about their behaviour. While this seems really obvious it is a very common reason for challenging behaviour in young children. It is best to explore other options and choices with a child after the child has had quiet time (come out of the red room) or become calmer after conflict. If biting someone who is in your way is to be discouraged then what are other possible choices for the child if the same situation occurs again? Jenny Roberts a specialist who works with troubled children, especially autistic children, in family homes around the world believes this to be true. In Jenny's own words if you have a troubled relationship with your child:

"Go back to basics is my simple direction to parents struggling with their child."

Learn how to BE with your child without conditions and develop their emotional intelligence; trust that everything will be okay.

❖ Realise that sleep and pockets of stillness are very necessary to stay balanced for today's living.

❖ Give up a few behaviours of your own first to get started rather than expect your children to do all the work.

❖ Let them see that it is easy. If you change they can too.

❖ See that the problems with your child are all about you - Your ways of relating, listening and thinking.

❖ How you choose to let go of the problem is easier when you have a process to help you.

The Kids CODE process Jenny has developed over the last 15 years working as an Occupational therapist with parents in crisis with autistic children teaches them how to create the necessary space for change to happen." (Jenny Roberts www.parentswantinghelp.com)

The third concern around expressing pent up painful feelings is one that creates many problems in the Western world. We are generally uncomfortable about the healthy diffusing of emotion. A growing toddler is supposed to be developing his or her capacity to become independent of its parents; being frustrated and angry when he or she cannot get their own way is not only normal, it is healthy in our modern world. Throwing a tantrum can be embarrassing and challenging for adults! However, the child is diffusing built up emotional energy and, given a safe place to do so, without anyone being shamed is really helpful for the child. With four sons I learned how to ensure tantrum-free shopping trips: as soon after a sleep as possible, after food and a drink, taking their favourite toy with us so they had something to keep them happy, and staying away from confectionary and toy aisles. The next chapter on emotional healing has more tips on how to help children diffuse built up emotion.

Un-diffused sadness and grief are other built up emotions that may be expressed as anger. Men have come to me for help because they are experiencing irrational anger. We have identified, for example, that they were unable to attend their mum or dad's funeral when they were children. Unexpressed energy in the nervous system can cause emotional problems, physical problems and challenges in close relationships. One man I worked with had grown up in Africa. His parents were of British descent and believed that children were very much to be seen and not heard. The children were sent to boarding school by the age of five years. This emotional abandonment impeded the man's capacity to love his partner and his children, so he became an alcoholic to numb the pain. He had also created an armour or protective defence around his heart to protect himself from further emotional pain. His chest was so hard it was like he wore a metal breast plate - it was one of the most defended hearts I had ever worked with.

Emotional damage not only creates an unconscious defence to protect a person from further pain it can create a physical body structure that supports the unconscious defensive patterning. Our voice, posture, the pace at which we walk, how we smile and even how we kiss all hold clues to emotional wounding we may have experienced as children. We can continue to live with these defences and survive most that life has to offer. Or we can make a choice to change, when we experience new moments of deep pain and suffering.

Susan Thesenga in her insightful book The Undefended Self: Living the Pathwork of Spiritual Wholeness explains that we create a mask to protect our true nature. Eventually we believe we are our mask.

"When people are emotionally sick, it is always in one way or other that a mask self has been created. They do not realize they are living a lie. They have built a layer of unreality that has nothing to do with their real personality."

Susan Thesenga. The Undefended Self: Living the Pathwork of Spiritual Wholeness 1994, p123.

We all yearn to experience deep connection and to belong in a loving, safe social group. This is what humans are biologically wired up to do.

"Emotional literacy improves relationships, creates loving possibilities between people, makes cooperative work possible and facilitates the feeling of community. We all thirst for emotional stimulation, above all for love and to give and receive love."

Claude Steiner. Achieving Emotional Literacy

For me, when I was younger, I created an illusionary world in which I wore a powerful mask of detachment and superiority that prevented people getting close to me. My mask prevented me from being hurt by rejection or abandonment. From the outside it appeared that I was confident and very capable. On the inside I was very lonely; I believed that my worth and value came from how hard I studied and how good my academic results were. What happened was that when I failed my first essay ever at university my mask cracked. I had nothing real to fall back on – no friend, no family. I tried to take my life within twenty minutes of getting the failed mark. I had fooled everyone but my true self.

As Susan Thesenga writes,

> "The deep longing that exists in every human heart for a more fulfilling state of consciousness and a larger capacity to experience life must sooner or later impel us to look within ourselves."

> The Undefended Self: Living the Pathwork of Spiritual Wholeness 1994, pix.

My search began in a small way and I am still searching for ways of being more authentic, more honest and more in touch with those aspects of myself that are hidden within me. The more I heal the less I require of the pleasures of the material world – less busyness and fewer possessions, public acknowledgements or financial rewards. At the same time I value the simple things more, like a shared smile, a moment of truth with a child, a rainy day and a heartfelt hug. I appreciate more the things I most value, the love of my husband, my four sons and those in my inner circle of life. My mind is more peaceful, I laugh and pray more often; I am truly honoured to live a life that is blessed.

We are all dysfunctional to some degree given that early emotional wounding affects us physically, emotionally, mentally and cognitively. Often we are not aware of its influence. Emotional overwhelm, illiteracy or exhaustion from struggle may be important elements in the following challenges in life:

❖ obesity
❖ low achievement

❖ relationship conflicts
❖ depression
❖ mental illness
❖ family violence
❖ loneliness
❖ poor health
❖ alcohol and drug abuse
❖ anxiety disorders
❖ slow recovery from loss experiences
❖ low resilience to life's setbacks
❖ disconnectedness
❖ suicide

Take, for example, obesity, especially long-term obesity. In almost all of my experiences with overweight children and adolescents I have found a deep layer of emotional pain underneath the need to eat compulsively. A very high number were the victims of sexual abuse at a young age. Simply introducing physical exercise programs to beat obesity will probably create more stress in the lives of these children. We are also enormously understaffed to manage the needs of emotionally damaged children. Medical practitioners struggle to find health professionals to send troubled children to; this is a world-wide trend.

Ongoing problems of poor health, loneliness, depression and low resilience could all be improved with a better focus in our education systems of developing personal and social life skills. Around the world there are some excellent programs used. However, the push to achieve academic grades over and above the emotional and social wellbeing of children means that the programs are too few, only happen for a short time and sometimes introduced too late. I deeply admire the work of the Virtues Project with Linda Kavelin Popov and am delighted to see how it has become a positive agent for change around the world.

Increasing opportunities for pastoral care of students in schools will help. This is one of the reasons why I am a passionate believer in the school chaplaincy program "Youth Care" in Australia that provides for chaplains in schools. That extra safe person in the school who has a flexible timetable and time to spend with students to really be present and listen is invaluable. Research has shown that schools with school chaplains have less truancy and aggressive behaviour.

The biological need for all humans, from pre-birth until old age, is to feel connected and loved. If this need is fulfilled in the first two years of a child's life then that child will have a better chance of being able to grow up a loving, empathetic person who is able to create relationships that are pleasurable and positive. If we could give pregnancy, birth and early childhood the holistic focus and importance that it deserves, to provide the best template for preventative care, Joseph Chilton Pearce believes that:

"With our present knowledge of brain-heart interaction, conception, pregnancy, childbirth and child development we could bring about the most immediate and dramatic revolution of our history."

(The Transcendence of Biology 2002, p233).

To achieve this feeling of being connected would require a huge mind shift globally: to truly honour the creation and arrival of a new child with awareness and commitment to being open hearted and loving. We would have to shift away from the current medical model where doctors govern pregnancy and birth. We would have to return to the social or 'tribal' focus of caregivers, a group of mainly women who, in the first two years of a child's life, offer constant love and reassurance. This would allow the prefrontal brain to grow naturally. We as a human race could develop the higher intelligence that we are now capable of by experiencing with the complete nurturing of the heart intelligence. Men fully supporting women during this time would give the women the opportunity to nurture a child in a safe place that is free from fear and where his or her physical needs are met. This is a return to natural function parenting that supports the child's development - in the window of opportunity that nature creates for the optimal growth of the whole brain and the whole child. In this way we may reduce the violent and inhumane treatment of others around the world and provide the best form of preventative therapy we can apply. Get the first two years right and we will have healthier and happier future leaders making decisions that affect mankind rather than those who have the consciousness that sees force and power, usually with violence, as the only way to achieve peace.

Being Born is Important

Being born is important.
You who have stood at the bedposts
And seen a mother on her high harvest day,
The day of the most golden of harvest moons for her.

You who have seen the new wet child
Dried behind the ears,
Swaddled in soft fresh garments,
Pursing its lips and sending a groping mouth
Toward the nipples where white milk is ready-

You who have seen this love's payday
Of wild toil and sweet agonising-

You know being born is important.
You know nothing else was ever so important to you.
You understand the payday of love is so old,
So involved, so traced with the circles of the moon,
So cunning with the secrets of the salts of the blood-
It must be older than the moon, older than the salt.

Carl Sandburg

One of the most disturbing trends I have noticed over the last ten years is the number of children, teenagers and adults who are experiencing emotional overwhelm.

Overwhelm drains the body, depletes the nervous system and often triggers depression. There is just too much emotional pressure being put on children, which creates the perception for them that they are unable to cope with life. We have created a fast paced, individualist, shallow world where supports are hard to find; people are less physically, emotionally or mentally capable of managing life effectively. The following are some of the situations that can contribute to emotional overwhelm:

- ❖ car accidents
- ❖ bullying and harassment
- ❖ nasty, malicious gossip
- ❖ failing at school
- ❖ depression
- ❖ other mental illnesses
- ❖ death of a loved one
- ❖ loss of job
- ❖ abuse of any kind
- ❖ teenage pregnancy
- ❖ betrayal
- ❖ criminal activity
- ❖ alcohol or drug abuse
- ❖ gender confusion
- ❖ discrimination
- ❖ serious illness
- ❖ personal injury
- ❖ family disharmony

- ❖ sudden unexpected life change

- ❖ unresolved conflict

- ❖ pressure of expectations

- ❖ perceived failure

- ❖ being late

- ❖ being overweight

- ❖ relationship ending

- ❖ living outside of an honour code

When more than a couple of these situations happen together a person runs a real risk of experiencing emotional overwhelm. People turn up at a doctor's surgery describing non-specific symptoms but few seek professional psychotherapy to get the help they really need to move forward in their lives. The most effective way for someone to move forward following a serious life challenge is to ask for help from family and friends, to contact their doctor and to see a professional to help them explore the emotional aspects that may be contributing to a sense of being out of control or de-railed by life.

> "When we deny our faults and selfishness, we stay trapped in trying to appear better than we are and to place the blame for our difficulties elsewhere." (p9) "...when we create the mask of the good girl or boy, or the powerful man or woman, the striving student, or the self assured teacher, the needy child or the competent adult, the naïve seeker or the worldly cynic, our masks are an attempt to rise above our failed faults and our pain, to deny our ordinariness and our pettiness."

> Susan Thesenga. "The Undefended Self" 1994, p9.

It is the search for truth that sets us free from patterns of denial. That is why we need an objective perspective as provided by a counsellor to explore our patterns, rather than a friend or family member. Such a search for truth increases our capacity for self acceptance and self awareness and opens the way to authentic self love. To live from the place of the undefended self brings us better health, wellbeing, caring and loving relationships. It facilitates our journey on our own personal pathway and helps the world to be a better place. This journey allows us to explore unexpressed emotions, especially within our shadows, to explore the distortions we have formed about ourselves and the world. It opens moments of great insight as we come to terms with the light within our higher self.

This century can allow the journey to wholeness to become more socially acceptable and will help us resolve the global shadows that have created the senseless wars of the last century, against others and our natural world. The turmoil in our children's lives may well provide a catalyst to seek personal healing. The emergence of shallow, unsatisfying lives will gather momentum until we wake up and move towards wholeness and authenticity. The 'un-wellness' of our children may force those still in denial to recognise the lack of truth in their lives. I began my healing journey because I wanted to be a better mother to my sons. I did it for them first, and myself second – we are all winners! I have ended a generational pattern of emotional distance to help my sons and hopefully they can take the healing on through their gene pool.

The fear-based mentality of our world has been created by pressures of modern living. The worst disasters around the world are now seen instantly. The media uses tragedy more than ever before to sell papers and to obtain high ratings on TV. Showing the worst of humanity disturbs our children; they do see it too. The children's nervous systems are very sensitive and different to adults. Young children are stressed by loud noises, being sick, being left unexpectedly and falling. When events happen one after another their nervous systems starts to exhibit stress, which creates physiological effects in a child's body. To release that anxiety and stress children need to be reassured and treated with tenderness. [This is explored more in the chapter on Helping Kids to Heal.] How can we tell if a child is struggling with life? How can we tell if their nervous system holds an unhealthy level of stress?

Some possible symptoms are:

- ❖ bed wetting
- ❖ chronic nail biting
- ❖ sleep walking
- ❖ nightmares
- ❖ reverting to outgrown behaviours
- ❖ irrational tears and crying easily
- ❖ anger outbursts
- ❖ fighting among siblings and friends
- ❖ becoming dependent and clingy
- ❖ poor school performance
- ❖ teacher concern
- ❖ rigidity – wanting to get things 'right'
- ❖ complaining about stomach aches and pains
- ❖ irritability
- ❖ talking loudly
- ❖ being tired and listless
- ❖ headaches
- ❖ eating disturbances
- ❖ bowel problems
- ❖ poor body language

If your child exhibits several of these symptoms and also has really disturbed sleep patterns then please seek professional help, sooner rather than later. Some fears, if left unchecked, can become phobias or the beginning of thought disorders and panic attacks. A really helpful and easy-to-read book for parents is called Fear-Free Children, by Dr Janet Hall. Learn to trust your own intuition too, and stay tuned into your kids. Children can wear pretty amazing masks - just like their parents!

Every stage of a child's growth and development brings gifts and challenges that need to be embraced rather than overcome. Each child grows and develops in his or her own unique way; what works for one may not necessarily work for another. The emotional wounding that occurs is to some degree a valuable part of a child's journey to becoming his or her authentic true self. To heal a dysfunction or a distortion in how a child sees the world is partly the responsibility of the child and partly that of the parents.

The greatest gift we as adults can offer to children and teenagers is to love and accept them when they are behaving appallingly, are ugly and when they are impossible to live with. I have worked with many families experiencing major trauma because their teenager is about to leave home, forever, as they find it impossible to live under the same roof as their family, anymore. By taking the families through the layers of unexpressed emotional pain we find the love that has been buried under unkind words, incorrect assumptions and lots of lies.

Once their hearts touch again the conflict simply dissolves. We can then create a new way of being that is based on mutual love and respect rather than fear and manipulation. This takes an independent observer to ensure that those involved stay in truth and take turns at really listening. It is amazing how powerful it is to be really heard in the company of those we love. So often the assumptions loved ones have made about a certain experience are so far from the truth. Clearing the decks and being honest in an open and respectful way is something that can heal the worst conflict. Every time I hear of another woman or a child who is killed or maimed in a family violence incident, I cringe knowing that emotional illiteracy will be behind the violence – emotional illiteracy that could have been healed.

Please never give up on your child and seek help before rather than later. Know that love can be identified and restored once emotional honesty has been achieved. The journey to emotional wholeness takes a lifetime and only the truth sets you free to be the best 'you' that you can be. It is worth the effort and benefits all those who you love and who love you.

"The need to feel in command of ourselves and our own corner of the world is central to human beings as are the needs for self-esteem and to belong. This need for autonomy is, to my mind, the core reason that we cannot use controlling forms of discipline with children." (Dr Louise Porter, p52)

Key Points

❖ There is no such thing as a perfect child or a perfect parent

❖ We all do the best we can for our children, given what we know and the skills we have

❖ Emotional intelligence begins with foetal awareness

❖ Early wounding is known as a source of dysfunction

❖ The emotional world of each of us seems to shape our physical bodies and influence our energetic wellbeing

❖ Being present to our children builds a loving connectedness

❖ Children need to diffuse emotional energy safely

❖ We all create defences and masks

❖ Emotional overwhelm is common in this modern world

❖ The first two years of life are essential for our children's emotional, mental and social wellbeing

❖ We live in a fear-based world, which adds to childhood stress

❖ Each stage of a child's life brings gifts and challenges

❖ We all benefit from emotional healing

Children Learn What They Live
By Dorothy Law Nolte

If children live with criticism,
>> they learn to condemn.
If children live with hostility,
>> they learn to fight.
If children live with ridicule,
>> they learn to be shy.
If children live with shame,
>> they learn to feel guilty.
If children live with encouragement,
>> they learn confidence.
If children live with tolerance,
>> they learn to be patient.
If children live with praise,
>> they learn to appreciate.
If children live with acceptance,
>> they learn to love.
If children live with approval,
>> they learn to like themselves.
If children live with honesty,
>> they learn truthfulness.
If children live with security, they learn to have
>> faith in themselves and others.
If children live with friendliness,
>> they learn the world is a nice place in which to
>> live.

>> Dorothy Law Nolte. Children Learn What
>> They Live, 1972.

Chapter 5

Helping Children to Heal

"Children throb with a natural connection. But the slings and arrows of outrageous fortune start hitting early.
Competitive siblings. Tough schools. Harsh media. Dangerous streets. Social injustice. All the noise of modern life. Hunger and pain. Each of these events, every childhood injury, physical and psychological, creates tension in the physical body. The result is that by the time most of us are teenagers we have lost that bubbling, continuous ability to feel life's natural beauty."

William Bloom. The Endorphin Effect, p50

Serious harm and abuse cause damage to children at a deep level. Prolonged verbal, mental and emotional abuse creates serious emotional processing disabilities that impede a child's growth throughout their life. Physical abuse, particularly if it is sexual, can result in enormous psychological damage and increases a child's potential to become an addict, a paedophile, a criminal, an abuser or a person likely to harm his or herself. They become vulnerable to contemplating suicide as a solution to problems when they are older. In reality these children are victims of life. This chapter begins with the plea that we need to vigilant in protecting our children from serious harm.

Discovering a child who has been the victim of serious abuse gives you the opportunity to seek professional help for them – yet know that taking this action requires commitment, time and energy. If, after the first visit, the child is keen to see the chosen therapist again then that is a good sign. If they are reluctant, then the therapist may not be the best person for that child. Find someone else. If you are also a parent of the child you may be helped by seeing a therapist yourself, so that you are able to support your child and yourself in the healing process. Unexpressed rage and hatred toward a perpetrator sours you and causes mental and emotional stress. Telephone help lines are available to point you in the right direction and to assist you in getting professional help (see the back of this book).

This chapter explores ways that parents, carers and teachers can help children who have been wounded or abused. In today's world there can be long waiting times to get professional help. Sometimes the wounding can appear minor and yet when handled inappropriately, it can cause long term problems. We as non-professionals –parents, teachers and other child carers – can help children overcome the challenges of life especially those disappointments, stresses and times when kids get irrationally upset. How do we support a child who is a chronic bed wetter, is afraid of dogs or is being bullied at pre-school?

A healthy place to start is with the nervous system. Emotions effect both the sympathetic and parasympathetic nervous systems and they can become overloaded and stressed. This can cause an increase in the cortisol levels and this can now be measured using a saliva test. The healthy diffusion of emotional energy helps a child to feel better, calmer and allows them to feel safe again. Essentially, children need to be reassured, nurtured and soothed as soon as possible after an upset or a moment of crisis. This allows them to diffuse energy and to feel soothed quickly and then they are free to feel happy within themselves. Research has shown that children who were reassured and emotionally supported as babies and young toddlers are better able to self-soothe or reassure themselves as older children. All children have these needs although sensitive children may appear to need them more.

Breath work and colour

In the Western world, breathing has become a rushed and shallow experience. It is a wonder that our bodies and our brains work at all! By being aware of taking a deeper breath, better still three deeper breast, we actually slow our thinking and mental processing. We give our minds vital time to have awareness about the possible choices we can make in our lives.

Try for yourself. Breathe normally and observe the busy nature of your mind as you read the words on this page. Take a deep breath and notice what happens – you create a slowing of your mental processes, even if just a little.

By pausing to take three deep breaths we can completely change how we are thinking and feeling, simply because we slow down the rapidity of a chaotic mind. Pausing to ponder and think about a question or an event allows our mind to interpret the world from a place of awareness rather than from a place of unconsciousness, or as an automatic reaction. It can create emotional pauses in our mental processing that allow us to make better choices about how to behave. We do not have to react, which is set up largely as a consequence of our earlier life experiences. With children, the same reactive processes take place except with more noticeable results. As children are immature and inexperienced they react to events without thinking – maybe with yelling, hitting or a tantrum. Children can have an unmet need that is as simple as feeling hungry, thirsty, sick or unloved!

Teaching a child when they are young to pause and take three breaths can help to stall unacceptable behaviour. The space made can also give you time to come to a better choice on how to manage the situation. It may be that you get a drink, a piece of fruit or simply bend down and offer the child a hug! In this way you are helping the child to understand what it is they need, which they are responding to, and it will encourage them to ask for what they want!

My work with children has taught me that colours can represent feelings in their world. Some negative or 'yukky' expressions are:

Red   anger and frustration
Orange   hurt
Grey   sadness
Black   fear
Brown   disappointment, feeling let down.

By using a child's imagination and the power of the unconscious mind, children can breathe out the red colour of anger and frustration from inside them. When it has all gone they can then breathe in a colour of calmness, like green or blue, or a bright yellow colour of joy and happiness or even a bright colour with sparkles in it. This works quickly and well. It is really effective in changing the mood of children less than 10 years of age. Encouraged simply because it worked when they were a child, a breathing strategy continues to work throughout adolescence and adulthood. Colour breathing is simple and anyone can do it - as long as the intent is to improve how you are feeling!

Calming the Angry Ant is on my Just for Kidz pack and uses this breathing technique. Teachers tell me it helps calm everyone in the class, including the teacher! The three tracks on *Just a Little Time Out*, which are all only 15 minutes long, use different breathing techniques that can easily be applied to everyday life. Breathing in slowly to the count of four, holding for a little, and then breathing out to the slow count of four is another good breathing technique. Try this while waiting at traffic lights, in queues, or if you are being kept on hold on the telephone!

I also really like the three sighs technique. You simply take a deep breath and then let out a sigh. Repeat again and again with increasingly loud sighs. The final sigh can be quite orgasmic – or just another normal sigh! You feel calmer, clearer and less stressed.

To model the quiet power of deep breathing is good for your children – you remind them, encourage them and show them the immediate benefits of emotional balance and improved thinking. It is a good idea to ensure your child does not make deep inward breaths through a blocked or snotty nose – not a good sound, especially in a classroom or around home during the winter months!

Positive safe touch

Touch has been contaminated by our fear-based world. We have let our children down by withdrawing one of the most important ways to offer love and reassurance, especially for children under 10 years of age. In removing safe touch we have negated our capacity to mother our children. This is important in times of crisis and suffering. *Mothering* is what our children need to develop healthy mental, physical and emotional competencies. Mums, dads, teachers, carers and non-biological 'family' can all provide healthy mothering. I believe that most of the problems of our angry, disconnected youth stem from a serious absence of positive mothering. Positive touch is an essential part of this basic need.

Clinical studies at the American Academy of Paediatrics found that touch therapy helped premature newborn babies to gain weight. It also improved asthmatic children's breathing, assisted in balancing glucose levels for diabetic children and lowered stress levels, improving the immune system. Researcher Tiffany Field PhD believes that "touch is as important to infants and children as eating and sleeping." (Denise Dewar 2005).

The Western world is far removed from a community or tribal approach to raising children. Extended families have largely disappeared. Instead we have created a huge industry in childcare. At times childcare is portrayed as being important in children's development. With large numbers of children grouped together, however, it is impossible to be able to meet the physical touch needs of every child. Children who are in casual day care (less than five hours a week) will not have serious problems because of this as these children spend most of their time with family at home, so that their needs are more likely to be met.

For fulltime working parents this is an area of concern. However by being aware of the importance of lots of physical touch and giving your child all you can does help. It also helps to find a day care centre where the carers have good mothering skills, not just good practical skills. A sure sign that you have found one is when your child is keen to return! Ask around and find a day care that has a good reputation for loving kids, has a small ratio of children to carers and the carers are comfortable with positive touch. Then you should be OK. Do not beat yourself up about it if you are one of those parents who have to work! Simply learn ways to fill your child's physical touch needs so that you can be assured your child will be touch satiated.

A wonderful teacher who is an advocate for more positive touch in schools, Denise Dewar, writes:

"Our dilemma, the importance of touch and physical contact, is not fully understood or accepted within our culture. We know that our children need to feel safe and comforted when distressed and yet we live in a society that has gradually pushed physical contact into a negative, unhealthy light, rejecting its importance, so as to make it easier to protect ourselves. As educators, both parents and teachers can do something about this."

Denise Dewar. Hands on Learning ,p 1,2005

I completely agree with Denise. As a high school teacher I practised positive touch by using the odd pat on the head, a touch on the arm, a ruffle of a boy's hair, or, when I knew a student was struggling with life, a quiet shoulder rub while they were working. A retired principal told me that he believed a lot of boys' aggressive and inappropriate behaviour was the result of touch deprivation, especially in the early years of adolescence. As a coach of basketball teams I found that the boys really connected with me once they were off the court, away from the pseudo-rough play antics that happened on the court. I would often send a letter to parents at the beginning of the year warning them of my propensity for positive touch, giving them the opportunity to remove their child if they were uncomfortable with my hands on approach. Usually this resulted in requests from other parents to get their child into my classes!

We do need to seriously reconsider the fear-driven perception we have around the safe touch of students. The same retired principal told me that a lawyer had spoken to him about the legal perspective of being sued for inappropriate touching. You can only be pursued legally if you have touched someone without their approval. This did not have to be verbal consent, tacit approval was sufficient. What this means is that unless a child pulls away, or looks unhappy, you have their tacit approval. When a child falls over or hurts his or herself and comes running with arms up for a hug we have their tacit approval. Commonsense needs to prevail. Denise Dewar writes:

> "At one workshop we were discussing the 'dilemma' teachers faced when hugged by a child. One of the teachers said that they had a 'Hands Up' policy, where the teacher had to put their hands in the air if a child hugged them so that everyone could see where their hands were and that they had not initiated the contact. This just blew me away! What are we saying to our children by behaving like this? Fear has become the basis of many of the decisions we are making within our schools! I believe that as teachers and parents we need to

know the benefits of touch and that as children they need to recognise safe touch and how to accept or reject physical contact."

Denise Dewar. Hands on Learning 2005

Young children need to learn the difference between safe touch and unsafe touch early on. They also need some guidelines on what to do if they become the victim of unsafe touch. As reported in Children of the Lucky Country (2005, p57), which is co-written by Professor Fiona Stanley, Sue Richardson and Margot Prior from Western Australia,

"69% of abuse cases involved a natural parent, 7% were relatives, 6% a step parent, 5% a parent's de facto partner, 5% a 'friend' or neighbour."

This statistic has to ring enormous warning bells for the Western world. Over 92% of all abuse is perpetrated by someone a child knows well, and yet there is almost no education on teaching our children about this danger. Only stranger-danger education is available yet that accounts for less than 10% of all child abuse. We are letting our children down big time by keeping them ignorant about what is acceptable, appropriate behaviour and what is not. The ramifications are enormous and there is a real need for bringing safe touch awareness into our schools, as early as possible. In this way, children who are being abused can know the difference between love, affection, unhealthy gratification and manipulation.

Children need to know how they can tell if people are being trustworthy and safe. I recommend the nurturing of children's intuition and more is written about that in the chapter "Building Intuition and Inner Guidance." To be betrayed by a loved one is deeply damaging to a child and has life-long consequences. The majority of women in prisons have been sexually abused. That wounding led on to high levels of addiction, abusive relationships and criminality. In my experience, sexual abuse is also a significant factor in self harm and suicide. No medication, illicit drug or alcoholic binge can heal the shame and despair that many victims of abuse feel. Some keep their abuse a secret for years.

Dr Arthur Janov, author of Biology of Love, argues in his book that the absence of loving care early in life causes increased levels of stress for a person. The result of this deprivation is high levels of cortisol that *change the structure of the brain*. Brain scans taken of extremely violent young men show huge spaces in the pre-frontal lobe. Early childcare centres, pre-schools and primary schools could hold the key to improving the future mental and emotional lives of children, through implementing safe touch programs. The brain has plasticity and can grow the necessary neuro-patterns, once it has experienced loving care and nurturing. It cannot create the patterns without first-hand experience.

It may be that children are already leading the way. Teachers tell me that young children are reaching out to them more and more. They want to hold their teacher's hand, sit closer and to be hugged. Once again, Denise Dewar explains the yearning to be touched:

> **"For some of my children this may be because they lack that physical contact from home and for others it may be the direct opposite, at home they are nurtured and loved so they develop a connection between feeling safe and cared for, and touch."**

Denise Dewar. Hands on Learning 2005

It only takes one genuinely trustworthy person to use safe touch to reframe how a child sees the world and to reshape how their brain perceives safety and tenderness. It is especially important for indigenous children. They often come from extended families where there is a lot of touch and when they arrive into our schools there is none. I have found indigenous children are mainly kinaesthetic learners and they need physical movement and activity more in their learning, like most boys. They respond best with teachers capable of safe touch and comfort with activity based learning. Surely it's worth involving those working in childcare and education in a safe touch training program for children under seven years of age because it costs so little and yet could change so much.

Positive respectful communication

> In NLP (Neuro Linguistic Programming) it is considered that:
>
> COMMUNICATION IS MADE UP OF
>
> 7% WORDS
> 55% PHYSIOLOGY
> 38% TONALITY

What this means is that maybe as little as 7% of our communication between people is verbal, the rest is non-verbal. Our physiology is expressed by how we carry ourself, our body language and our natural defences. These behaviours are determined both consciously and unconsciously by our core belief system. In these changing times one of the areas causing us the most angst and confusion is our changing belief patterns and our perceptions. The tone with which we speak has a great influence on how our words are received.

Making a conscious effort to 'request' rather than 'demand' from our children immediately alters the tone of our voice. If you think children should be seen and not heard then this will also come through in the non-verbal aspects of your communications, both with and around children. If you believe that children are miracles and that they deserve to be respected and honoured, then that too will come through. Children are pretty good at sensing non-verbal communication – maybe better than adults. Differently from previous generations, they often will be disrespectful to adults who are disrespectful to them. The judgemental way that many adults see children or students dictates the level of communication that takes place. If we assume that a scruffy looking teenager with body piercing is going to be more of a challenge to teach than a well dressed one, then we express that belief within our behaviour and physiology. This happens all the time for many indigenous students. They are never given a chance to form their own unique relationship with a teacher; rather it has already been shaped by the teacher's prior experiences and attitudes to indigenous students.

Dr Ross W Greene in his book The Explosive Child (2001) explores inflexible, explosive children and how families can help these children behave more calmly. He writes: "When patterns of communication are maladaptive, dealing with an inflexible-explosive child will be much harder" (p224). One of the patterns of adult behaviour that he has observed to cause conflict is the pattern of 'speculation', that is 'psychologising' or 'mind reading'. You can see this when a family member makes statements about another family member, often inaccurately. An example is, "John is always aggressive after dinner".

Making assumptions involves making judgements. It is a sure way of creating resentment in the other person involved. It also threatens the other person's autonomy, regardless of age. Overgeneralisations, sarcasm, exaggerations, ambiguity, frequent criticism and lecturing are other verbal patterns that are sure to cause conflict! With explosive children, or highly spirited children a supportive network can help families work through their challenges. Dr Greene affirms that time pressures contribute to frustration levels in families. If we were able to calm down and slow the busy pace of our lives then maybe our children would not feel so pushed and pressured. They would not be so emotionally volatile! If we as parents are able to work at being less stressed, less rushed and calmer, then our children will follow. They are our emotional barometers, even if we disagree about that!

Marshall Rosenberg in his wonderful work Nonviolent Communication (2000) explores how we can improve our communications and create more harmony in our relationships. Furthermore,

"Compassionate communication is a process language which focuses our here and now awareness on feelings and needs, and actions to meet those needs. The model is a practical way to put the intentions into practice."

Marion Badenoch Rose PhD. The Heart of Parenting, in Byron Child Magazine 2004

An essential concept behind non-violent communication is that whenever we try to make anyone behave in a certain way, through demanding or coercing behaviour, we evoke resistance. This is because humans have a universal need for autonomy. The resistance that builds up becomes resentment or rebellion, at any age. Non-violent communication involves four processes:

1. observation
2. feelings
3. needs
4. requests.

Non-violent communication embraces a holistic approach to all communication within all relationships – at home, at school, in our community and politically. Unfortunately, being respectful of others is almost like speaking another language, often because of past conditioning.

"Most of us grew up speaking a language that encourages us to label, compare, demand and pronounce judgements rather than be aware of what we are feeling and needing. I believe life alienating communication is rooted in views of human nature that have exerted their influence for several centuries. These views stress our innate evil and deficiency and a need for education to control our inherently undesirable nature."

Marshall Rosenberg. 2000, p23

Unmet needs form the core of much of our emotional pain. By being aware of this we can help our children discover what is troubling them and then help them to ask for that need to be met. This simple model is incredibly powerful as well as being full of commonsense. So much of the violence in our modern world is the result of others forcing their needs and wants onto others, without consideration for how those others feel. The enormous disquiet apparent in communities where people live under the threat of violence can be traced back to unmet needs. The over-riding assumption that there is only one way to see things is erroneous. In situations like this a process of mediation that allows everyone to be heard and for all needs to be considered. Encouraging non-violent communication is important.

For more excellent information check out the books by Marshall Rosenberg, Chick Moorman's Parent Talk and Teacher Speak, and The 10 Commitments. Maybe you could consider doing a basic level course of NLP or a program in non-violent communication? Some further suggestions on how to practice positive life-enhancing language with yourself and others, especially children, are given.

What is life-enhancing communication?

The way we have been taught to speak or learned to speak has a huge influence on how we think and program our unconscious mind. The continuous use of negative non-conscious language prevents us from achieving many of our positive outcomes and goals. It also contributes to us sustaining less than resourceful emotional states and behaviours.

When we use generalisations instead of specifics we disengage our emotions. The unconscious mind takes little notice and thus manifestation is unlikely. Remember that our unconscious mind takes notice of specifics that are emotionally charged and it takes language literally.

Negation language	Life-enhancing language
Isn't it a nice day	It is a nice day
Wouldn't you like to go?	Would you like to go?
Don't you like Maths?	Do you like Maths?
I love you but.........	I love you and...
I want, I wish, I need	I require, I choose, My choice is......
I should, ought, have to	I choose, I will I would I will
I must, I've got to	I will
I might, I am supposed to	I will
I'll try	I will I am I can
I hope	My choice is.........
At least	At best, at most
Probably, perhaps	I will, I choose
Maybe	Is
It's hard	It's a challenge, It's an opportunity

(Adapted from Gary De Rodriguez 2003)

Avoid using **why** questions. Use sentences that encourage:

- ❖ How might we resolve this?

- ❖ What do you think needs to happen now?

- ❖ What questions do you have about what we have just done?

- ❖ What can I do to help you complete this task?

- ❖ Sounds like you have a problem.

- ❖ How can we work together to get the best outcome here?

- ❖ There is a conflict here – how can I help you sort it out?

- ❖ Please make a decision to stay with us or go to the time out area. CHOOSE. DECIDE. PICK.

- ❖ Please consider making a different choice.

- ❖ Act as if.....

- ❖ Check yourself...... do you have everything to do this?

- ❖ Check it out inside...... does it feel right?

- ❖ What's your goal? What's your intention?

- ❖ Make a picture in your mind. Positive picturing..

- ❖ I'm willing to help you complete this task.

- ❖ Avoid using always or never.... or it's easy! Or it's going to be hard or tough as a predictor!

- ❖ I know you can handle it!

- ❖ Every problem has a solution.

- ❖ Use 'next time' rather than 'don't do this...'

- ❖ Different people have different needs...... (it's not fair).

With our rapid 'time-poor' world I feel our capacity to communicate effectively with each other has deteriorated. We constantly e-mail and SMS one another, in an abbreviated and speedy way. Many children and teenagers have TV's and computers in their bedrooms and spend hours in their rooms experiencing virtual reality relationships instead of real ones around the dining table. And often these brief speedy messaging forms are misinterpreted. It is getting harder and harder to teach children at school the codes of language that are required to excel in tertiary studies. We seem to keep in touch more and yet we keep in touch in a shallow way. No wonder we are finding it hard to express our emotional states, and to manage stress. No wonder more and more of our children and teenagers are running away from home feeling unloved and unimportant. To feel loved and valued, our young need to feel connected and heard. They interpret how we feel about them through our verbal and non-verbal communication. Often they misinterpret our actions and our words! So be mindful of how you communicate to your child and maybe try asking them how you are doing as a parent!

Being present and really listening

The First Duty of Love is to Listen

When I ask you to listen to me, and you give me advice
You have not heard what I asked of you.
When I ask you to listen and you tell me why I
shouldn't feel as I do - you are trampling on my feelings.
When I ask you to listen and you feel you have to find
solutions to my problems - I feel let down, strange as it
may seem.
Please listen. All I ask is that you listen - not talk or do
or advise - just LISTEN.

Advice is cheap. I can get that anywhere.
I can do for myself. I'm not helpless.
Maybe discouraged and faltering, but not helpless.

When you do something for me that I can and need to
do for myself, you contribute to my fear and reinforce
my weaknesses.
When you accept as a simple fact, that I feel what I feel
however irrational it may sound to you, then I can quit
trying to convince you and I can then explore this that
irrational feeling.
When that's clear, the answers are obvious and I don't
need advice.
My irrational fears make sense when I can discover
what's behind them.
If you listen and understand I can work things out for
myself.

So I ask again. Just listen - and if you too have
something to say be patient,

Then I'll listen to you.

Source Unknown

The notion of being fully present when your child feels wounded or upset follows on from positive respectful communication. This is so important. Kids know when you are fully present with an open and understanding heart. Are you present for the small stuff not just the big stuff? They can tell when you are really listening. If your child comes home from school noticeably out of sorts and showing signs of distress, how you support them is critical. Often our first reaction is to question or interrogate them, yet this is best avoided! My suggestions are:

- ❖ as you drive home with them, send them loving thoughts;

- ❖ once home, ensure you have met their physical needs of hunger and thirst;

- ❖ create a safe place away from their siblings;

- ❖ build rapport in a way that is appropriate to that child, they are all different;

- ❖ open with "you seem to be not yourself this afternoon", or, "my Mum radar is going off that something is troubling you." Avoid using terms like, 'want to help', 'fix' or 'sort it out', as these invalidate. The worst is 'what's the matter with you'!

- ❖ if the child likes safe touch ask if you can give them a hug, back rub or stroke their head;

- ❖ if they are still processing their emotional world and not ready to share let them know that when they are ready will be OK by you, and then leave them alone; maybe remind them to breathe deeply;

- ❖ leave for 20 minutes at least and then take them a cup of Milo, hot chocolate or juice and a small plate of cut-up fruit or a cookie;

- ❖ when they begin to chat do not interrupt; nod and um, validate their feelings with 'that must have been hard for you', 'you must have felt frustrated';

❖ let them vent off their anger and frustrations, if they need to, without hushing them or judging them; let them talk their way through whatever they need to - this healthy diffusing.

❖ do not offer solutions, advice or try to fix it for them;

❖ help them to determine what needs of theirs were unmet in the conflict, maybe ask how they plan to resolve what has happened;

❖ if you can see something that may help them then ask: 'are you open to some Mum feedback or input?' and only give it if they say yes;

❖ when they seem calmer ask if they are OK, suggest that they give the problem some more thought and that you will reconnect later that evening to see how things are looking. This gives them time to sort through the situation from a more rational and balanced place; it helps them solve their own problems. Let them sleep on the problem and see how it looks in the morning.

❖ once they have vented their feelings I always try to use humour!

❖ if possible have your child lie down and hold their head gently with your right hand at the back of their head or on their neck; place your left hand on their forehead. This is very calming and reassuring. It helps them integrate emotional conflict and diffuses their emotional tension. They often sigh when they finish talking about what happened and how it made them feel. Ask your child to hold Mum or Dad's head the same way when you have a headache or feel stressed; it works like a charm;

❖ if you have promised to reconnect later then ensure that you do. Always finish on a light note, a laugh, hug or by doing a daggy thing like talking to a favourite toy or teddy; this is important as it helps their brain to be in a relaxed place before they sleep.

The Power Of Words

A group of frogs were travelling through the woods, and two of them fell into a deep pit. All the other frogs gathered around the pit. When they saw how deep the pit was, they told the two frogs that they were as good as dead.

The two frogs ignored the comments and tried to jump up out of the pit with all of their might. The other frogs kept telling them to stop, that they were as good as dead. Finally, one of the frogs took heed to what the other frogs were saying and gave up. He fell down and died.

The other frog continued to jump as hard as he could. Once again, the crowd of frogs yelled at him to stop the pain and just die. He jumped even harder and finally made it out. When he got out, the other frogs said, "Did you not hear us?"

The frog explained to them that he was deaf. He thought they were encouraging him the entire time.

This story teaches two lessons.

1. There is power of life and death in the tongue. An encouraging word to someone who is down can lift them up and help them make it through the day.

2. A destructive word to someone who is down can be what it takes to kill them. Be careful of what you say. Speak life to those who cross your path.
The power of words....it is sometimes hard to understand that an encouraging word can go such a long way. Anyone can speak words that tend to rob another of the spirit to continue in difficult times.

Author Unknown

Unintentionally we can kill a conversation or a dialogue we are having with someone. To make a meaningful, honest connection, have the intention of really caring about the person you are speaking to, stay present and match the rapport of that person. The experience is then positive for both of you. If you are not sure what to say, perhaps the person has just suffered a bereavement, then simply say that you do not know what the right thing to say is at that moment. Stay present with an open heart and they will feel your loving concern, which is actually what you intended. It really hurts when people avoid others because they don't know what to say. And yet they wish they could show their caring. Be honest and everyone wins.

Being really heard

❖ Let me put this down so I can give you my full attention.....

❖ Wait a second while I turn off the TV, radio, or computer so I can really hear you...

❖ This is not the best moment for me to give you my full attention. I will finish what I am doing and then come to your room. Is that OK?

❖ Turn your body toward them

❖ Make eye contact, but don't overdo it!

❖ Be comfortable with their silence and allow them the respect to communicate when it suits them

❖ Stay present both physically and mentally

I recommend that you really listen and do not ask questions. Remember if you are trying to fix them, rescue them or be a wiser person than they are then the sentence beginnings given will come across as patronising. So, be sure of your intentions.

The following are some beginnings of sentences that can help you communicate with someone who is distressed.

❖ Tell me more
❖ I am listening

- ❖ What you are saying is important to me...... tell me more

- ❖ What happened?

- ❖ How did you feel about it?

- ❖ I appreciate what you are saying

- ❖ I am trying to understand how you must have felt

- ❖ Are you saying that......

- ❖ Am I understanding you correctly that.......

- ❖ Do you mean to say that......

- ❖ I get the sense that you are frustrated, angry, disappointed, or really sad.......

- ❖ You seem upset.

- ❖ What needs of yours are not being met?

- ❖ How can I support you at this time?

- ❖ Thank you for letting me know

- ❖ Thank you for trusting me enough to confide in me

- ❖ What is your preferred solution to this conflict?
- ❖ What may be a learning opportunity you can take away from this experience?

I firmly believe that ineffective communication is behind and underlies all family and community disharmony. Unfortunately, where there is ineffective communication and emotional illiteracy conflict escalates. This is why emotional and social competencies are so important and need to be nurtured in our children, starting at as young an age as possible.

The healing potential of positivity

We are living in times with large amounts of new knowledge and research and intellectual property are valued enormously. Many parents and teachers suffer from a sense of inadequacy because of the thousands of books and programs that have been produced, as a way of making us better informed – including my book! For this reason I recommend that parents and teachers explore awareness and consciousness when helping children to be healthy, socially comfortable and happy to be themselves. Our belief system determines our behaviour whether intentionally or unintentionally. In the 60s and 70s two Harvard researchers, Rosenthal and Jacobson, did a study on the impact of classroom teachers' belief patterns on student performance.

The Oak experiment was when Robert Rosenthal of Harvard University did a study of 650 students and 18 female teachers. The aim was to show that the IQ test would identify the 20% of students who not only rated with highest IQ but who would also make rapid and superior progress throughout the year. The gifted students did perform superiorly …..yet the 20% were actually chosen randomly!

Rosenthal had done an earlier experience using rats where students were told that certain rats had been genetically bred to be superior in performance. Two groups were given 30 rats: group A were told they had the superior stock and group B were told they had the inferior stock. The rats were trained in the same environments and in the same ways yet the ones believed to be smarter "achieved achievement scores far above the supposed unintelligent rats". Yet the rats came from exactly the same gene pool and stock base.

Rosenthal's conclusion was simply that the minds of the experimenters influenced the performance of the rats and the students, both positively and negatively. This became known as the 'Pygmalion Effect'. Larry Dossey MD discussed the influence of the non-local mind, and the work of Rupert Sheldrake suggested that we are influenced by the non-local mind of significant people in our lives, like parents and teachers. This 'self-fulfilling prophecy' has validity in education particularly where students who are seen as being at educational risk usually do end up educationally disabled. It seems their demise is a consequence of both the teacher and the student accepting the label that has been assigned, often by people who are well meaning.

I have given this background so that you can better understand the concept that we carers help children create their realities. If you see your highly spirited son as hyperactive and having attention-deficit hyperactive disease (ADHD) you are supporting him to create the belief that he does have ADHD. Once he believes this then his mind creates the behaviour that matches the belief. The same goes for kids who are not ready to read by the first year of school. They see themself as flawed, dumb, and often develop a hatred of reading. Even if their reading ability does kick in the child still believes they are dumb. The result is that they cannot read easily and they behave accordingly.

It is so easy for parents to develop corresponding beliefs that support the assumed 'reality'. An important thing that parents can do is ensure that they see their children as unique, special and valued, even if they have delayed reading ability or lots of energy. Spend time visualizing your child in the preferred way. And avoid speaking about them as struggling, delayed or a pain! This is essential, even well out of their ear shot. It is about how we each create our beliefs. Remember the experiments that were carried out – students (and rats) performed to how they were perceived to be and not how they really were!

Mary Sheedy Kurcinka explored the devastating effect that labels can have on kids and their parents:

"Most of us find ourselves facing an array of labels spoken and unspoken that affect how we think, feel and act toward our spirited children. If we are going to build a healthy relationship with them, we must lay the labels out on the table, dissect them, and then redesign those that make us and our kids feel lousy. The lousy ones cloud our vision and hide the potential within."

Mary Sheedy Kurcinka. Raising Your Spirited Child: A guide for parents whose child is MORE, 1991

In her wonderful and resourceful book Kurcinka gives positive labels to replace the negative ones. This is to help reshape people's beliefs and unconscious expectations. Some of her suggestions are:

Demanding	Holds high standards
Unpredictable	Flexible, Creative Problem solver
Loud	Enthusiastic and zestful
Argumentative	Has Strength, holding strong opinions
Stubborn	Assertive, persistent
Nosy	Curious
Wild	Energetic
Anxious	Cautious
Picky	Selective

I believe that many of the children diagnosed as having ADHD are wrongly diagnosed. Many are highly spirited, energetic children who have been labelled as such early in their childhood. Once labelled, their parents, teachers and others treat them as ADHD. What else can they be? I firmly believe that we should try the following before taking a child to be tested for ADHD:

❖ take off any label and call them highly spirited;

❖ ensure they are getting plenty of sleep

❖ practise positive, respective communication;

❖ teach them how to manage their energy field;

❖ make sure they are not eating bread with the preservative 282;

❖ try giving them supplements of fish oil tablets;

❖ teach them calming and centring techniques;

❖ allow them plenty of play outside in the fresh air;

❖ see them as the new normal – kids who learn

fast, see the world differently, and who deserve unconditional acceptance for who they are and not who others want them to be;

❖ ensure they feel loved and that their love cup is filled despite any society stereotypical behaviour towards them – this includes close connection to a loving adult;

❖ avoid passive technologically-driven entertainment, play and toys, like TV, computers and game boys;

❖ avoid too much talking and too many commands and directions.

If you have tried all these and you see no improvements then please take your child to a paediatric health professional for diagnosis.

How many parents with young children are secretly dreading the teenage years? Guess what you are doing? You are supporting the belief that they will be awful and challenging! I really looked forward to my boys' teenage years. This was 'by accident', as I enjoyed teaching teenagers. My youngest son now heads towards his seventeenth birthday and the older three are no longer teenagers but I have to admit the teenage years were wonderful years, with lots of laughter, growth and genuine connection. The boys are each unique and enjoy the ride of life even though they all have moments they wish they hadn't. I pray every day for my sons' safety. I never allow my mind to imagine disasters of any kind, especially around cars and city living. So far this has worked.

Having an optimistic, positive mind set toward your child and his or her potential is really important in helping them to grow in a healthy way. What mental representation do you have of your most challenging child? Are you expecting them to get into trouble at school? Maybe you are expecting them to be crabby and disrespectful to you when they come home? On the other hand, look forward to them walking in the door alive and well – be deeply grateful that they have their health and a roof over their head.

Please be aware of the thoughts patterns and beliefs you hold in your mind. Be aware and conscious that you have the power to choose positive life-enhancing thoughts that allow you to support your child and a positive version of who they can be and are.

Create a family solution-seeking process

The most harmonious families I know use family meetings to make big decisions. These decisions may be where to go for summer holidays and how to run the family home. Doing this helps children develop negotiation skills and makes them feel valued and respected. A family solution-seeking process also helps to resolve problems and conflicts. A simple, easy to follow process that may work for your family is described by Chick Moorman and Thomas Haller. They suggest seven steps.

❖   See the problem as an opportunity.
❖   Define the problem.
❖   Brainstorm possible solutions.
❖   Reach consensus.
❖   Commit.
❖   Set a date to evaluate.
❖   Evaluate.

Chick Moorman and Thomas Haller. The 10 Commitments: Parenting with Purpose 2005

The first step is really important; see any problem as an opportunity to learn or to grow. It changes the problem immediately from a punitive focus of allocating blame to one of finding a solution that works for everyone. In this way you help your family build its capacity to manage and resolve conflict. They can take this with them in life and when they live with others having been taught really valuable life skills.

No child is too young or too old to be involved. Allow your children the respect of being a part of family life regardless of age. This helps to build their inner sense of value and worthiness. It teaches them how to see the world from other people's perspectives and builds empathy – a key component in emotional literacy and competency. Involvement also has a bigger purpose. Solution seeking and problem solving takes place in the area of the brain called the frontal lobe. This area is the output and control centre for behaviour; it is also the area that has 'holes' in it in the brain scans of very violent individuals.

The frontal lobe is where we make choices, choosing from options, comparing possible outcomes and managing our behaviour. When we are in the 'red room', or the brain stem, we are likely to express emotion through yelling, kicking and slamming doors. This is our survival centre and it is where our basic functional autonomic nervous system exists. However, to resolve any issue we need to calm down and move to the multi-coloured room, the limbic brain. This is where our emotions are created. Once we can identify and understand what emotions we are feeling we can then move to the blue room, the frontal lobe. This is the part of the brain where we are capable of processing at a higher level, which is something unique to humans. We help our children develop these functions when we give them opportunities to work out solutions to problems. Those individuals who have a low emotional competency tend to stay in the brain stem (red room), and maybe the multi-coloured room. They seldom move to the blue room to consider balanced solutions to problems. Because of this they consider that the only way to end conflict is with violence; and that is what they do, over and over again. As Glenn Capelli and Brealey wrote:

"The blue room is where our higher order thinking occurs. It is where we understand, comprehend, and store important memories that have been learnt through experiences."

Capelli and Brealey. The Thinking Learning Classroom 2000, p99

Many problems can be solved creatively using cooperation and negotiation. With careful guidance you can help your child become a creative problem solver well before the adolescent years. You can use the skills to help maintain family harmony, fairness and respect. Family members are then capable of being able to respond from their own inner authority.

"The new children have a keen system of justice; they respond well to democratic approaches in which they have a voice in decision making and poorly to authoritarian parenting styles."

Linda Kreger Silverman. Creating A Supportive Family in Children of a New Earth Magazine Summer 2003, p46

Innovative healing techniques

In the early chapters I explored the elements of personal healing, made up of loving care, emotional diffusing and the need to change the core concepts that support the wounds. Many of the strategies in this chapter overlap. Several years ago I was intuitively drawn to a seminar on Emotional Freedom Techniques (EFT). What was espoused during the seminar seemed too good to be true! EFT is a new energy psychology that assists people of all ages to overcome irrational patterns of dysfunction, both quickly and effectively. It is especially good with children and men! If you have a chance, attend a seminar and discover for yourself how you can help your children overcome simple things like irrational fears, negative attitudes and feeling overwhelmed with negative emotions.

A beautifully illustrated book written by the two psychologists Steve Wells and Jo Wiese, called Rose and the Night Monsters, tells how EFT can work with children. It is a story of a little girl Rose who is really scared about having a sleepover at Grandma's. The pictures show how magical tapping completely took away Rose's fears about monsters. For anyone who has not experienced EFT this sounds unbelievable. I love the technique because it is quick. By using it you give your family a tool to use later in life when they have a family and wish to cancel any irrational fears that appear in their children's lives. I have used EFT for myself so that I can settle at night and go to sleep, get rid of headaches and to prepare myself for really large conference presentations. I have also used it to help students lose their fear of public speaking and to prepare for examinations. It is a tool for life that I encourage you all to try. I believe it is a skill all counsellors and chaplains should learn because kids and teenagers feel so much better after EFT, and quickly.

Another healing therapy similar to EFT is thought field therapy. It uses the same tapping technique and is the process I use to help people release phobias and deep-seated patterns of dysfunction. Its creator was Dr John Callahan who was a well respected psychiatrist. He was concerned that traditional psychotherapy was effective for only a low percentage of his patients and was very slow and time consuming. Thought field therapy can create almost miraculous results and the lowering of tension in a person's nervous system is discernable using a heart rate monitor. Young children see the therapy as a magic tapping dance, a game that is fun.

I am a huge advocate for both of these energy therapies. When used by caring and committed therapists they do help people make very noticeable positive changes in their lives, quickly. They are amazingly simple and can be learned over a weekend. I recommend all parents to learn at least one of them and teach simple aspects to their children. Anxiety and fear can be dissolved in minutes through these tapping therapies. The best way is to learn how to use these techniques yourself and control your own levels of nervous tension and stress. They are also excellent at clearing serious phobias that can be life debilitating like fear of public speaking, flying, spiders and water.

Neuro Linguistic Programming (NLP) also has some excellent innovative techniques that help children who are struggling. Many of the techniques are explored in NLP books that are available in local libraries. The techniques that I like for children are:

- ❖ the magic eye scramble

- ❖ reframing

- ❖ positive visioning or preferred future or solution

- ❖ life enhancing language strategies

- ❖ embedded commands

- ❖ time lines

- ❖ circle of confidence

- ❖ the resource triangle.

The power of mental rehearsal and creative visualization

Creative imagining using the most favourable outcomes is considered an essential activity for fast tracking personal achievements in all areas of life. This has been briefly touched on before. I wish to reaffirm the importance of this approach for helping our children to develop positive mind patterns and beliefs. I firmly believe that with more awareness of the power of inner thought patterns, visualization and language, especially for children before ten years of age, we can help turn around the frightening escalation of failure and low achievement. We can give our children the tools for life that allow them to manage their negative feelings states and their emotionally destructive patterns BEFORE they get to puberty when everything accelerates and life becomes even more unpredictable.

"I'd prefer to see parents spending time with their children learning to visualize, rather than spending time in front of the television set or reading bedtime stories. It's important to teach yourself and your children manifestation techniques with visualization."

Doreen Virtue. The Care and Feeding of Indigo Children

In 1998 I was given a small class of low achievers in English. They were all boys. I decided to work at changing both their mental and emotional perceptions of English classes and their inner beliefs and perceptions about how well they would perform at the end of term. We created 'the Best Report Ever' visualization. It involved taking the students into a quiet relaxed place and imagining them taking home their very best report ever – it guided them to imagine the best report ever - with good grades and positive comments written by teachers. They also imagined how Mum reacts, how Dad reacts and how proud the boy feels within himself. The students enjoyed the activity as they were able to feel positive about themselves; and the body followed the mind. About four weeks into the term a maths teacher asked me what I was doing with those 'grommets'. He was wondering why they had started handing in their maths work. What the boys hadn't realised was that their inner perceptions of their potential had changed, without coercion or threats. Every one of those boys took home the best report they had ever achieved! They were further surprised because they improved in all their subjects and not just English. A key aspect to remember with visualization is that the brain cannot tell the difference between vividly imagined and real, and so it thinks it has already done what it has imagined. For the boys the brain thought it had taken home this excellent report at least eight times, so the automatic change in behaviour is effortless!

Parents often tell me how the relaxation CD they bought for their stressed teenager has not only calmed them at exam time but has also helped change how the teenager sees his or herself. Their self esteem has grown. The repeated use of positive creative visualization techniques changes our unconscious belief system without effort. We often sleep better as a bonus. This is why men who had to listen to a calming visualization because their wife was suffering stress suddenly find people telling them they are easier to work with and seem happier. Making change without suffering is the best possible way to change!

The truth sets us free

Emotionally and spiritually we create tension and unease when we are acting out of alignment of our truth. When we avoid telling someone how we really feel, or we
hide a secret misdemeanour for years we create tension in our nervous system. When we share the secret with someone, or we tell the truth, our nervous system is eased and dissolves the tension it was holding. This is the key aspect of counselling – telling the truth, of "slaying the dragon within." The good news is that using the principles of creative visualization, setting ourselves free and telling the truth can be just as helpful on the inner level of imagination as it is in the real world. This is how I help people resolve unfinished business with loved ones who have died, and with people who they have lost touch with. The meditative state is a powerful tool for healing.

In 1998 at the Jack Canfield Facilitator's seminar I did the truth process. This process (see below) was shared with a beautiful woman from Santa Barbara. We both chose to do the process about our fathers who had died. I thought I was "over" my Dad's death, as he had died four years before and that I had no unfinished business with him. As we were guided through the following, I found I had so many unexpressed emotions especially as a little girl, that I was able to come to a new state of healing and peace.

This process can be done as a letter that once written can be destroyed. It will still set you free of much unresolved emotional pain. Please take an hour or two and try this.

Truth Letter Exercise

Sometimes we can resolve issues with people by writing an honest letter to them....sometimes we do not even need to give them the letter, but the mere process of acknowledging what troubles you is enough to resolve it inside yourself.

Dear...........
I am writing this letter to release my resentment and negative emotions and to discover and express any positive feelings that I might have towards you.

Anger

I don't like.........
I feel angry.........
I hate it when.........
I can't stand.........
I resent.........

Hurt

It hurt me when.........
I feel hurt that.........
I feel sad when.........
I feel awful about.........
I feel disappointed about.........

Fear

I'm afraid that ....
I feel scared when.........
I'm afraid ....
I get afraid of you when.........

Remorse, Regret, Accountability

I'm sorry that ....
Please forgive me for.........
I'm sorry for ....
I didn't mean to..........

Wants

All I ever wanted.........
I want you to.........
I want.........
I deserve..........

Love, Compassion, Forgiveness, Appreciation

I understand that ....
I appreciate.........
I forgive you for......
I love you because ....
I love you when.........
Thank you for ....

Adapted from 1997 Self Esteem Seminars, Santa Barbara, US with permission from Jack Canfield. www.jackcanfield.com

In conclusion, I wish to affirm that kids respond best to loving care from the people they love the most. Really listening, being fully present and staying positive about life, love and living all help a child build a positive sense of self. Yes, children need a lot of reassurance and encouragement. They need a home that is safe and a life that is consistent and fair. These are essential elements in the healthy healing of our kids. Having a circle of people who care around a child ensures that someone is close by who can help them when life is unfair, bites them or the wheels fall off. Resilient children bounce back from set backs quickly – and they have learned that life is not perfect, and yet that they can overcome problems. The three key protective factors that a longitudinal study in the Bronx discovered about resiliency, that helped children from one of the worst social environments to become effective and successful in life were

❖ sense of humour
❖ healthy detachment
❖ one significant adult who cared and believed in them.

When helping a child to heal, remember these three factors and avoid " awfulizing", blaming, invalidating and complicating. Keep things simple and reassure their capacity to manage and overcome the challenge that is facing them. Remember a child's capacity to make choices and to accept responsibility for his/her actions is essential for healthy emotional, social and spiritual competency later in life. This is how they grow in competency. Help them find their own inner voice of truth or "wise counsel" early in life and remind them that it is always waiting to help them to heal from emotional, physical and spiritual pain. If you can also find the same voice within yourself, then healing will be ever sweeter and deeper.

Key Points

❖ Early abuse can damage a child for life

❖ Serious abuse needs professional help

❖ Breath work helps to diffuse emotions

❖ Positive safe touch is essential for young children

❖ Teaching children about safe touch is important as over 90% of incidences of abuse come from someone they know

❖ Positive respectful communication helps children feel valued and heard

❖ Unmet needs drive much of the emotional conflict in families

❖ Being fully present and really listening helps children to heal, feel loved and valued

❖ Life-enhancing language supports the growth of healthy minds, hearts and souls

❖ Be aware of the harms caused by negative labelling of children

❖ Stay as positive as possible in your mental processing – thought fields influence others

❖ Explore the whole ADHD picture before

medicating your child

❖ Create a family solution-seeking process for your family

❖ Give children opportunities to problem solve and resolve conflict

❖ EFT, thought field therapy and creative visualization can help children to heal

❖ Mental rehearsal is a valuable life skill for children

❖ The truth sets us free

❖ The inner voice of truth will help children to heal

Chapter 6

Building Intuition and Inner Guidance

"Thoughts have a higher dwelling place than the visible world, and its skies are not clouded by sensuality. Imaqination finds a road to the realm of the gods, and there man can glimpse that which is to be after the soul's liberation from the world of substance."

Kahlil Gibran 2001

I discovered an interesting piece of knowledge while researching brain development in early childhood. It was that in the first two years of life the brain stem or the reptilian part of the brain is still growing, and this is where 'goodness orientation' is shaped and formed. The need for healthy bonding, love and attachment has been known for a long time and we now have documented with brain scans the disastrous affects of deprivation of these essential baby needs. We only have to recall the frightening images of the children in the orphanages in Russia following the Chernobyl disaster to see how completely debilitating the absence of tactile and emotional bonding has on the healthy development of the child. The brain scans are from these children.

Goodness orientation was new to me and yet it makes a lot of sense. A new baby is unable to communicate verbally and yet it has an enormous ability to open hearts and to challenge adults. When a baby is able to feel protected, safe and cared for then the dendrites that are extensions of the nerves in brain matter are able to grow. Memory of a kind is imprinted in the brain and can be recalled from an unconscious level later in life. The senses smell, touch and sound have the ability to bypass the cognitive parts of the brain and become part of those memories.

I remember seeing my boys, as school boys, go all soft and cuddly when their faces came in contact with our sheepskin floor mat. They had all slept on sheepskins as babies and the strong memories had an instant impact on their physiology, even though they were now older and 'tougher'. The same goes for soft touch and stroking, which is also experienced in those first two years. Stroking restless boys softly on the forehead induces calming yet this strong effect is almost involuntary or unconscious. These are deep memories that can still be accessed. Logically the reverse must be so. If a child has been deprived of safe gentle touch and loving care then the memories of unmet need stay deep in the brain. The orientation to being gentle and loving will also be absent and maybe this can be part of the explanation for some children being more emotionally illiterate than others?

The goodness orientation may also be explored by using the term intuition. John Miller in his book The Holistic Curriculum explained intuition as 'direct knowing'. This is in contrast to linear thought which involves a sequential, observable process. Frances Vaughan (1979) described four levels of intuition – the physical, emotional, intellectual and spiritual levels. Essentially, intuition is a knowingness that stands outside logical, rational thought. Intuition occurs to assist an individual to make choices that are of a positive nature, especially around situations of personal safety. My son Ben was once chopping some kindling for the fire when he hit his finger with the axe! As we were driving to the hospital emergency department I asked him if he remembered having any thoughts just before he brought the axe down. His reply was that he did, and the thought was that it wasn't a good idea! He continued anyway.

Over the years I have asked many children and teenagers who have hurt themselves, or made a decision which they later regretted, if they had a thought or a sense that this was something they would later regret. Overwhelmingly they have all had an intuitive thought that they chose to ignore. Indeed, in research Andrew Weil (1972) has come up with the hypothesis that:

'The intuitive consciousness or what he calls the non-linear consciousness is an innate normal drive analogous to hunger or the sex drive."

This has also been my experience. As a child I spent a lot of time in nature, which allowed me to develop a healthy imagination and a deep comfort for non-linear thinking. My four years at university caused a distortion in my psyche because the required cognitive, linear and logical way of thinking conditioned me to question my intuition and my inner knowing. I came to think that if what I thought could not be supported by evidence then it was not valid, or important. These were the darkest years of my life. My suicide attempt after failing a politics essay was the result of a serious disconnection to my spirit, thanks to the unbalanced structure of how I perceived my university education. The message for me was to keep a balance between the two levels of thinking – the logical rational and the intuitive non-linear. I never experienced that darkness again as I returned to my poetry writing and spending time in nature. The failed attempt at suicide was a moment of awakening that I now see as a gift. Because I have experienced the depth of disconnection and deep despair that so many of my teenage clients experience, I am able to understand these teenagers from an empathetic place. We are not able to reach this place of understanding depression and thoughts of suicide from a text book.

Our fast paced, overstimulated world is full of visual, auditory and kinaesthetic stimuli. The overload of stimuli is contributing to a weakening of the gift of intuition, which is our inner guidance. Intuition can become stronger when children calm down and practice stillness in their lives. Their sense of self and self esteem also becomes stronger and more positive. Our inner guidance is really the best friend we have. It strives to help us become the best person we can be and keeps us safe, healthy and on a positive course in our lives. It is important that children are given opportunities to develop their intuition and to hear the silent voice within. The relaxation activities and visualizations that are now being introduced into classrooms around the world are an excellent way of doing this.

Sharing within families also provides positive learning. One of my sons felt rejected when he returned to his primary school after the summer holidays, because his teachers had separated him from his two best friends by putting him in a different classroom. He was so upset that he refused to stay at school that first day. Back at home we chatted about how he felt and explored that he did have choices. His emotions were running pretty high despite the chat. I encouraged him to go outside for a while so that we could have another look at the situation. When he came back inside I asked him to sit quietly and consider the question "Do I stay or do I go?"

First, I encouraged him to empty all thoughts from his mind so that he could take note of the next thought that came up. A few moments and it was clear to him that it was time to move on. We had already explored the option of moving to a new school, leaving his old friends, so I knew this was his intuitive voice accepting that option. He did change schools and this was really important for his social development. It enabled him to create a different persona for himself within a year. To do this can be challenging to strong-minded almost teenage boys when they are surrounded by their mates. The new school was keen on school camps and community-based programmes, which I now believe helped to shape the social conscience that set him on the path to become the lawyer he is today.

"Each of us has a wise part within, an intuitive part that knows what is best for us. Learning how to contact, listen to, and trust that inner authority are important skills. They are invaluable when life presents us with problems whose answers are not found in the back of the book."

Chick Moorman. Parent Talk 2003

A simple shift in focus can strengthen the intuitive voice within children. It allows them to balance their rational and intuitive thoughts. Creating more quiet time and spaces to simply 'be', within the pressures of our chaotic world, is enormously important for our children. It keeps a connection to their inner knowing. I have found that children who played freely in the natural world as young children tend to have strong intuitions, more so than children who have lead more confined childhoods. Once again, the passive, highly visual world of TVs and computers starves the intuition and makes it harder to find.

The theologian Caroline Myss PhD wrote:

"The intuitive sense of connection is moving us as a planet toward a holistic understanding of health and disease, of the environment and its biodiversity and of social priorities for service and charity."

Caroline Myss. The Anatomy of the Spirit 1996, p271

I see a narrowing of the gap between medicine, scientific and spiritual disciplines. Rupert Sheldrake's fascinating scientific studies around telepathy and morphic fields is an excellent example. He has shown that when there is a very strong emotional connection between participants in a study situation, be they people or pets, then an overlap in their non-local minds can become apparent. This is what happens when a dog waits at the door as an owner comes home. It became apparent that the dog would move to the door to wait when the owner first turned his thoughts toward home, even when arrival times were random. The dog did not wait until the owner was pulling into the driveway or when the train pulled up at the nearby station - another example of intuition or non-logical knowing.

A key element to the ability to tune in to another is emotional attachment. Breastfeeding mothers experience this when they are away from their babies and their milk lets down spontaneously. It turns out their baby has woken and is crying, although they did not know it at the time - once again an example of the non-rational thinking mind.

My brother is an exceptionally good emergency doctor. Wayne also has an extensive background as a country general practitioner or GP. He was appointed to the emergency department because the hospital could not fill the emergency positions when it opened. Country general practice was seen as great practical training for emergency medicine. He too has found and shares my passion for the emotional and spiritual exploration of life, and for meaning, which might be a little challenging at times because of his scientific background.

One day we were chatting about the notion of holistic medicine and he became defensive, explaining that he 'wasn't one of them'. I asked him what he would say to a person who had a debilitating illness that persisted in being hard to diagnose. His response was that he would suggest they took a holiday and had a serious look at their life, perhaps make some significant changes. As I argued that this was holistic medicine he became less defensive and shared the following story with me. They had an emergency at the hospital when a gentleman came in experiencing a heart attack. Wayne and a fully trained emergency doctor were on duty (to be fully trained in a specialty you have to complete six extra years of training in Australia). Following the initial examination, my brother decided to inject straight into the heart with the appropriate medication. Soon the man was in recovery and well on the way to being alive and well. The other doctor in attendance asked Wayne how he had come to make the decision so quickly and was able to act so decisively. Wayne replied that he had made a logical rational decision based on what he observed. He then ran his decision past his gut as he knew that if it felt good it was the correct decision.

The fully trained doctor confided that he felt that his extra training had made him focus only on the logical and rational consequences. The result was being overly cautious and tentative. Wayne is recognised as very competent in his field with his intuition and intellect in fine balance. Now he has stepped back from full-time emergency medicine because he was spending more time on the telephone finding beds than he was working with patients who needed his expertise. Sad but true. He uses similar techniques to make decisions on the stock market.

Children have a strong intuitive sense; and it is adults who play havoc with it and often distort it. Have you seen children pull away from some family members? Maybe they don't want a hug from an uncle or a grandad. When we make a child hug someone they feel uncomfortable about, we are putting their intuition in doubt. Children have a 'yukky' barometer. They 'just know' how they feel around some people. As adults we need to be careful to honour that so that the children do not question their intuition later in life.

I have concerns about the stranger danger programs that well-meaning people run for children. Only 10% of perpetrators of child abuse are strangers. I especially disliked the TV programs where 'fake strangers' came to family homes. The parents watched from a nearby car to test their children. If we make children fear all strangers, instead of any adults who make them feel 'yukky' or uncomfortable, then what happens when they become genuinely lost? How many familiar people or policeman do you see walking around shopping centres or suburbs of a city?

One of my sons became lost when we were visiting family in Perth while he was still young. He had experienced the stranger danger program at his pre-school. When we re-located him, he told us he had run away from everyone who came to help because they were strangers! He was looking for a policeman. Fortunately he saw a lady who looked like a friend of ours and went up to her. She helped to bring him back safely.

Instead of disempowering children's intuition we should encourage and strengthen it. We can do this by taking children to places where it is unsafe under our supervision and see how they feel. Make them wary of dark lanes, isolated parks and playing alone away from home. Teach them how to scream if approached and what safe house signs look like. I would also teach children the power of prayer and to ask for help from the Divine.

I have found that children have a strong sense of their own safety when playing on play equipment or out in nature. One of my boys was a tree climber. I knew that I had to keep quiet when he was climbing because my fear could influence his own innate sense of safety. He never fell out of a tree. He only ever hurt himself on mechanical things like motor bikes and skateboards! I have seen parents pull children off climbing frames because the parents were frightened that the child may fall. If we distort a child's inner knowing of their ability we can limit their understanding of themselves - not just at that moment in time but in the future as well. It is hard to restore a child's confidence and the need to be able to take learning risks once interrupted or impeded.

A child's sense of safety does not mean that children will never make poor decisions. Life teaches through experience. For this reason it is important for children to be able to learn through unpleasant experiences as well as good. Indeed, traditional indigenous communities believe that experiential learning for children is best, as children learn for themselves. A child who picks up a hot coal will only ever do it once! At the International Spirit of Learning Conference in Northern New South Wales a very wise Native American called Chuck shared in his address the importance of allowing children to interpret their world through experience. This sits well with the premise that undirected play, with as little parental supervision as possible, is how children learn best.

"Our highest endeavour must be to develop individuals who are able out of their own initiative to impart purpose and direction to their lives."

Rudolph Steiner. (taken from Byron Child Magazine 2005;15:32

A lot of children's learning comes from modelling others. In today's technological world much of this type of learning comes from virtual experiences, rather than real experiences. Children model on characters from TV programs like soapies and reality programs, far removed from real life. Nothing beats real life with its varied experiences as much as is possible. This provides the perfect environment to grow a healthy intuition that can guide any individual through life. Overexposure to TV and computers stifles a child's natural intuitive abilities.

I often use the term higher self, the higher level of our mind, when sharing how the intuition works for children. The explanation I use is that our minds can be seen as twins. One is noisy, often critical and judgemental, and likes to follow linear apparently rational thoughts, even though these sometimes turn out to be irrational. The other twin is much quieter and needs to be tuned in to in order to be heard. It often gives short guidance, very different to that of its twin. A simple way to teach children to solve problems or make a tough decision is to have them imagine that they can put the problem on a plate. They then hold the plate up to the sky and ask that their higher self, or God, solve it for them. They can then imagine it, the problem, being taken away. A solution will be received in some form within the next few days. This technique has saved me hours of sleeplessness and has never failed to give me the guidance that helps me in my daily life.

Children and adults' intuition can be improved by selecting images that may be of favourite animals or birds. For me, this means rainbows, happy white clouds, a full moon, the flowering trees that I love, blue wrens, white doves or pigeons, ducks, owls, roses, wildflowers, wisteria, English lilacs, kangaroo paws or happy children and dogs. When I am visiting a new place I know I am safe and protected when any of my images actually appear. When there is a complete absence of these things, dark skies and nothing beautiful, I leave fast. Encouraging children to seek 'reminders of goodness' gives their intuition an avenue to express its inner guidance.

I had a really frightening experience once when visiting Sedona in the US. My sister and I came across a National Park called Secret Mountain that was full of natural beauty. It had bubbling streams, lush greenery and many birds. I even saw my first woodpecker! As we were leaving we were told where there was a medicine wheel right off the usual tourist route. We followed our directions along a dirt road and I became aware that my body was feeling cold and very heavy. The sky became overcast and the scenery was dry and rocky. When we turned the next corner we drove past a big pick-up truck that had four rifles lined up in racks on the back window. The driver stood next to the vehicle smoking and watched us as we drove by. My body went into complete alert and I started to shiver. As soon as we could we turned around and made our way back to the main road. The driver of the pick-up had begun to follow us so that we passed each other going in opposite directions. I 'know' that if we had kept going our lives would have been threatened. A well nurtured intuition is an important asset in anyone's lives.

A well-developed intuition is an enormous asset especially in a teenager's life with the high-risk situations that many teenagers find themselves in. Before going into a party or accepting a ride from someone I check how my intuition is feeling. Parties can change quickly from being safe and enjoyable into uncontrollable fights and chaos. Teenagers have shared with me how they had intuitively known when to leave a party, BEFORE any conflict started. They found out about the trouble the next day. A real concern is that alcohol and drugs inhibit the power of the intuition. That may be a reason why there are so many accidents among the adolescent population. Weak intuition and inexperience can have deadly consequences.

A fifteen-year old once shared a story about an intriguing sense of 'knowing', in one of my classes. While she was at home in her room her father was working on his tractor down in the paddock. She became aware of feeling uncomfortable and uneasy. When she went out into the garden her unease became stronger. She clearly remembers the message, "something's happened to Dad", and headed off down the paddock as quickly as she could. She soon discovered that her Dad was injured and was able to run back home and arrange for help, then returned to her Dad's side to wait until help arrived. Uncanny and yet true. From that point on in her life she believed that she had a guardian who kept watch over her.

I clearly remember my Mum being very intuitive when I was a child. On one occasion she drove out to a very back paddock, many kilometres away, to discover that my Dad's truck had broken down. He was walking home to get some help. My Mum also knew when I needed assistance in my life and would always act upon her instincts without question.

I am grateful that I have such a keen intuitive sense as it has helped me to come to the aid of others, at times when my conscious and logical mind was unaware that something was seriously wrong. There is a strong interplay between intuition and the natural world for me. The bush is my second home. The seasons resonate with me, my life journey and my connection to the natural world empowers my intuition. I can feel quite scattered and disconnected if I am unable to spend time in nature, daily. Even if it's a city park, a lake or a pond I replenish myself and reconnect to my goodness orientation in nature. I sense that the alienation so many people living in cities experience is driven by disconnection from the natural world. Rachael Kessler writes of the many ways to build connectedness. One way is through a:

"**Deep Connection to Nature**   For some it is the beauty and majesty of nature that calls forth awe and wonder that satisfies and feeds the spirit."

Rachael Kessler. The Soul of Education 2000 p 52

When I taught at an inner city school back in 1979 I was concerned that city students knew so little about their country counterparts and how it was to live in the country. The result was that I took around twenty-five students to stay for a few days at my family's farm. There they witnessed sheep shearing and also played basketball with students in a nearby town. They were fascinated with the process of shearing wool from a sheep and with the acres of space. Most of them had never been camping before and so they were challenged in many ways. My family farm was near a place called Wandering, in the South West of Western Australia. In October in spring it is very beautiful with green crops, fat sheep and lambs and many wild flowers in the bush. At that time of year it is very sunny during the day, around 20 degrees centigrade, however during the night it can drop to minus one or two. This was exactly what happened! The students had never been so cold in their lives and many sat around the camp fire all night to keep warm, rather than sleep in their sleeping bags. During the day they saw a dam that looked inviting. Anyone who knows about farm dams knows how cold they are, even on a hot summer's day. A couple of the boys dived in for a quick dip and it would have been the fastest swim they have ever had in their lives.

Later the students shared how amazing the few days had been for them and how they loved the quiet and beauty of the countryside. They wanted to stay and enjoy some more, not having missed the shops, traffic and the fast pace of city living. Unfortunately, very soon the students forgot the calmness and beauty of the country.

Intuition and being able to access higher awareness and guidance is one of the best ways of disempowering our inner critic. The incessant voice of the inner critic begins very early in life. It is always reminding us of our inadequacies, imperfections and that we are basically not good enough! One has to first be aware that the inner critic exists before being able to witness its diatribe, and step back from it. By teaching our children that the inner critic exists we help them to realise they are not the only person who has one. They can then create strategies that allow them to detach from it. Once again, play is a beautiful way to build detachment from the inner critic, non-competitively and creatively, if possible.

The state of transcendence that we all yearn for is really a state where the inner critic is completely disempowered. We can feel expanded and free of criticism and judgment. This mind-body state of bliss is free of anxiety and worry and allows us to feel safely expanded, 'out of the ordinary'. In moments of such transcendence we see ourselves with clarity and in the most positive way imaginable. No wonder we yearn to find transcendence. No wonder many seek it by using alcohol, drugs and medication. The strange paradox is that this state of freedom is an inner journey of acceptance and release. When induced from outside it is transitory, brief and often has unpleasant side effects. When transcendence comes from within, perhaps with deep relaxation, a meditation or time of stillness in nature there are no unpleasant side effects! Yes, achieving this state requires a little effort and time to create and yet the benefit is long-lasting and does not risk our health. Children love the state of transcendence and often, if allowed, they can step into this place while in self-absorbed play.

Homes and schools are full of more external stimulations than ever before. Is it any wonder that our children are struggling with hyperactivity, anxiety and emotional unpredictability? Essentially, technology does not nurture the inner world of children. Children's intuition may very well be stunted by its use, especially with high levels of contact before they are 10 years of age.

The importance of intuition and a capacity to 'sense' another person's emotional and attitudinal space is something that all of us have, at least to some degree. People who are able to hold genuine warmth and unconditional acceptance and support of others are very important in each other's lives. William Bloom calls these people:

> "life's true heroes. They carry a supportive and positive attitude that endures, especially in times of crisis. They do not drop away when the going gets tough or when there is a period of failure and struggle. They remain constant, seeing the best, supporting and accepting even when things are at their worst. They are good leaders, companions and friends."

William Bloom. The Endorphin Effect 2001

Boys in our schools perform better with teachers who care about them. This has been shown in studies. Maybe the boys are able to intuitively sense whether people have the warmth that Bloom writes about. They then behave accordingly. Perhaps some of the inappropriate behaviour we observe is the result of children responding negatively to adults who are themselves struggling to find their own 'goodness within'?

A chapter on intuition and inner knowing would not be complete without mentioning synchronicity. More and more, people are becoming aware of the flow of reality and the incredulous ways that our own realities and lives connect and influence others. I am told many stories, from ordinary everyday people, about coincidental events that they have found both inexplicable and mysterious. I remember someone once saying, "Coincidences are miracles where God chooses to remain anonymous". When we take unexpected turns and find ourselves in the perfect place we are surprised. What if that was our inner guidance working, our intuitive sense bringing us to the place where our heart and soul wanted to be and not our intellect?

I have a special friend in my life who, when she was seventeen, was to attend a concert with three others. The concert was in the city about five hours from her home town. For some inexplicable reason she wasn't able to go. The friends were all killed in a car accident just half an hour from home, caused by fatigue. I am sure you have heard of stories about people who have missed planes that later crashed and others who delayed visiting a place where a tragedy then occurred.

Being able to cultivate a healthy intuition in our children may very well save their lives one day. It is easy to help them nurture their intuition if you start before they are five years old, definitely before they are ten! To tap into inner guidance it helps to do three things:

❖ become centred and fully present
❖ breathe deeply and slow the body and the mind
❖ actively seek the quiet voice within.

Nurturing our intuition allows us to both consciously and unconsciously access our wisdom within. The fact that we are doing that at all means that we know we have a higher intelligence. It also helps us to know that answers from the inner well come in many ways and shapes. Sometimes it is a single word, sometimes an image of a person or a place, or a clear sense of a choice to make. Often the choice does not appear to be rational. The reason for that is probably so that you can see the difference between the intellect and intuition!

When making life's big choices, I encourage students and adults to list all the rational options they can think of. I then ask them to 'go within'. It helps if they do this in a safe place, perhaps in a natural place that is familiar to them, and where they will not be distracted. Tapping into intuition is also why it's helpful to suggest to a troubled person that they 'sleep on it' before choosing a solution. Taking a gap year works well for many teenagers before they embark on a tertiary study course. It gives them a chance to explore the world and experience life from a different perspective before committing themselves to three of four years of study. Changing later can be expensive and very challenging. To have a pause before making important decisions helps, regardless of age or experience.

The younger children are when we encourage them to ponder, or to 'check it out within', the more natural this intuitive process becomes. Doing so may later help them to make better choices in exams, around their friends and in social commitments.

At times, my intuition is a source of great mirth in our family and with my boys. They have seen my 'reading' or sense of 'signs' as something completely wacky. Yet, I allowed them to make their own decisions from the age of sixteen, without lectures or nagging from me, because I honoured their own intuitive good sense. I do remember a time when one of the boys decided to go to a big party on someone's property where there was no supervision. Everything inside me wanted to shout "NO, don't go, it's unsafe!" I kept my lips sealed knowing that they had to begin making choices themselves. On the night before the party my son came and said really casually, "Mum I've decided not to go to that party – is it OK if we have a movie night here instead for my friends?" I am surprised he did not hear me yelling "YES, YES, YES!" inside my head. I was so relieved. My intuition was also the reason why I was OK when my boys went surfing the day after a shark had killed a surfer in the same area. My intuitive warning signs were as quiet as a mouse. They also told me, "We have more chance of being killed in a car going to uni every day than by a shark!" It didn't hurt that I prayed as they left, though. I believe that the times when we are in real danger, the real life-threatening situations in our lives, are very few. Most of the time we frighten ourselves with our imaginings. That is why our intuition is able to have such a quiet voice. When it needs to be heard you know! That is, if you have nurtured it and cultivated it over your life.

Please help our kids to develop their intuition and to access that wise part of themselves that is within. Children are only able to tap into this source when they are calm, grounded, centred and able to have silence and stillness in their day. The chaotic lives of children shut down this gift. Stress also is a big killer of intuition. I know I sound like a broken record sometimes, but keep the noise down, the TVs and computers off and encourage children to be in the natural world as often as is possible.

Key Points

- ❖ Goodness orientation forms in the first two years of birth

- ❖ Everyone has an intuition

- ❖ Quietness and time in nature build intuition

- ❖ A key element to telepathy is having a strong emotional bond

- ❖ Real life experiences build intuition

- ❖ Virtual reality stifles intuition

- ❖ The higher self is like a quiet twin

- ❖ Favourite symbols and things reflect intuition

- ❖ A well-developed intuition is an enormous asset, especially in a teenager's life

- ❖ Weak intuition and inexperience can have deadly consequences

- ❖ The intuition can dis-empower the inner critic

- ❖ Transcendence is a state we all seek

- ❖ Natural transcendence allows us to connect more fully with our inner wisdom

- ❖ The intuition helps kids to discern who is safe and has genuine warmth

- ❖ Synchronicity and intuition go hand in hand

- ❖ The intellect and intuition speak different languages

- ❖ Help our kids to develop their intuition and to access the wise part within themselves

Chapter 7

The Gift of Imagination

"For as long as he could remember
Wombat had wanted to be in the Nativity.
Now, at last, he was old enough to take part.
So, with his heart full of hope
And his head full of dreams,
He hurried along to the auditions."

Mem Fox. Wombat Divine, 1995.

Those delightful moments of joy that children experience within their imaginations are important parts of being young.

Do you remember that horrifying moment when you learned that Father Christmas was not true? Or maybe you remember a time when a grown-up tried to tell you that wishes never come true or when you were shown how a magic trick really worked? If you can remember any of these experiences you will also recall disappointment, sadness and the poignant moment of grief that accompanied that moment. Sadly, imagination is being killed off in our Western world by busy parents, overuse of technological creations like television, computers, videos and DVDs and the pressures of consumerism.

Children's imaginations, especially when a child is not yet seven, help them experience joy. They are totally unaware of the concerns of later life. More than that, a child's imagination can nurture, protect and insulate them from many of the harsh realities of the adult modern world that surrounds them. It can feed their growing spirits and build on emotional and social competencies that will help them in adolescence and adulthood. Imagination and the holistic growth of healthy, happy, resilient children have suffered greatly in the last couple of generations. Modernism, the rise of a popular culture that honours 'fast and quick' living, the 'must have' mentality and family and community disintegration have all taken their toll on children.

I firmly believe that a rich imaginative childhood is essential for the evolving brain. It helps to create the neuronal templates that ensure emotional stability, social awareness and the spiritual strength to cope with life in this chaotic, constantly changing world.

In a simplistic way the imagination helps children explore and interpret life experiences as they strive for a sense of meaning. This search for meaning is not a logical process for children. We need to remember that they do not see the world as we do, and thank God for that! One of Australia's best professional speakers, Glenn Capelli, has a beautiful term to describe the way children see the world. It is 'neotony', a unique way of seeing the world that enables them to stay curious and full of wonderment and spontaneity.

We lose something when we only see the world through the eyes of an educated, sensible and logical adult. To demonstrate how children search for meaning from within their imaginary world let's run through the following scenario.

A little girl lines up her dolls and teddy bears. She then assumes the voice of an adult and proceeds to teach her 'students' about the importance of being tidy. Watching carefully we notice that she is modelling a significant adult in her life. She copies the voice, body language, words and intonations that she experiences so strongly in her life. And she copies so well! Sometimes she uses a growly voice to scold an inattentive doll: "Are you listening to me?" She may then immediately become tender and console the wounded doll, reassuring it with kind words and a hug. I have noticed this pattern of events many times. Interestingly it is the child who makes up the part about consoling, probably in response to what they wish had happened to them when they were scolded. In this play they are able to explore their emotional worlds and attempt to make sense of how adults behave and how their world could be improved.

It is accepted in Neuro Linguistic Programming that each person creates unique filters in childhood. These filters shape and influence how we interpret future life experiences. They become unconscious and help us to delete, distort, generalize, store or suppress experiences. Yet our bodies retain the memories which influence future behaviours. Knowing this can help us to understand, in part, how some children, teenagers and adults behave irrationally and unpredictably at times. Their minds are running experiences through their filters and they then react to the experience. The person concerned does not pause or think about making a choice – he or she responds quickly and impulsively according to unconscious beliefs that were formed as a result of prior experiences, either good or bad. The thought processes that stem from the influence of the filters on our conscious and unconscious minds are the real problem: Indeed M Scott Peck well respected psychologist of "The Road Less Travelled " fame believed:

> "Over the years I came to believe, and again I'm leaving out the biological aspects, but that psychological disorders are all disorders of thinking. So narcissists, for instance, cannot or will not think of other people....What we used to call passive-dependent people don't think for themselves. Obsessive-compulsives tend to have great difficulty thinking in the big picture. And I would say that if you have a patient or a client who has some real difficulty, psychological difficulty, look for the problem in their thinking. There is some area where they are not thinking correctly. "

M Scott Peck from his web site www.mscottpeck.com Conversations

If this is the case it is also true that it is difficult to change unconscious negative beliefs: firstly, we may not be aware what the beliefs are; and secondly, the child has created filters that we are unsure about and mind patterns that support those filters.

The imaginary world allows children to re-create the experience and gives them the opportunity to 'reprogram' how they have wired filters to support their belief system. Take our little girl and her dolls again. By imagining that the naughty doll was consoled by the person who held the power at the time she could re-program herself to believe that even when being scolded we are still loved and that the act of reassurance is important.

Thinking can be changed as a consequence of hearing a story that resonates deeply within a child or a person. It can and does happen however is impossible to measure. Rich literary backgrounds for children that encompass myths, legends, fables and stories that include fairy tales and metaphors help them to create healthy social and emotional constructs that help them to in life.

"The beauty of literature is that it talks in a direct and moving way to the imagination instilling a love of language, and awakening in the soul a sense of what it means to be fully alive."

Kevin Donnelly "Exploding the Literary Canon" The Australian Newspaper Oct 8-9 2005

One of the key attributes of emotional intelligence is the capacity for empathy. This can be really challenging for a teenager whose childhood took place in a toxic environment; they have no experience of empathy in their home. It can still become a part of their programming if they are able to explore and express empathy through the imaginary world and through creative visualization. Remember, the brain cannot tell the difference between vividly imagined and real experiences and so a person can be empathetic if they are able to experience it on the imaginary plane.

This is why regular use of creative visualizations that build empathy, positive social behaviour and life- enhancing language transforms negative filters and beliefs. Visualizations can change the unconscious mind when used repetitively and with a strong emotive component to the activity. Another way to change the unconscious mind is for a young person to spend time in the company of a person who models the opposite to their belief system; over a period of time their belief system changes. I once had a teenage boy with a reputation of being rude and disruptive join one of my school classes in the middle of the year. He tried to be disruptive in his first class so I chatted to him after the class and told him how I cared for all my students. I told him that I believed there was something special and unique within every student and that I wanted to support him to become the best person he could be. The class had already evolved into a class that worked together both cooperatively and collaboratively; they accepted the newcomer on the same terms. He was able to meld into the class and embrace this different way of being. He never behaved inappropriately for the remainder of the year. The boy also found his sense of humour and welcomed help from myself and other students, which was necessary as he was almost illiterate.

A negative mind set can be changed if the environment and the people within that environment function sincerely from a different space. The famous English scientist Rupert Sheldrake would have said that the "morphic" resonance of the classroom had been largely responsible for the student's change. By this he meant that the minds of all members of the classroom had created a collective memory of how to behave in that unique social grouping; it is this that had transformed the new member of the class, once he felt safe and liked. (Rupert Sheldrake. The Sense of Being Stared at from Behind, 2004)

Children's imaginations can create new ways of seeing the world and of coping with things that challenge them. Indeed, Marjorie Taylor in her book Imaginary Companions and the Children Who Create Them explained that children who had imaginary friends as younger children appeared to be mentally and emotionally more stable as adults. Rather than store, suppress or distort their experiences, they explored them with their imaginary friends. This allowed the child to diffuse any unexpressed emotion and to find a sense of meaning out of their experiences. Professor Susan Harter and Christine Chao from the University of Denver argue that children may fashion their imaginary companion in one of two ways: one possible way is to create an imaginary friend who is helpless and incompetent and who makes the child feel strong or better by comparison; or they may create a friend who is extremely competent so that the child has a powerful ally, which bolsters their self esteem.

> "Think of the imaginary companion as providing a window on your child's thoughts and feelings."

Marjorie Taylor 1999, p159.

Marjorie Taylor believed that the main reason children created imaginary friends was simply to experience fun and companionship. Essentially they can be great boredom beaters and, for a lonely child, fill the need to have someone to play with. These views support the role of imaginary friends in the healthy development of a child's personality. Furthermore, most imaginary friends disappear before six years of age.

From the age of two we use the imagination to process life experiences, achieve mastery of our emotions, enrich our social understandings, develop communication skills and create wonderful possibilities for our future lives. Even though young children's imaginations are more fertile than those of adults, teenagers and adults can still use the imagination for support. It can support our emotional and mental wellbeing right through life.

Now to explore the notion of daydreaming and how this impacts on children and teenager's lives. Many a classroom has dreamy students in it. They are often called space cadets. I have always been fascinated with these students and have chatted to many. I have found they usually have the following characteristics in common.

- ❖ They have experience of a parent or teacher who frightened them, often with shouting or verbal abuse that included sarcasm, shaming or harsh criticism.

- ❖ They are gentle, sensitive individuals with a deep love of nature and animals.

- ❖ They are usually unaware of drifting into that dreamy state ('unplugged' from the surrounding environment).

- ❖ Their dreamy state is not always a daydream that they can remember.

- ❖ The spacey state protects them when they are in an unsafe environment.

- ❖ They often missed important learning in classes, while they were 'unplugged', and miss important instructions.

- ❖ They are often introverts who enjoy their own company and being in quiet places, especially safe bedrooms.

- ❖ They show significant improvements in achievements when given gentle reminders to focus on what is happening.

- ❖ They are usually well liked by their peers and friends.

- ❖ They agree that their spacey pattern helps to protect them emotionally from toxic, critical people.

There seems to be a fine line between being dreamy and thinking deeply about life in general. I am a deep ponderer, or thinker, and often get my best ideas and intuitive thoughts when in this state. I believe, however, there is a difference between the spacey, dreamy ungrounded state and the thinking state that is in touch with one's intuition; this is a grounded state. Being grounded means being fully present in our body, energetically connected to the surroundings and able to act on thoughts that come to mind. Dreamers are ungrounded. They are living their lives from a place of safety and out of touch with reality. Unfortunately, they are also disconnected from their hearts when in this space and are incapable of experiencing deep joy and happiness. Dreamers avoid deep emotional pain, which is one of the main reasons why they created the pattern in the first place.

> "Children sometimes find a special place of spiritual sustenance in their own back yard – a bliss station as Joseph Campbell called it –"
>
> Tobin Hart "The Secret Spiritual World of Children" 2003, p58.

Do you remember a special spot you had as a child where your imagination was free to play and you were uninterrupted? It is really common when working with adults to discover they had a place of great comfort in their childhood; they retreated there, away from the world, to play, be, and to gather strength. This place may exist only in our imaginations, as "a gateway in our consciousness that opens into the depths of mystery" (Hart 2003:59). Depressed children and teenagers have closed this gateway and it appears to be locked away. Yet the gateway holds the joys of mirth that are only possible through the consciousness of a child – where the shining eyes of a happy child are to be found. This gateway is closed by busy lives, being out of touch with our hearts even when in the presence of children, and with prolonged suffering.

It is important that we bear witness to a child's way of experiencing the world and that we allow a childlike way to flow through us, to imbue us and to change us. A child's delight at their first touch of a cat's fur, hearing thunder or experiencing a colourful sunrise can soften the hardest adult heart - if we simply stay fully present in the moment. [Being in touch with awe and mystery will be explored later in the chapter on spiritual intelligence.)

Children under seven years of age have an exquisite imagination. It is fertile and woven closely into their real world so that the two constantly merge, ebb and flow together. Young children who are asked to breathe out their worries as part of therapy sound like steam trains. When you ask teenagers to do the same you can barely hear any breath at all! Imagination is an enormous source of comfort and protection for children.

Today children have rapidly increasing levels of childhood stress. This may show as sleep disorders, depression, attention deficit hyperactivity disorder (ADHD), obsessive compulsive disorders, autism, hyperactivity or emotional instability. Maybe we need to look at how life has changed in our modern world. 'Baby boomers' born in the 40s, 50s and early 60s were raised in a time of very little TV, lots of free play and a strong God consciousness. The God figure was portrayed as a powerful omniscient being who watched over us at all times. There was a sense of protection. This is summed up in the following prayer and was relevant even for those who did not go to church.

Now I lay me down to sleep,
I pray the Lord my soul to keep.
See me safely through the night
Wake me in the morning light.

Imagine how comforting it was for a child to have this powerful all-knowing Being watch over them at night. Then along came cultural diversity, 'political correctness' and a shift away from traditional religion with a diminishing influence of religion, especially Christianity, in our mainstream schools. The spiritual archetype weakened and children were left to fend for themselves at night, and during the day, without God watching over them. This is a simplistic description of the changing influence of a publicly accepted norm about God in our children's lives. At the same time as the weakening protective archetype, stress-related illness and sleeping difficulties have become common in children, frighteningly so. As a result, I have introduced an imaginary figure, a three metre high guardian angel or super hero, into my work. The children create the figure for themselves so that it can watch over them at all times. That was the start of my Safe-n-Sound visualization technique, found in the Just for Kids CD pack. Children created guardian angels with names as diverse as 'Sunshine' or 'Julie'; many boys have super heroes called 'Bob' or 'Bruce'. Some children have empowered one of their toys to superhuman status so that they can protect them. Their fertile imaginative world allows these angels and super heroes to feel real to them. Children also transferred their guardians and protectors into real-life situations, similar to having an imaginary friend. In some cases bullying from others stopped, children were able to sleep over at their friends' places more easily and they were less likely to have emotional outbursts and unpredictable behaviour. The Sleepytime visualization was created to help children get to sleep more easily and to sleep more soundly, preferably in their own bed at home! Using the imaginary world to re-create a powerful protector combined with beautiful music and the voice of someone who loves children is a combination that works a treat.

> "Despite having a bed time routine my four year old daughter has always had trouble settling to go off to sleep. We had tried many tactics including 'sleep school' when she was a baby. This did improve things but still she could be awake two or more hours after she had gone to bed.
>
> The results from the Sleepytime CD were dramatic and instant - the first night we used it she was asleep in no time. She is now familiar with the pattern of relaxation and the CD is only required occasionally. Still at two months after the introduction of Sleepytime my daughter is asleep within minutes rather than hours!
>
> We no longer have a problem with 'monsters' either as her imaginary guardian angel that the CD has helped her create makes her feel safe. Our whole family has enjoyed the dramatic and positive change in her sleep habits all thanks to Sleepytime!"
>
> Peter and Michelle De Cort, Victoria, Australia, 2005.

Some of the picture books that children enjoy have animals like a hippopotamus eating cake on the roof, possums that eat lamingtons, in Australia, a turtle called Franklin who is afraid of the dark, and a bear called Winnie-the-Poo who loves honey, and his friend Christopher Robyn. These are wonderful books to have in childhood and they build a rich soil for the imagination. Fantasy stories have been happening since time began. Now we have the technology to create colourful stories complete with animation, making it easy to surround children with positive experiences while they are young.

Young children also benefit from non-picture books that have stories that are rich in cultural and archetypical concepts. A noted US psychologist Bruno Bettleheim

"…..not only are myths, legends, fables and stories an essential part of our cultural heritage but such works epitomised by fairy tales also speak in a profoundly important way to the young child's need for emotional, psychological, and spiritual well being."

He goes on to write

"The deep inner conflict originating in our primitive drives and our violent emotions are all denied in much of modern children's literature and so the child is not helped in coping with them. The fairy tale by contrast takes these existential anxieties and dilemmas seriously and addresses itself directly to them." The Australian Oct 8-9th 2005 p 23

When my sons were young we read ancient fairy tales, like those the Grimm brothers wrote. The boys enjoyed the stories where 'witches burned in ovens' while I was concerned that this was frightening for them. The human mind functions on so many levels, including the non-local or collective consciousness, the universal mind. This extended form of the mind essentially gives us knowledge and wisdom that defies rational description. I have already mentioned Dr Rupert Sheldrake's notion of fields of morphic resonance, invisible fields that exist around us and which are able to influence us. In a very simplistic way this means that there are things we simply 'know' and that resonate as truth for us, particularly from our ancestral past.. Whether the knowing comes with us when we are born and is in our genes or by some other pathway, it is still real. Maybe our modern world's children's literature is missing something as Dr Bettelheim suggested above. Maybe it is not feeding the collective consciousness that was innately more honest about the dark sides of life?

Be mindful of exposing children less than seven years of age to too many passive imaginary activities. There is plenty of time for movies, videos and DVDs after they turn seven. Nothing replaces story telling with real people and real books when children are young – as these stimulate their own pathways of imagination using all their senses and in the company of someone who is safe. When we put young children in front of television all the creativity is being done for them. We are making their imaginations lazy and zoning them out. In Marjorie Taylor's work she found that children with rich imaginary worlds including imaginary friends "were more imaginative in their free play" (Taylor, 1999:41). She also discovered that children with imaginary companions watched significantly less TV than children without imaginary friends (Taylor 1999:45). Taylor believes that children watching TV substitute an externally generated fantasy world for their own creative world. Children who watch a lot of TV may also have less time to be participating in imaginary play. Essentially a young child's imaginary play is an activity where they entertain themselves. Children who always need an external source of entertainment are less able to entertain themselves later in childhood and in life. This is when parents may really regret the overwhelming presence of technological distracters or 'baby sitters'!

At this point it is important to mention the parental concerns around young children and fantasy play. Many parents are concerned that imaginary play, especially with imaginary companions, may be a sign that their children are mentally impaired and unable to cope with the real world. Some parents actually believe that imaginary play encourages children to tell lies and fabricate things in a dishonest way.

Some fundamentalists fear that their children may end up in some form of spiritual bondage as a consequence of being too attached to an imaginary figure. On the other hand, parents may believe that a strong belief in Santa Claus means that their children will go on to question the existence of 'God' when they finally learn that Santa is not a real figure. Research does not support any of these concerns and it is important to remember we are exploring the imaginary development of children under seven years of age.

Brain research supports the healthy pursuit of the imagination because it stimulates growth of neuronal pathways that subsequently continue to develop as a child matures. We cannot analyse a child's imaginary world from the perspective of the educated, logical mind of the adult. Rather, "Imaginative thought is an integral part of every day cognition and human experience" (Taylor 1995:163); it is woven into the threads of our lives, without conscious thought or intention, and enriches our lives. It is more than a form of escape or a source of entertainment; imagination plays a very important part in the creation of a preferable future. Its role in modern thinking and consciousness is undisputed.

Thomas Moore writes that

"Tradition teaches that soul lies midway between understanding and unconsciousness and that its instrument is neither the mind nor the body, but imagination." He goes on to explore the notion of soul and of living in the absence of soul. To him, the symptoms of loss of soul are:

- ❖ emptiness
- ❖ meaninglessness
- ❖ vague depression
- ❖ disillusionment about marriage, family and relationship
- ❖ a loss of values
- ❖ yearning for personal fulfilment

❖ hunger for spirituality

Thomas Moore. Care of the Soul 1992, pxvi.

The above symptoms are familiar; they are rampant in our children and youth. Previously these symptoms were only found in teenagers and adults, particularly those struggling to find a sense of purpose or meaning in life. The fast pace of life and quick and often shallow methods of communication create space between people, especially those we love.

As we search for answers to things that are supposed to remain a mystery and try to push children into rational and predictable thinking before they are ready, by criticizing the role of fantasy and imagination, we may unwittingly create the disease of 'loss of soul'.

"Politicians and educators consider more school days in a year, more science, more maths, the use of computers and other technology in the classroom, more exams, more tests, more certifications for teachers and less money for art. On all these counts soul is neglected....".

(Thomas Moore. Care of the Soul 1992, p52)

Creative play, imaginary companions and fantasy stories and books that use the ancient archetypes of good versus evil may very well be the best pathways to ensuring the emotional and mental wellbeing of all of us, not just our children. [Creativity is explored in the next chapter.] Stories that are rich in imagination and quality fantasy allow us to take a break from our world and at the same time remind us through our ancient memory that we are all connected. We all yearn for the same things; we all seek fulfilment and peace. We all seek authentic love and a sense of belonging and to live a life of value and worth. This is what we are able to seek in the world of the imagination.

"He looked down at his wand, which he was still clutching in his hand. If he was already expelled (his heart was now thumping painfully fast) a bit more magic couldn't hurt. He had his Invisibility Cloak he had inherited from his father – what if he bewitched the trunk to make it feather light, tied it to his broomstick, covered himself in the Cloak and flew to London? Then he could get the rest of his money out of his vault and ...and begin his life as an outcast. It was a horrible prospect, but he couldn't sit on this wall for ever or he'd find himself trying to explain to Muggle police why he was out in the dead of night with a trunkful of spell books and a broomstick."

JK Rowling. Harry Potter and the Prisoner of Azkaban 1999, pp29-30.

The amazing phenomenon that is the Harry Potter series of books, by JK Rowling, has set the literary world of children and adults on fire. The lovable lad Harry Potter steals the hearts of millions of readers who eagerly await the arrival of the next book so that they can explore more of his exploits. Indeed, Harry Potter and his friends have been able to push the technological world aside for a time and to allow the imaginary world of millions to be fed and nurtured. Why has there been such an amazing response to this lad who has abilities we would all like to have just a little of in this world? Maybe Harry Potter fills a place in the starved minds and souls of people both young and old. JK Rowling has written an exceptional series of books that honour our ancient yearning for good to triumph over evil. This is in a world with terrorism and war still. Maybe the child within us remembers how much it loves a good, rollicking story and it simply wants more, more MORE!

In times gone by the Narnia series of books, which include The Lion, the Witch and the Wardrobe, and Tolkien's The Hobbit and The Lord of the Rings have similarly fed imaginations. Many of these books have become bestselling films, often for those who enjoy having themselves scared witless in the company of others. Personally, I prefer the written story and find the film versions of these great stories way too scary.

There are differences between quality films and those that disturb the psyche of our children. Harry Potter may be a great read for a seven-year old; however, the enormous visual effects of the same story given sound and special effects can be quite disturbing and even frightening. Good films are examples of rich imaginative stories that feed a deep part within our psyches and that somehow are more than just stories. For this same reason I do not advocate that children watch movies about aliens, ghosts or those that are based on natural disasters like earthquakes or volcanic eruptions. The ability to discern between what is imaginary and what is real is not fully developed in the younger child. This means a child may develop irrational fears because the films based on natural disasters are more realistic than those based on a children's book.

The work of the scientist Candace Pert extends our understanding of how our emotional world is experienced throughout our whole body. A mind-body connection to every moment of life is now well recognised. Candace Pert and her colleagues show that neuropeptide interactions take place in two directions: every change in physiological state is accompanied by a change in mental emotional state, either consciously or unconsciously; and conversely, every change in emotional state is accompanied by a change in physiological state. The regulator of this process, the place in the brain where the mind and body meet, is known as the limbic system. The limbic system is that part of the brain concerned with emotions and memory responses. It is known by some as the 'emotional brain'. In her book Molecules of Emotion Candace explores how the emotional domain within us is largely a molecular drama that takes place constantly and largely unconsciously. This is why imaginary stories and films are important in all our lives, as they can allow us to come to a place of emotional understanding and closure through the eyes of someone else's suffering or story.

Good imaginative stories reinforce the core truths that we know from within our higher consciousness. That is: good eventually conquers evil, even in our darkest moments we are never alone, hope can overcome fear, and within everyone there is a place of goodness that can be found or lost. Thus the search for the hero within is true for everyone regardless of culture, age or gender. Joseph Campbell wrote about this search using metaphors and most philosophers search for and seek the same place of truth. Essentially we are all searching for answers. The imaginative world is important in helping us explore options, possibilities and choices for who we are and how we can be.

Some animated films also search for the hero within. The Lion King was a hit with my youngest son - he watched it fifty-one times. He is the one who kept count! Other films were Pocahontas, Shriek, Finding Nemo and more Lion King films. Hopefully we will continue to see these quality animated films that have a strong story to tell, which is the key to an excellent fantasy film. Special effects do not create a successful film unless they honour a part of the 'collective consciousness' or memory. This is the same for both children and adults. Quality animated films have an important part to play in nurturing our inner world, for all of us, and in nurturing heart and soul.

Maureen Garth was an Australian writer who created beautiful imaginary journeys or guided meditations for her daughter. These have become part of thousands of children's lives across the world. Starbright, Moonbeam, Sunshine and Earthlight all begin the same way: in a star prelude children are invited to feel cleansed with the light of a beautiful star above their heads. Maureen then invites a guardian angel in to guide the children on an imaginary journey that allows their imaginations to direct what happens while feeling safe and relaxed. Many children have heard these beautiful stories and they are very quick to embrace the notion of a guardian or super hero who watches over them and protects them. I am sure Maureen would be delighted with how many families have her guided meditations. She has provided a very special legacy for her daughter.

Another wonderful resource that is useful for parents and teachers uses the imagination to teach children about emotions and feelings. This is the wonderful Forest of Feelings by Jo Browning Wroe and Carol Holliday. The story takes place in a magical forest and weaves beautifully around the adventures of Rusalka, Ben and the imaginary creatures in the forest as they set out to save the forest from ruin. It also promotes the archetypes with good finally conquering evil through the efforts of decent people. The rich, imaginative background used with a strong story allows children to explore emotions about the actions of others. It is a powerful teaching tool.

Children are particularly influenced by creative visualization because of their rich imaginations. Using creative visualization is also an excellent way to stimulate the imagination and to allow children the benefits of quietness and stillness in which they can explore other ways of being, without interruption from our busy world. Running through a creative visualization with a child and then chatting to them about what they saw, where they went and what they heard and felt is a great connecting activity. It is also a beautiful way to build empathy and consideration for others. On my School Mastery CD there is a track called I Can Read Easily which was created to help reluctant readers overcome negative attitudes to reading, especially if they are experiencing difficulties and are not ready to take up reading. A child's readiness to read can kick in at any time in the first four years of schooling. If they hate reading, avoid doing it and fight with Mum to get out of reading after school then they may very well stay away from reading for life. Teachers often report that after as few as two uses of I Can Read Easily, children are keen to listen to stories again and to have another go at learning to read themselves – with no pressure, no coercion, and no tears!

Undoubtedly, the gift of the imagination is a powerful source of comfort, distraction and escape. The imagination also helps us to process life experiences, manage and balance our emotions, enrich our social understandings, explore our spiritual world, develop communication skills and create wonderful possibilities for our lives. It is alright for children to have imaginary play, friends or explanations to help shield them from the often awful, harsh realities of the adult world.

Children's imaginations need time and space to develop and a willingness on the part of adults to really honour this gift, not expensive toys. Adulthood comes early enough into our lives and a rich imaginative childhood helps build resilience and coping skills that will last for life. Maybe with more honouring of the imaginative world of children we can reduce the chances of the following. A Columbine student who experienced one of the many high school massacres in the US wrote:

REFLECTION

The paradox of our time in history is that we have tall buildings,

but shorter tempers.

We have bigger houses and smaller families;

more conveniences, but less time;

We have more degrees, but less sense; more knowledge but less judgement;

more experts but more problems; more medicine but less wellness.

We have multiplied our possessions, but reduced our values.

We talk too much, love too seldom, and hate too often.

We've learned to make a living, but not a life.

We've added years to life, not life to years.

We've been all the way to the moon and back, but have trouble crossing the street to meet the new neighbour.

We've conquered outer space, but not inner space.

We've cleaned up the air, but polluted the soul.

We've split the atom, but not our prejudice.

We have higher incomes, but lower morals.

We've become long on quantity, but short on quality.

These are the times of tall men and short character;

steep profits, and shallow relationships.

These are the times we worry about world peace,

 but have domestic warfare;

more leisure, but less fun;

more kinds of food, but less nutrition.

These are the days of two incomes, but more divorce.

Of fancier houses, but broken homes.

It is a time when there is much in the show window

and nothing in the stockroom.

A time when technology can bring this letter to you instantly

and a time when you can choose to make a difference.

(Source World Wide Web)

Key Points

- ❖ The imagination is supposed to be a positive part of being a child

- ❖ The imagination can nurture, protect and insulate a child

- ❖ It can nurture the growing spirit

- ❖ It can build emotional and social competencies for later life

- ❖ Imagination helps children explore and interpret their life experiences

- ❖ It can create new ways of seeing the world

- ❖ It can create new ways of seeing oneself

- ❖ Imaginary friends are usually beneficial to later emotional and mental wellbeing

- ❖ Dreamy students have developed this pattern to protect themselves from fearful situations

- ❖ Having a special place to escape the world is healthy

- ❖ Young imaginations are very fertile

- ❖ The imagination can help our children feel safer in our adult world

- ❖ Fears around children's imaginative worlds are largely unfounded

- ❖ The imagination feeds the soul

❖ Good quality films support growth of children's inner worlds

❖ Creative visualization is good for children

❖ The imagination is a gift in our lives, one that can sustain us through life

Chapter 8

The Healing Potential of Creativity

"Doctor doctor giver of meds
giver of advice, giver of life
Prescibe me a cure for this world
In which I find myself trapped,
Unable to break free, find peace.
Write me a script
That will make me understand
The bodies of babies discarded on the streets of China
Perverts harbouring mountains of kiddie-porn multimedia
My friend's innocence stolen at 9 years of age
Tanks powering down the streets of Israel
And children blown to shit when they throw rocks at them….."

Excerpt from The Problem by teenager Linnea Pierre. A Circle in a Room Full of Squares edited by Suzanne Covich.

Creativity is suffering in our consumer driven, technological, time poor world. Opportunities that allow individuals to express themselves, away from feeling competitive or judged, have been devalued by a world that values success, mainly in terms of wealth, fame and status. More than ever before children and adults are feeling pressured to achieve and excel with the result that creative pursuits are losing ground. In school systems around the world the opportunities for the arts are decreasing, which has almost forced the arts to be an extracurricular pursuit. Thomas Moore writes,

Art broadly speaking is that which invites us into contemplation — a rare commodity in modern life. In that moment of contemplation art intensifies the presence of the world. We see it more vividly or more deeply. The emptiness that many people complain dominates their lives comes in part from a failure to let the world in, to perceive it and engage it fully.

Thomas Moore. Care of the Soul, p286

Creativity can emerge when we allow the world in as we contemplate life, ourselves and what makes us unique and different from others. Thomas Moore believes that creativity is about soul. It allows us as humans to connect our inner and outer worlds. Creativity allows the mind, body, heart and soul to come to a gentle place of truth and wisdom and is really a search for wholeness. In this busy world there is less time than ever before to honour creativity in our lives, leading to fragmentation and separateness. This is so for children too. We need to strive, even fight, for creativity to hold a place of value and importance in the lives of modern children. Maybe in this way we can heal some of our disconnected and confused children and teens? We can provide the doorway home into our hearts so that we can become more compassionate towards ourselves and others and create the opportunity for personal freedom for those who are lost in the chaos? We can only but hope.

The search for authenticity and wholeness is universal. As Rachael Kessler explored in her excellent book The Soul of Education there are seven gateways to education of the whole child. They are the:

- ❖ yearning for deep connection;
- ❖ longing for silence and solitude;
- ❖ search for meaning and purpose;
- ❖ hunger for joy and delight;
- ❖ creative drive;

- ❖ urge for transcendence;
- ❖ need for initiation.

These seven gateways provide keys to exploring the world of a troubled child or teenager – what is missing in their life? Interestingly the pursuit of creativity often opens all the other gateways simply by opening an individual's creative expression. Why is this so? Without being too intellectual or philosophical, I believe creativity takes a person out of their head-mind into the heart-spirit; from a place of logic and rational thought into the garden of possibilities and freedom. It allows for the free expression of a person's uniqueness, originality and authenticity.

Our education systems are allowing less and less time for the creative pursuits. The results are less tangible, harder to assess and measure, and funding is being directed towards the mainstream content of the three 'Rs'. Even in our pre-schools there is less free play and artistic expression than five years ago. Certain prerequisites are mandated for first grade rather than encouraged and this causes pressure on the pre-schools, which is deeply concerning. From birth, children have an innate creative drive to explore and interpret the world. This innate drive is being disturbed by the presence of many commercialised toys, TV and overprotective parenting that does not allow babies to crawl around on the floor following their own instincts. Yes, babies and young children do put a lot of unhealthy things in their mouths and they do sometimes tumble down stairs and get their fingers caught in drawers and doors – rich very real learning experiences that allow their brains to develop their imagination and to be creative. This is how children used to grow and explore – with the courage to be able to express themselves authentically through their play, sport, love of music and the arts.

Healthy creativity in children and adults has four main elements, the first of which is an active imagination. As has already been explored, many of the modern passive activities that use screens numb children's imaginations and stunt their capacity to explore their imaginary world in a positive way. The second requirement for creativity is the courage to express oneself as honestly as possible. Courage is needed because you may be judged. Even pre-schoolers are sensitive to judgment and criticism and will curtail their creativity if they feel they risk being judged unfavourably. The third requirement is freedom, when we are allowed and also encouraged to express ourselves however we like in whatever form suits us. The final requirement is very simple – opportunity – in the home, at school and even in the work place. When all four of these attributes are present children can experience the healing potential of creativity. They can diffuse excess energy, unexpressed emotions and experience safe transcendence by connecting deeply with their inner selves. Problems can be externalised, a sense of powerlessness and their fear about how the world appears to them expressed. This frees them to be open to joy and delight – and we see those shiny eyes that we so love in children.

Abused children are often rendered completely silent and mute by their painful experiences. Yet these children can re-gain their voice through drawing or sand play. A recent article in the Australian newspaper (September 10-11, 2005) featured some very dramatic children's drawings that showed how children expressed the trauma in their lives. As the head of the Australian Childhood Foundation Dr Joe Tucci stated, "Children are often more comfortable with pencil and paper than they are with adult constructs of conversation". One of the pictures was drawn by a 9-year old girl. She had been sexually abused by her uncle and then rejected by her parents following her disclosure of the abuse. The girl drew a child with no mouth, fingers or feet; someone completely unable to speak, fight or flee. The child in the picture was paralysed but the tears she cried formed puddles on the ground. Such a powerful drawing showed how much pain the girl was experiencing inside.

When I work with children and teenagers I often begin by asking them to draw for me. Many children reach for the black coloured crayon, or maybe the grey or brown crayon. They draw pictures with no colour in them and draw themselves as very small or tiny figures. When we had finished our time together and I have introduced them to colour, they often ask to draw another picture, because they wanted to draw in colour again. It is this picture they take away with them, often screwing their first picture up as it 'wasn't them' any more. I am also able to use the first drawing as a way of distancing a young person's problem, from inside them to outside them. It is easier to talk about the sad girl in the picture and what may be making her sad rather than asking the girl sitting in front of you. That externalising of the problem was beneficial when helping them explore solutions to the conflicts in their life. A similar approach could be taken with sad toys, which needed to get help to make them feel better.

Children often need someone outside their lives to help them understand what is happening and to work out possible ways of healing their challenges. In this way they find their wise counsel within, just the same as for adults. My role as a child's counsellor was more often than not to remind the child that he or she was lovable, they were acceptable and could manage whatever was happening in their life. Reassurance is a powerful healer for young children.

Often helping the parents was harder than helping the wounded child. Ignorance is not bliss and unintentionally damaging children can create enormous guilt. Being able to give parents new knowledge and positive empowerment from a place of compassion and humility is not easy. However, we all want to do the right thing for our children.

Just what is the right thing at any given moment is a challenge, that's what makes it interesting! Remember, there is no perfect solution and we all get it wrong sometimes. The depth and frequency of abuse is what does the serious damage to babies and young children. Anne Manne writes,

> "The unequivocal message from our contemporary knowledge of early childhood development is that children are vulnerable, and that there are circumstances from which they are unlikely to recover. The earlier and more extensive the trauma the less likely the recovery."

Anne Manne 'Motherhood' 2005, p165

Children have great capacity to bounce back from minor disasters and challenges, especially when they have consistent cherished caregivers in their life. So rest easy and give your children plenty of opportunity to express themselves creatively, whether they are feeling good, bad or ugly! They can do all three in the same hour some days.

How many opportunities are we offering our children to be creative, original and to be expressive, as they wish?

- ❖ Are you comfortable with dirt, mud, paint, water and glue?

- ❖ Do you have an area around your home where your child can get down-and-dirty with their creativity?

- ❖ Do you have a strategy that helps your child keep their creative 'mess' outside, like a cleaning bucket or bowl and towel?

- ❖ Do you join in with your child when invited?

- ❖ Do you keep the 'creation' as your child leaves it or do you quickly clean it away, as soon as possible?

- ❖ When did your child last make a cubby – inside or outside the house?

- ❖ Have you brought home any big boxes lately for your child to play with?

- ❖ When did you last watch ants or butterflies with your child?

- ❖ If your child is likes music is it all on CD or do you allow them to make their own sounds and rhythms on pots and pans?

- ❖ Do you have TV-free days?

- ❖ How many sand castles and sculptures have you made?

- ❖ How many mud pies have you cooked?

- ❖ How many dozen pipe cleaners or pop sticks have you bought?

- ❖ How many sidewalk chalk packs have you been through?

- ❖ What does your fridge look like?

- ❖ Have you ever made capes for your child to wear?

- ❖ Have you hand painted kids T-shirts with them?

- ❖ How many framed 'kid's bits' do you have?

- ❖ How many homemade kites have you made and flown?

- ❖ When did you last have races with leaf or bark boats?

- ❖ When did you last make fresh play dough?

- ❖ When did you last have fresh sand in the sand pit?

- ❖ How often have you danced with your child?

- ❖ Have you made cookies using shape cutters with your child?

- ❖ Have you made homemade chocolates with moulds?

- ❖ When did you last have a treasure hunt in the garden or park?

- ❖ When did you last play hide and seek with your child?
- ❖ Have you kept kisses or wishes in a jar?

❖ Has your child grown anything from seed?

❖ When did you take your child to the library to pick out story and picture books they wanted?

❖ Do you have a box of dress-up clothes?

❖ When did you take your child camping - away from the technological world into the natural world?

This list of questions is not intended to be a checklist to assess your parenting. It is more a list of suggestions of ways to help young children with opportunities for creative expression. Notice these suggestions seldom cost much money – more the commitment of time and energy by you the parent or carer, someone they love to spend time with. These opportunities have scope for free expression so that children can direct the experience as they wish. This not only allows creativity to flow without being inhibited – it also allows a child the chance to make choices and to direct his or her own life for a change. Play leaders in children's wards of hospitals are also important. They allow children to choose their activities, whether they want to play puzzles or do face painting, and this sense of empowerment helps the children cope with all the procedures and painful tests they have to endure and over which they have no say.

My work with teenagers in high schools showed me how shut down their creativity was. I noticed how 'safely' the students wrote in creative writing activities, how restrained they were, not letting their imaginations run at all. Over time and with the careful use of many of Edward De Bono's thinking strategies, we used challenging writing activities that stretched their imaginations and I noticed their creativity open up. What I realised later was that the students needed to feel safe with me before they could express themselves freely. The results were stunning. Not only that, what I discovered from these students many years down the track was that they found they had grown in their understanding of themselves and of life with these creative writing activities.

We underestimate the potential for self growth and exploration that can take place when we let ourselves undertake a creative pursuit. I remember taking a class of restless 14-year olds outside onto the lawn and offering them the opportunity to simply 'improve on a blank page'. The activity was a spontaneous response to a lesson that had not been flowing. I recognised later that it was mainly for my benefit as I felt scattered and a little frazzled. In the twenty minutes outside the students settled and become thoughtful and pensive. As I did not have any expectation of what I wanted them to achieve, I believe it set them at ease to write with complete freedom. The creativity was amazing. Some reflected on being an ant, an insect or a dead leaf. Some wrote about what life was to them. Some drew pictures or patterns. Some wrote about the bliss of silence and stillness. Not one of them abused the opportunity for creative freedom. The insight and wisdom they shared has always stayed with me. Freedom from assessment had also given them a new kind of permission to express themselves creatively, without concerns about length, style, neatness or what form of expression they chose.

Creative expression has healing potential as it provides opportunity to search for meaning and understanding; from where we are, without any expectations or conditioning to interrupt the flow of ideas and thoughts. This flow allows our higher consciousness to express truths and perceptions from our own higher counsel. It is not the voice of our mask or lower self. Our higher counsel cannot be heard when we are in a state of stress, uncertainty or confusion. In my dark moments as a teenager I wrote poetry – lots of it. Much of it was dark and depressing, however, the mere act of expressing myself made me feel better.

Writing fictional stories also has healing potential. I learned about myth writing during my diploma in transpersonal studies. I was staggered at the depth of healing that could occur as we set out to write a myth that represented our life in some way. This exercise demonstrated to me the depth of meaning that we can reach on a symbolic or archetypal level and which can help transform us. My understanding was further expanded when I explored indigenous healing and the power of story telling, especially by tribal medicine men. It showed me the higher consciousness that exists within all of us and which needs an opportunity to express itself in order to help us heal or to reduce our suffering.

Storytelling helps families and communities to deal with crises, or where there has been a breakdown of order. In my exposure to funerals I have been fascinated with the importance of family stories in assisting the grieving process and in celebrating a loved one's life. Stories act like glue that holds the links between the past, the present and the future together. They help us feel connected to family, especially ancestors who are no longer present; they define a place of belonging even during challenging times and events. Everyone needs to have a sense of belonging. Stories are wonderful teaching tools in homes, families and communities because they:

❖ personalise presentation and content to connect

❖ presenter or storyteller and the listeners or audience;

❖ open to the intuitive knowledge of the audience;

❖ tap the resources of the unconscious mind;

❖ energise, calm or cause personal reflection.

Stories are magical because they speak to us metaphorically in a way that we relate. We are guided by symbols and ceremony and use them to interpret meaning deep within us beyond speech. Stories can open us to the symbolic dimensions of experience and the multiple meanings that coexist. They give extra shades of meaning and can engage our unconscious minds in ways that bring resolution to problems, shift us from distressed emotional states to more positive ones and offer self healing. Share stories in your family from when your children are as early an age as possible. Share fairy tales, picture books, imaginary and real stories from your past and your family's past. Share the funny stories and the sad ones and allow your children to become the story tellers too. If you are nervous about how to start with true stories then you could begin with Chicken Soup for The Soul books by Jack Canfield and Mark Victor Hanson. They have books for the Kids and Teens Soul and my favourite would have to be their first book.

The following is a story I wrote about a bush fire in the area in which I grew up.

Bushfire in Pingelly, Western Australia (WA)

Just before Christmas in 1997 a nasty bushfire formed outside Brookton, a town in the South West of WA. Due to high temperatures, very strong winds, and extremely dry conditions the fire rapidly turned into a fireball and headed towards Pingelly about twenty kilometres away. Local fire fighters were powerless to stop it and did the best they could to get people off their properties and into safety. Several locals narrowly escaped with their lives and many were hospitalised following the fire.

The fireball miraculously did a right hand turn on the outskirts of Pingelly just before reaching the huge fuel tanks on the outskirts of the town. Tragically one young lady lost her life while trying to get to safety. The town was stunned by the total annihilation of the countryside, the thousands of dead stock, ruined fence lines, loss of property and machinery.

The mood in the hospital ward where the injured men were following the fire was very quiet and subdued. Many were still in shock and struggling to come to terms with the disaster.

There was no laughter and people spoke in hushed tones even though they were having a quiet beer or two.

Tex, one of the local Aboriginal workers from one of the farms went to visit his boss in hospital, a thirty something year old man who received nasty burns fighting the fire. His boss told him about the fireball turning on him and of how he grabbed a bag and dived into a dam....the fireball went over him and it was so furious that it took all the oxygen and he could hardly get a breathe. He told him that he had to keep having to duck under the water because of the heat, but he had to keep coming up to try to get some air. He had to gasp for every last ounce of oxygen before having to escape under the water to get away from the ferocious heat. It had been life threatening and very scary.

Finally Tex said,
"That's bad boss....Hey boss you was very lucky..... now did you feel any yabbies in that dam??"

One by one the whole hospital ward full of the fire casualties all broke into laughter. It was a turning point for them to finally start to let go of the horror of the experience and to begin healing their bodies and their minds.

Tex then went on to tell his boss about his fire experience. "Hey boss, I was comin' out from town and saw all these black fellas in a paddock and I thought them's was my cousins...and when I get to them , them's not my cousins, them's black whitefellas'!!" The local farmers were so covered with ash and dust that they had looked like Aborigines. He had thought that was so funny. The laughter continued and the men continued to chat amongst themselves. Such is the healing power of stories and laughter.

Creativity and humour must be cousins! I have noticed that when people gather to paint or draw, write or do patchwork there is always lots of laughter and delight. In the retreats that I run we have several creative activities and they always end up with lightness. I sense that when people gather together in a safe place with like-minded people and the intention of being creative then the natural benevolence and good will of humans comes to the top. This may also be why creative craft work is so important in aged care facilities, hospitals and institutions.

I do voluntary work in a local maximum security prison and have found that the art department in the education unit has an incredibly important role to play in the lives of those on the inside, especially those with long sentences. I asked the art teacher about a whole wall mosaic there. She told me that a prisoner had worked on the wall over the length of his stay. He had placed the final piece – a circle mirror – in the centre of the work the day before he was released. It was an exceptional piece of work that marked his journey during the time of his imprisonment. The bright centrepiece showed a great sense of hope. The metaphor of the man-in-the-mirror is strong: the person you have to love and respect is the one in the mirror – yourself.

Another story from that same prison is about the writing group. They wrote a play called 'Revelations', a story about a released prisoner. The play was performed inside the prison and was well received. It not only gave the men a life-enhancing experience, it also gave one of them a new career away from crime – acting. The play also contained powerful messages against walking the path of criminality that may benefit someone out in the real world. Creativity can be enormously helpful in opening us to new possibilities about who we can become, no matter where we are when we start. Creativity can be beneficial and healing although it can be really difficult to see how at the time. The healing power may only be apparent looking back retrospectivity.

Many people find creative pursuit to be a natural transcendent experience, especially when they become deeply absorbed. An individual enjoys being themselves without props, distractions, noise and stimulation! These moments of deep absorption are healing, validating and allow the benevolent force of the Universe to connect mind, body, heart and soul simultaneously. This state of natural transcendence is exquisite and does not need anyone else around - whether it occurs in the midst of painting, singing, writing or thinking creatively. It is sheer joy and has a timeless quality to it so that it seems like time stands still – completely still. Maybe it does. Have you ever seen a child in this state of absorbed play? It does not happen when they are watching a screen or they are being guided or supervised by other older children or adults.

Natural transcendence is a state that people are fortunate to discover by themselves when they are young. They can again seek that place of 'being', at one with the inner and outer worlds, later in life because they know how it feels. Teens and adults who have never experienced this natural moment of transcendence may keep seeking that invisible, wonderful 'something' through risk taking, and sedating or mind-altering substances.

Creative expression has a healing quality of its own for adults as well as children. It allows us to access the right brain, a place that many rarely visit in their everyday work environment. It can allow us to diffuse simple frustrations. My friend is a builder and when he was in his office speaking on the telephone he doodled on his desk pad. These doodles evolved over days and they almost became works of art. He laughed about them and joked that he should probably be 'locked up' yet these doodles were a great way for him to creatively express himself. And he unintentionally expressed some of the frustrations and stresses he experienced in his building business. It was simple, healthy and very inexpensive.

Safe and inexpensive creative pursuits that can diffuse excess emotions or simply re-focus back to now are:

❖ gardening

- ❖ sewing
- ❖ cross stitching
- ❖ knitting crocheting
- ❖ cooking
- ❖ mosaics
- ❖ painting
- ❖ drama
- ❖ dancing
- ❖ story telling
- ❖ joke telling
- ❖ singing
- ❖ dancing
- ❖ clay work
- ❖ ceramics
- ❖ journal writing
- ❖ scrap booking
- ❖ flower arranging
- ❖ making teddy bears
- ❖ doll making
- ❖ renovation.......minor not major
- ❖ chanting, humming
- ❖ drumming
- ❖ sand play
- ❖ fabric painting

- story writing

- calligraphy

- inventing

- meditation

- wine making

- beer making

- creative visualisation

- music

- making love to someone you love

- bush walking

Remember the four elements to creativity and it is simple:

1. healthy imagination;

2. courage to let go;

3. freedom;

4. opportunity.

Beginning a new hobby can provide a very exciting opportunity to find yourself and your creativity. Your children model themselves on you so you will be showing them that life can be an exciting journey of possibilities when you take the risk of going on a new creative journey. You may find a secret potential within you that opens up a whole new life direction for you. Creativity makes you more interesting and expands your life force. It is just as important for men as it is for women. There is an enormous healing potential in creativity, as long as you don't go looking for it but allow it to come and find you. The gifts are hidden from view, from the conscious rational mind, which makes them 'cup filling' and transforming. See what happens when you get creative in your home.

> "Tradition teaches that soul lies midway between understanding and unconsciousness and that its instrument is neither the mind nor the body, but imagination."

Thomas Moore Care of the Soul, pxiii

Key Points

- ❖ In today's world, creativity is struggling
- ❖ Creativity allows the mind, body, heart and soul to come to a gentle place of truth and wisdom
- ❖ Creativity needs
  - o healthy imagination
  - o courage to let go
  - o freedom
  - o opportunity
- ❖ Creativity has healing potential
- ❖ Abused children are often rendered completely silent and mute by their painful experiences.
- ❖ Artistic exploration can help children to heal from emotional wounding
- ❖ Creativity can allow for self growth and exploration
- ❖ Creativity can open individuals to the wise council within
- ❖ Creative pursuits can be inexpensive and fun
- ❖ Storytelling can be powerfully healing

❖ Creativity often opens up laughter and lightness

❖ Creativity in groups is bonding and connecting

❖ Creativity helps people to heal physically and emotionally

❖ Creativity can open up natural transcendence

❖ There are many creative pursuits that are inexpensive and yet soul feeding

❖ Creativity has hidden benefits

❖ Creativity allows the gift of imagination to enter our lives

Chapter 9

Encouraging Character in Children

"If others know that a person can be relied upon to speak
honestly, to act in times of crisis, to contribute with generosity,
to use wisdom in making decisions, and to be faithful to family
and friends – that person has earned respect."

Jamie Sams, Earth Medicine

It seems that in this chaotic world we have lost sight
of what is really important in raising our children. We focus so
much on the grades our children achieve and their physical,
musical, artistic and mental abilities that we seldom recognise
or celebrate their humanity and the depth of their unique
character. It is only when we see an absence of this dimension
that we bemoan the fact and complain about our young
people. When we see senseless violence against the old, the
defenceless and the innocent we are horrified. When we see
young people hopelessly addicted to alcohol, drugs and other
forms of self harm we are saddened. We see young people
living lives that are aimless, with no purpose or meaning, and
we wonder why? Yet we neglect to focus on development of
character, the ability to be a valuable member of a social
group and to support the growth and development of
everyone within a group. Our consumer driven world holds
sporting heroes and actors (especially impossibly thin ones!) in
places of high status and value regardless of their true
character. Mindless magazines keep the world informed of
their infidelities, their alcohol driven excesses and their drug
addictions as those that is something to aspire towards!

Someone with a depth of character acts with honour, respect, concern, unconditional regard and the courage to hold ground when confronted with choices that compromise being true to self.

Indigenous tribes historically focussed on the development of the character within their children as well as their physical growth. Responsibility for the development of a child was shared by everyone in the tribe. Physical growth was important and children were taught new skills when they were ready. They were also taught the gifts of the spirit and the heart. These are what we loosely term values, virtues, social manners and etiquette. Without these templates young people are often unaware of how to behave and what to value; they basically live a life that is code-less.

Many years ago I spent a year teaching in a metropolitan high school that was considered to be rough and tough. I was given a class of Year 10 students who were listed as 'at risk'; they were the biggest challenge I ever encountered in my teaching career. These students had a range of cultural differences, coming from Greek, Italian, Macedonian and Indigenous backgrounds. They also had low literacy skills, were enmeshed in a strong gang culture and hated school. I was a country person who was very unfamiliar with city life, especially when surrounded by a marginalised group of first generation migrant children. My twelve months with this class showed me that we held completely different values and beliefs.

We saw the world very differently and had very different interpretations of life experiences. I felt that my best option was to give these students life skills to help them make better choices in their lives. Over time we came to trust each other and we explored many of the perceptions they had about life and living. We detached many layers of victim mentality. We built a new understanding of cultural acceptance and learnt about socially acceptable ways of communicating, using manners, positive language and positive assertive behaviour. The end of the year culminated in dinner at a French restaurant. We had spent many weeks exploring French words, dining etiquette and manners. I still have a clear picture of those neatly dressed young adults, excited and enthusiastic about showing off their new skills. It was a fun night and I saw first hand that, with more information and knowledge, all young people can make better choices: socially, personally and interpersonally. On the last day of the school year this class of 'animals', as the principal had called them, presented me with a huge bouquet and a silver platter. It had engraved on it,

**"Thanks for everything.
From your favourite class of stirrers."**

What this group of fifteen-year olds did not know was that they had been my teacher. I had come with many stereotypical beliefs about kids who belonged to gangs, were sexually active before fifteen and who abused alcohol and drugs. They taught me to see within, to avoid judgements and to look for the good within all of us. I was and still am deeply grateful to them.

An understanding of values and virtues is essential for children to develop the qualities that build character and provide a sense of humanity that will bring out the best in themselves, others and our world. Emotional intelligence adds to those tools that build character. Without knowledge of values and virtues children will always struggle with knowing how and why to behave positively in any given situation.

How do we best teach manners to our children?

Model those manners! Use them every day, with respect.

"We should say 'please' and 'thank you' to our children, and say 'sorry' when we know we have done them a wrong. We also have to display good table manners ourselves."

Jane Bartlett, Parenting with Spirit, p190.

NB: The wonderful work of Suggestopedia is a great way to understand how to communicate to children without using power as a means. It models such a rich and respectful way of teaching that not only do students learn faster they have fun. To learn more about this way of encouraging learning and positive communication, research Lonny Gold's work via his web site http://www.going-for-gold.net.]

I am a huge fan of Linda Kavelin Popov, one of the co-creators of The Virtues Project. She has a method of teaching virtues in homes and schools that is excellent and teaches children the foundations of character. I am delighted that schools around the world are moving more in the direction of having a values-based program as part of their school curriculum. Even though a child may be attending a faith-based school, they can still have significant gaps in their understanding of social norms and of manners. They can also have different perceptions of what honesty is, or punctuality. It is essential that children are given both the knowledge and opportunity to experience good manners and appropriate language in a stable, safe environment. When they do get it wrong they are best helped by someone who is kind and caring.

Being shamed, yelled at or criticised only builds fear and anxiety; it often confuses a child who is trying to learn how to be caring and considerate!

Jenny Mosley, from England, has another amazingly powerful way of building character. It is described as 'circle time'. Jenny's model helps schools to create an environment in which social, emotional and behavioural skills are developed. Essentially what Jenny has created is a method that honours and respects everyone – parents, teachers and students. It is a democratic and creative approach that demonstrates the extent of what can be explored and solved when everyone feels valued and safe. The model is deceptively simple and yet is a powerful, safe way for young children to learn to listen, share, problem solve and to feel heard. These are essential attributes for the development of healthy self esteem. The building of connectedness and a sense of belonging are also incredibly important in the development of resilience. And the communication skills learnt are invaluable for life.

I have used class circle time to gain feedback where wanted as part of classroom learning, to defuse social issues in the school yard and to resolve confusion about world events and major disasters. I was able to use this strategy successfully with the difficult class in the city. Jenny's model is especially important in the school years from early to mid-primary; it gives children an opportunity to explore values, social norms, effective communication and how we can help each other with issues and problems.

"In schools children and staff become trapped within negative cycles of low self esteem. With children it is often their initial poor or inappropriate behavioural responses that ensure they experience little or no learning or social success.

The issue of self-esteem in pupils and staff alike is crucial to the effectiveness and happiness of a school."

Jenny Mosley, Turn Your School Around

www.circle-time.co.uk

When we help children develop positive values about themselves and how they live we help them expand their understanding, not only of themselves but also of others and our world. It is essential that we raise children's awareness that humans do live in social groups. We can do this by nurturing their understanding of family, the classroom, school and community. Encouraging kindness to others provides them with a positive trait that they can build into their lives. I was blessed that my beloved Dad was a wonderful teacher in this area. He was a committed community man who helped create a local recreation centre, sporting oval and golf course. He served on the local council for over thirty years of his life and gave of his time generously. As a child I remember helping him make sandwiches when there was a bush fire and going to help harvest a crop because a farmer was sick, injured or unable to.

The quality of concern for others is imprinted deeply within me. Cultivate this concern early in children's lives and we help them to act with kindness. All win and the inner feeling of joy is tangible and lasts for ages. Our rapid-paced living has decreased acts of service, because people are simply too busy. Many sporting groups and service clubs now find it hard to attract volunteers to help run the programs that assist in the development of healthy children and communities. If you want your child to be a person with character and personal worth then you need to model that pattern of behaviour; find opportunities to do so.

"When a child's environment does furnish a model, it follows that the nature of the intelligence or ability awakened and developed in the child will reflect the nature of the child's model. Likewise though to an indeterminable degree, the nature or extent of governance a child displays over the impulses of the more primitive systems in his or her brain will depend upon the nature of the governance exhibited by the model caregiver."

Joseph Chilton Pearce, The Biology of Transcendence: A Blueprint of the Human Spirit.

Pearce discusses the importance of development of the adolescent brain, during a secondary prefrontal development stage, where there is a critical window of opportunity for growth in maturity, particularly in emotional and social functioning. This begins at fifteen and continues to around twenty-two years of age, opening the heart's latent capacity to function. In Pearce's words,

"If no nurturing or modelling is given, the powers of the heart can't unfold – they will be dormant for life."

Joseph Chilton Pearce, The Biology of Transcendence, p54.

These critical years of pre-frontal development are essential in the development of an emotionally competent adult. They also coincide with important years at school when the focus on teenagers is mainly on their cognitive ability and development.

How important are heart-centred teachers who model emotional and social maturity, compassion, positive life values and healthy senses of humour? They are essential to the future health and wellbeing of the next generation!

I remember when a troubled fifteen-year old boy joined one of my classes and it was obvious he had a low level of literacy. He appeared confused because when he tried to be disruptive and discourteous the other students looked at him as if he was strange; no-one spoke like that in our class. Within a couple of days he had settled into the new norm by becoming polite and positive. I could also see that he was comfortable as there were others in the class who were not frightened to show their weakness or vulnerability. Indeed, he was able to ask for help and his improved attitude meant that his grades began to improve. Another instance involved a boy who had been labelled a 'trouble maker'. Within two days of joining my class I asked him to take some excursion money to the front office. Returning, he ambled up to my desk and I thanked him for doing such a great job. I could see he wanted to say something and asked if he could help me after class. Once everyone else had left, I asked if everything was alright. His response was that he was feeling a bit weird - because no-one had ever given him a job like that before. No-one had ever trusted him before. How can we learn about trust and responsibility without experiencing it and how it feels, without being exposed to the inherently positive feeling of knowing that regardless of what you look like, spell like, run like or the colour of your skin you can help someone. You can make the world a better place in some way, because of who you are.

There are a number of ways children can learn and practise the gift of concern for others and to discover the benefits of loving service. For modelling service and community spirit:

❖ collect papers or mail for a neighbour when they are away

❖ care for friends' pets when they are away

❖ take soup to sick family, friends or neighbours

- ❖ help elderly people with tasks like shopping and gardening

- ❖ make crafty gifts that cost little and give them to people in need

- ❖ make cookies, scones or muffins for people in need, or for birthdays

- ❖ take small gifts of gratitude to teachers and carers

- ❖ phone and send cards or letters to thank people for kindnesses

- ❖ share toys and the like with friends

- ❖ practise random acts of kindness to others

- ❖ make a family friend a cuppa without being asked

- ❖ help with family chores without being asked

- ❖ pray for someone

- ❖ send rainbows of love and kindness to people and countries in need

- ❖ smile lots

- ❖ say hello to people at school or in the community who seem sad or lonely

- ❖ give a gentle shoulder rub to family or friend

- ❖ leave a loving note on family member's pillow to share why you love them

- ❖ with permission, gather blankets for a blanket drive

- ❖ knit a scarf and donate it to a charity

- ❖ pick up broken glass on the road or path

- ❖ give family and friends a hug

- ❖ feed the ducks.

A very obvious way to build character in children and teenagers is to watch an uplifting movie with them. Chat with them about if afterwards, what happened and the choices the characters made. There are some golden oldies.

- ❖ Dead Poet's Society
- ❖ Good Will Hunting
- ❖ Alaska
- ❖ Life is a House
- ❖ I am Sam
- ❖ Pay it Forward
- ❖ Braveheart
- ❖ Lion King
- ❖ Shrek

It is important to ensure that you are mindful of the appropriate ages for children to watch certain films, videos and DVDs and of the children's personalities. I find Star Wars, Lord of the Rings and Harry Potter movies way too scary for me and I am fifty years of age! My youngest son brought Finding Nemo home for me to watch one night and he had to warn me, "Now Mum, I have to warn you – there are some pretty scary crabs in this movie!"

Literature and books can build a deep sense of character. I grew up in a home without TV, which meant that I was deeply affected by the books around me. Today, the huge runaway success of the Harry Potter books brings many children and adults back to books and the archetypal battle of good versus evil that can shape the inner world of us all. A sense of victory when good wins over evil feeds the 'goodness orientation' that is within us all. The personal battles of key protagonists that are portrayed within quality fiction can also expand our perceptions of how people can choose to live their lives. As a former English teacher, I have experienced the changing beliefs and misplaced preconceptions of many of my students as we studied great texts, in a robust, open-minded setting. Drama and stage performances can also entertain and challenge us as we witness unfolding conflicts. The arts are enormously important in the healthy growth and development of character, for all of us and not just children.

Non-fiction texts, biographies and autobiographies are also important to expand our minds and hearts and possibly to shake any unhealthy beliefs around ourselves and how we live our lives So many excellent books are available in our bookstores and libraries. One of my favourites is Janine Shepherd's Never Tell Me Never. This inspiring book documents an Australian Olympian cyclist Janine's struggle to overcome a serious accident that happened during training. This incredibly powerful autobiography shows how resilient and strong Janine is as a person and, more importantly, the depth of her character as her journey to recovery unfolded.

Another excellent book is The Diary of Anne Frank, and fortunately this is still studied in schools today.

"The best remedy for those who are afraid, lonely or unhappy is to go outside, somewhere where they can be quiet, alone with the heavens, nature and God. Because only then does one feel that all is as it should be and that God wishes to see people happy, amidst the simple beauty of nature."

The Diary of Anne Frank

This young girl had incredible strength of character for one so young. It is the simple wisdom that she shared about coping with fear and injustice that leaves a powerful mark on every person who reads her testimony.

It is sad that with today's young surrounded by the technological explosion of visual special effects and simulated, virtual images they are less likely to read a book like The Diary of Anne Frank, because it is slow and visually dull. The growth of character that evolves through a book is more like real life than a film or TV show. A book allows the developing psyche of our children and adolescents to be opened and to draw some positive impressions with which to review their own lives. If you can, please encourage love of the written word in your child well before they develop an adulation of the film, DVD, computer and TV world.

Life is a journey of growth where each and every individual is presented with choices and options each day. Sometimes we make choices that create great suffering, other times we make choices that allow great joy and abundance in our lives. In the total journey of life both types of choice help to define us and shape our character and humanity.

"We tried so hard to make things better for our kids that we made them worse.
For my grandchildren, I'd know better.

I'd really like for them to know about hand-me-down clothes and home-made ice cream and leftover meatloaf. I really would.

My cherished grandson, I hope you learn humility by surviving failure and that you learn to be honest even when no one is looking.

I hope you learn to make your bed and mow the lawn and wash the car — and I hope nobody gives you a brand-new car when you are sixteen.

It will be good if at least one time you can see a baby calf born, and you have a good friend to be with you if you ever have to put your old dog to sleep.

I hope you get a black eye fighting for something you believe in.

I hope you have to share a bedroom with your younger brother. And it is all right to draw a line down the middle of the room, but when he wants to crawl under the covers with you because he's scared, I hope you'll let him.

And when you want to see a Disney movie and your kid brother wants to tag along, I hope you take him.

I hope you have to walk uphill with your friends and that you live in a town where you can do it safely.

If you want a slingshot, I hope your father teaches you how to make one instead of buying one. I hope you learn to dig in the dirt and read books, and when you learn to use computers, you also learn how to add and subtract in your head.

I hope you get razzed by friends when you have your first crush on a girl, and that when you talk back to your mother you learn what Ivory soap tastes like.

May you skin your knee climbing a mountain, burn your hand on the stove and stick your tongue on a frozen flagpole.

I hope you get sick when someone blows smoke in your face. I don't care if you try beer once, but I hope you won't like it. And if a friend offers you a joint or any drugs, I hope you are smart enough to realize that person is not your friend.
I sure hope you make time to sit on a porch with your grandpa or go fishing with your uncle.
I hope your mother punishes you when you throw a baseball through a neighbour's window, and that she hugs you and kisses you when you give her a plaster of paris mould of your hand.

These things I wish for you — tough times and disappointment, hard work and happiness."

Lee Pitts, Keeping the dream alive (World Wide Web).

It sometimes takes experiences of great pain and suffering for us to dig deep within ourselves and search for that which has as yet remained invisible. The shaping of our true nature or character continues throughout life. I have a friend who is currently serving a long jail sentence. I met him when I was running a life-skills program in a maximum security prison. He uses much of his time studying, learning and healing.

"The world is complicated and unfortunately the contribution of a few countries of late has set us back many years. I hazard a guess that people are going to be much traumatised over the coming years. It seems to me that life is indeed a constant emotional challenge that is somehow aimed at bursting our bubble. Thank heavens for it being this way; it would be a rather mundane old life of vanity and ignorance if it weren't for the ups and downs. The upsetting part of this trauma we face in the modern world, a world where the change to a new millennium presented us with an opportunity to change our ways, is that instead of learning from the blunders of the past, we have become worse than ever. We do not need to be doing what we are doing out there in the real world; we do not need to be at war with ourselves. What I believe is that humanity needs to turn toward the vitality of life, rather than continuing to hold on so god damned tightly to what we all seem to think we possess......I think we should be grateful for what we have had, for what we continue to experience now, at this very moment, and understand that we cannot imprison good fortune and hold it there. It is dynamic and it flows with the forces of nature, as indeed we all do……."

P.Berghella, Albany (2003)

This man now recognizes that he was walking a destructive pathway before he was locked away. He wonders who he would be now if he had not received his 'wake-up call'. He uses his time in jail to re-create himself and to learn from wise masters, the literature, theology and the arts. He has grown in character and will be a wise teacher when he is released.

The growth of an individual's character, their true essence, is a journey involving something that is often invisible and intangible. This something that Joseph Campbell called "the hero's journey". Character is shaped by life experience and cannot be seen from the outside or from physical appearances. It cannot be judged by prizes and accolades. Nor can it be judged by age or culture. Character can only be ascertained from how a person lives and interacts with others. It is shown by a person's capacity to be themselves and not imitations of others. It is a quality that is felt and experienced through the human body, mind heart and it creates a "knowing." My best understanding of a positive human character that is worthy of respect and honour is a person who uses their unique gifts to make the world a better place, while holding a place of unconditional regard for all. This means that people with disabilities and those who live in poverty or suffer horrific accidents can all be people of great substance and great worth.

The Endless Journey

"Every single child ever born
is a one off, unique special
human being.

Every child ever born is born with a mind,
a body, a heart and soul.

Every child ever born is born with the
gift of a free will so that the child
can choose the life journey they wish to travel.

Every child ever born is born with gifts and talents that are
unique to them so that they can fulfil their own potential.
Sometimes these gifts are hard to find.

Every child ever born will be hurt or wounded in some way as a
child. This wound will need to be healed before they can
become the best person they can be.

Every child ever born wants to feel loved, valued and
appreciated exactly as they are by the people
closest to them.

Every child ever born wants to make the world a better place by
using their unique gifts and talents
in a positive and peaceful way.

Sometimes life can seem to be cruel and we can feel very
unloved, unnoticed and un-special. Everyone feels like this at
some time in their life.

Sometimes in life our bodies will cause us pain and
disappointment. We all only get one body and it is up to us to
care for it as best we can with healthy foods, exercise and plenty
of clean, fresh water.

Sometimes in life our minds will cause us pain and confusion.
We all only get one mind and it is up to us to care for it with
healthy living, lots of learning and with positive kind
thoughts about ourselves, others and our world.

Sometimes in life our hearts can get really hurt when we lose
someone we love, when we feel rejected or when we
feel lost and alone.

We are the only one who can heal our hearts through kindness,
understanding and forgiveness. However we heal faster with the
help of people we love and trust. When we heal our hearts we
can truly feel at home within ourselves.

Sometimes in life our soul gets wounded and crushed by the
experiences we have. Once again you are the gardener of your

own soul and you must make the time to take care of this ancient connection to our other Home.

At the end of your physical life your beautiful soul, with all its life's learnings locked into its memory goes Home. Everyone goes Home.

Even though every child ever born can sometimes feel lost and alone you never are. You are always protected and guided by special guardians from Home. You are never alone.

Every child ever born is invisibly linked and connected to every other child ever born. We all want the same things, we all feel the same things and we all get hurt by the same things. We are all part of the whole 'being-ness' of Life on Earth regardless of colour, age, gender or culture.

We are all one.

Every child ever born lives on a
beautiful, wise and caring place called Mother Earth.
All of us are her children. She loves us all and she cares for us while we are here. She is our home while we are away from Home.

Every child ever born needs to know the truth.
You now know.

Remember you already are loved, special and unique.

Your purpose here on Mother Earth is to make this a better place in some small way by using your gifts.

We all go home when we have finished our life journey - no matter what.

Simply be the best person you can be."

Maggie Dent (2003) Audio CD

May we all hold a vision that every child has a unique potential for creating a character and humanity that will improve our world in some way. Let us release our perceptions of seeing academic and physical prowess as preferred over the experience of living life in accordance with the universal truths that honour all living things in a context of love and respect. Let us live with the perception that within every child is a calling to 'greatness', no matter how big or small. We are all responsible for helping our young to find their gifts and talents and to express them positively.

More often than not a knowing:

"To compose our character is our duty....
Our great and glorious masterpiece
Is to live appropriately.
All other things,
To rule, To lay up treasure,
To build
are at most but little
appendices and props."

Michel De Montaigne (1533-1592)

The philosopher and writer Joseph Campbell wrote beautifully about the hero's journey. This metaphor encompasses human life well. We have moments of greatness and moments of great pain and suffering when all seems lost.

Life is seldom smooth and conflict free. The more tools we develop over the years to help us bounce back, then the better quality of life we live. Resilience tends to be more evident in people of good character. It is the capacity to get up, get back into life and let the past stay where it is, in the past. Resilience is something we can help our children develop. Protecting children from pain and disappointment does not assist them in developing effective protective mechanisms or the mental and physical toughness for living life. This is why it takes 'a whole tribe to raise a child'; this is why the return to a family and a community model of raising our children is important. Birth and death are a part of normal family life and of home life, keeping medical and professional intervention in balance. When children are surrounded by all the things that make up the whole picture of life, as shared experiences, families can pull through disasters and enjoy celebrating the moments of success and positive change.

Kids Who Are Different

Here's to kids who are different
Kids who don't always get A's
Kids who have ears
Twice the size of their peers
And noses that go on for days.

Here's to kids who are different
Kids they call crazy or dumb
Kids who don't fit
With the guts and the grit
Who dance to a different drum.

Here's to kids who are are different
Kids with a mischievous streak
For when they have grown
As history has shown
It's their difference that makes them unique.

Digby Wolfe.

Since the beginning of mankind people have been birthing, raising children and dying. People have not always had university trained professionals, counsellors, medical equipment and drugs, cars, washing machines, mobile phones, computers, consumerism, technology and globalization. The main purpose in life was to continue the species. To achieve that people worked beside each other, for each other and for the future of their children. They accepted responsibility for the type of adult the children would become and they placed, almost accidentally, the holistic growth of children as their number one priority.

Because parents were so busy maintaining homes with no time saving products like washing machines, dryers, dishwashers, gas and electric stoves and microwave ovens children were able to develop how nature intended -by entertaining themselves with simple toys, plastic cupboards, pots and pans in quiet environments. They were not propped up in front of screens like TV's and force fed educational programs before three and bombarded by noise from the technological age. The so called benefits of modern living are the very things that may be frying our children's brains and what we think is good for growing babies may be the reverse – and may be what is adding to the increasing numbers of children with ADHD, autism and delayed development. One autism expert I spoke to recently told me that the first thing she does in homes of an autistic child is get rid of the three T's – TV, toys and too much talking! Our homes are overstimulated and in a hurry for rapid child development because everything else is so rapid. The first few years need to be quieter calmer and with as little external input as possible.

Today, we squeeze raising children in among busy lives. Children are sicker, fatter, sadder and more disconnected than ever before in the history of mankind. My prayer is that we change our focus and, no matter what research offers and academics profess, we permit our children to have natural childhoods. A natural childhood takes place in communities that honour family and share the raising of children in ways that are based on values, manners, resilience and a commitment to creating character. This is over and above attaining academic benchmarks, doing often meaningless homework and wasting life experiences by spending so much time studying for educational assessments; these count for nothing when real life challenges present themselves.

One of the privileges of working in the funeral industry is that you get to hear many life stories of unsung heroes. People who have overcome amazing odds to survive, who often had no education and who had raised wonderful offspring and made the world a better place. I know about true character because I have heard their stories told by people who loved and respected them. Few of these unsung heroes will ever win any accolades or prizes. Yet to me they rank above those who find fame as a result of being able to pretend they are someone else or they can play tennis or golf.

I want to tell you about one of my unsung heroes. I had a phone call to visit a 70 year old lady who had agoraphobia. She hadn't been to the shops or to afternoon tea with her family for over 15 years. She worked with me and learned how to calm her fears by using relaxing visualizations, deep breathing and praying. This lovely lady overcame her fears and happily re joined the world at 74 years of age. This special lady, tiny as she was, was a hero in my eyes. Her name was Peggy Williams and her wonderful supportive husband was John. Character takes many shapes and forms and can grow at any age.

It matters not what has happened in your past, your childhood or bad fortune. It is important how you deal with whatever comes your way, and how you move on in your life that really counts. If you forget how to dream of greatness, or how to re-create yourself following disaster, then you will surely stay in a rut and never realise your blessed potential. Remember the best revenge for a challenging childhood is to be happy as an adult. This is what true character is about.

Key Points

❖ Focus on development of character in our young

❖ Show children a code that includes how to behave acceptably in social settings

❖ Children learn good manners from the adults who model them

❖ Values-based education is essential in developing character in our young

❖ Circle time helps children in schools learn effective, compassionate communication and builds self esteem

❖ Kindness to others and acts of service are character-building qualities

❖ The arts help build strong perceptions of good character

❖ Encourage children and young adults to read good literature and non- fiction texts

❖ All life experiences build character when understood and appreciated

❖ Individuals build good qualities of character at any stage of their lives

❖ Good character crosses physical, mental, cultural and spiritual boundaries

❖ Good character allows a person to become the best they can be

❖ Every child has a unique potential waiting to be uncovered

❖ Seek the highest good within each person we meet, regardless of differences

❖ We are all responsible for helping our young to develop character, personal strength and wisdom – it does not happen by chance

Chapter 10

Boys and Emotional Literacy

"Emotional literacy is the most valuable gift we can offer our students, and urging parents and educators to recognize the price boys pay when we hold them to an impossible standard of manhood is important in today's modern world."

Clark Wight, Principal, Christ Church Grammar Junior School, Western Australia

It is a risk being born a boy. Statistics show clearly that boys and men are more at risk of the following:

- Injury as a result of an accident, sport or risky behaviours
- Failure at school
- Offences involving criminal activity
- Being killed as a pedestrian, in motor accidents or at work
- Alcohol and drug abuse
- Suicide.

An Introduction to the New Men's Health, Richard Fletcher 1995 (Men's Health Project, University of Newcastle).

When I first read the above I, as a mother of four sons whose ages at that time ranged from seven to fifteen, felt sick to my stomach! How was I going to keep them alive? How was I going to keep them safe? I also knew from my counselling work that troubled boys seldom seek help, or even acknowledge they may need help.

More and more boys in our schools are becoming aggressive, violent, inattentive and hyperactive. This is happening at younger and younger ages. Many boys are in emotionally charged situations that challenge and confuse them. Many boys are frustrated in school systems that are conditioned against boys, or that have teachers inadequately trained to meet the learning needs and styles of most boys. Unless you can build rapport with a boy you will struggle in your ability to really connect and communicate with him.

The whole emotional domain of feelings, theirs and others, is pretty hard for boys to understand. Irrational feelings that are hard to control cause much angst and confusion. The need for boys to mask their emotional state causes even more uncertainty and confusion. Many boys bury their anger and rage over many years until this unexpressed anger turns into depression, bitterness, sarcasm, irritability or pettiness. Unfortunately, they freeze out the positive feelings at the same time, which makes it difficult for them to maintain loving relationships. Adults who try to give advice to boys often unintentionally inflame emotions. If you wish to control boys' behaviours, overtly or indirectly, then watch out! Nagging and questioning boys will only add to the volatility of relationships. Boys, of course, learn to become selectively deaf very early in life and sometimes do this unconsciously, and as a result they miss valuable learning opportunities in classes.

I have noticed that the boys who cope best in school have strong auditory processing abilities. Auditory learners usually make up about 15% of the population. Professors Ken and Rita Dunn reported the following:

❖ Only a third of students remember even 75% of what they hear in class
❖ Tactile or kinaesthetic learners are the main candidates for failure in traditional school classrooms

- ❖ Tactile-kinaesthetic learners often drop out of school because they cannot focus well when forced to sit down, hour after hour
- ❖ Many people in schools are high achievers in linguistic and logical learning styles, so to them that environment works best
- ❖ Most underachievers are motivated by their peers to be so
- ❖ The overwhelming majority of boys are kinaesthetic learners.

(The Learning Revolution, Ken & Rita Dunn 1997 pp349-355)

Boys learn best through teachers who they like or who they think likes them. This is why it is so important to teach teachers how to build rapport with boys because that helps them feel connected, understood and valued. Despite what they show with their tough masks, boys are very much influenced positively or negatively by the perceived absence of acceptance and genuine care. Humour is an essential component in connecting with boys. It also helps prepare them for the world of manhood where men are the practical jokers and jesters. They will listen to you if you build a connection through humour or moments of lightness. They hate being told what to do, hate being lectured, nagged, shamed, yelled at and hate being coerced or manipulated to behave in a certain way. (Yes, we all hate these things and yet the traditional schooling model believed this was the best way to manage boys, especially in our schools and colleges!) They will respond with anger, frustration and resentment and when that emotional tension combines with a surge in testosterone, which occurs spontaneously and randomly, there is a high chance that aggression will follow.

Boys naturally like to be able to 'fix' things that do not work properly. I believe boys need extra reassurance that they will be able to cope and that they will get better and better at managing the seemingly irrational emotional challenges of life. Also, we need to let them know that asking for help is a sign of strength and not a sign of weakness. I just pray that there is someone who is non-judgemental, older and wiser, who they can share the confusion of their lives with, and that this person (possibly a teacher, a coach or a chaplain who the boy believes likes them) will not try to take the boy's problems from them or offer unsolicited advice.

The newer therapies like NLP (Neuro Linguistic Programming), thought field therapy and kinesiology are great for boys. They can diffuse intense anger and rage without having to talk about it much. In my experience with boys in schools and homes, I have discovered they need quiet spaces to help sort out their thoughts. I am sure that too many parents and teachers overcrowd their boys with too much talk and too many questions. It took me a while to realise that my boys settled better by playing by themselves outside, especially after a full school day.

"Silence is often an excellent way of letting our sons find their own solutions rather than us imposing our own." (Ian Lillico: Boys and Their Schooling, 2000).

How often does a boy get sent to detention, and told to "go and think about what you have done!" NLP suggests that this strategy may increase the likelihood of the boy repeating the experience as it is anchored in his visual memory. Also boys get shamed, yelled at, bullied and verbally abused more than girls in some misguided sense it will toughen them up. So often in boys who become suicidal there are core issues of serious shaming that came from childhood that have contributed to their mental crisis. When there is a conflict that ends in an inappropriate response like shouting, hitting or yelling we need to be aware that the boy will be functioning from his hind brain or brain stem. This is where our survival instincts are buried and much of our instinctive behaviour comes from. To move to the frontal lobe where we can process from a higher level of intelligence, where we can make choices and consider outcomes, we need time and also the removal of threat. Giving time out to calm down and reflect is a valuable thing to do at this point. Then the following request will bring a much more beneficial outcome: "Go and think about a different choice you could have made, that would have created a more positive and appropriate outcome for all concerned". How often do we as parents or educators try to resolve conflict at the moment it occurs? It is almost impossible for the children concerned to do this without some quiet time to calm and reflect. Brain research has discovered that it takes boys and men longer to move from the left brain (rational thought) to the right brain (creative thought) and this time delay happens often when they are asked to respond to an emotional question like " How do you feel about…?" Rather than it being a problem or something to be judgemental about, parents and educators can simply adjust their communications and interactions to allow for this gender difference.

Empathy is an extremely important emotional intelligence skill that boys struggle to develop without guidance. It can help boys make better decisions when they meet personal conflict. I firmly believe that boys respond to physical violence because they know no other way of 'fixing' the problem. One of the beautiful benefits of Jenny Mosley's circle work with children is the way that it builds empathy and creative problem solving. This especially helps boys to develop these aspects of the frontal lobe in the brain in a safe environment and well before puberty hits!
Australian Dr Arne Rubinstein has spent many years researching boys and the journey to manhood. He believes the following is true for boys:

Boy Psychology:

I seek acknowledgment.
I want it all for me.
Power is for my benefit.
I am the centre of the universe.

I believe I am immortal.
I take no responsibility for my actions.
I want a mother.

If you have lived with boys you will know about the "I want it all for me!" tendency. My number three son could demolish a one kilogram tub of yoghurt without even considering that any one else in the family might like some......until the last mouthful! And how many long term relationships have been contaminated with men wanting mothers instead of equal partners! No wonder the passion dies in the bedroom – what man really wants to sleep with his mother??

The journey to healthy manhood involves these concepts and beliefs evolving into the following:

Healthy Man Psychology:

I seek that which I believe in.
I share with my community.
Power is for the good of all.
I am just part of the universe.
I know I am mortal.
I take full responsibility for my actions.
I want a relationship with a woman.

(From www.menshealthandwellbeing.org.au)

This journey of maturation needs the input of healthy men who are comfortable with the innate process of evolution that allows a boy to grow into a healthy man. In many areas of the world today we have women in single parent families who have the main responsibility of raising a son. Women cannot take boys on the manhood journey and the role of supportive men in our families, our schools and our communities is essential in the development of boys into healthy men. As a mother of sons I have learned much about "letting go" and about allowing boys to keep secrets from their mothers without taking it personally. That will be explored in a later book I am writing called Dear Boys: the Healthy Mothering of Boys.

Quiet "downtime" is really important in the lives of children. In homes and classrooms where regular relaxation and silent time occurs, the most noticeable positive benefit is the improvement in boys' behaviour and concentration. Boys prefer quiet spaces to think, and yet they are often the ones making the noise!! I believe that boys who learn how to bring more silence and stillness into their lives manage the emotional roller coaster of adolescence better than those who have no idea how to become quiet and still. In the quieter moments the unconscious mind has a better chance to make sense of experiences, create more positive solutions to problems and allow boys to feel less overwhelmed. The constant activity and busy-ness of boys may also lead them to create stress-related illnesses later in adulthood. The magic of silence and stillness for boys must be taught as well as modelled, because it is not a normal activity for most boys. The earlier the better! Stress related illnesses later in life account for over 75% of all illnesses and this stress busting method can help reduce anxiety and tension in the nervous system. As boys do less emotional debriefing with friends than girls do , they are more at risk of emotional overwhelm that many numb with alcohol, drugs and risk taking behaviour. Clark Wight, a principal of a private junior school in Western Australia, believes that:

"we as teachers and parents need to listen to boys' voices. It is an opportunity to de-construct the 'boy code' —old rules that favour male stoicism that make boys ashamed about expressing weakness, vulnerability and their own emotions. It is about giving boys an opportunity to use their 'voice', to enable us to give the consistent attention, empathy and support they truly need and desire, as well as to give parents and teachers some tools to try and understand our sons and students even better."

("A Time to Connect: Being 10 and Moving Forward." 2005)

When boys are met with big emotional challenges, how you support them at this time is critical. They need lots of time to work out how to deal with the problem, quite often alone, and usually somewhere safe. Tell them you are there for them but take guidance from them on what you can do that helps. Do not assume anything! Ask them who they would prefer to see for advice or help.

Latest brain research has explained the "paper bag" stage of adolescent boys between 14-18. Many teachers and parents will know than many boys seem to lose the ability to speak clearly and they sound like they have a paper bag over their head and they respond only in grunts. This is also a time when they seem to be less motivated about manners, cleanliness, personal hygiene, effective empathetic communication, school work and how to be a sociable being! The brain apparently does a pruning of unused parts of the brain at this stage and so they actually can go backwards and you may wonder where they have gone! They struggle with decision making, self motivation and are prone to making very risky decisions. The good news is that the brain has two other significant growth spurts, the first one around 18 when they start to speak in sentences again and wash their hair a little more often. This is an age where boys make better decisions about work opportunities and education. Then the next growth takes place in the frontal lobe around 22-24 and this is when you suddenly discover that your parenting was not a complete failure! They become more emotionally mature, sensitive and much better at forming life enhancing relationships. Many young men decide to plan for their futures, and start thinking of others and now often re-connect to their siblings! Please hang in there until this age – and pray often. They will come out of the tunnel of adolescence and over 80% become decent human beings! Of course these stages of brain development can be seriously impaired by excessive use of marijuana, speed and amphetamines and binge drinking.

Yes, raising boys is a risky business. But just consider how dull would our world be if not for boys – with their energy, their cheeky sense of humour and their lust for life and adventure. Even though they do make most of the noise in classrooms and homes, they benefit enormously from silence and stillness, less questions and less commands, and more space, and being heard – they need people in their lives who are not afraid to love them, warts and all, and they especially value people who share laughter and lightness with them! They are biologically wired to work hard, mentally and physically, and to defend those most vulnerable in our world especially in times of crisis. If they have been shown how to behave in such a way.

Emotionally literate men who have a capacity to be aware, conscious and committed to leave the world better than they found it, are the key to healthy boys.

WHAT IS A BOY?

A boy is an explorer
from his very early days
who finds fun and adventure
in the most surprising ways.

He's a builder of wooden blocks,
a climber of apple trees,
a teller of jokes and stories,
with a grin that's sure to please.

He's a friend of little creatures
like puppies, frogs and bugs.
He's a player of almost any game.
A winner of hearts and hugs.

He's a dreamer of great dreams,
the future's hope and joy.
He'll bring you worlds of happiness,
that wonderful little boy!
(source Unknown)

Key Points

❖ It is a much greater risk to be a boy

❖ Boys get easily confused about emotions

❖ Boys are more inattentive and susceptible to hyperactivity than girls

❖ Boys learn best through teachers who they like or who they think likes them

❖ Boys are largely kinaesthetic learners and struggle if kept still and having to listen too long

❖ Boys benefit from quietness and space

❖ Avoid shaming boys as it damages their spirit and creates deep low self esteem issues later in adolescence

❖ Healthy maturation of boys needs healthy men – women cannot take boys on this journey to manhood

❖ Boys need an adult ally from childhood if possible, especially through adolescence

❖ We all need to listen to boys' voices and help them deconstruct the old boys code

❖ Brain development from 12 -22 explains much "it's a boy thing" behaviour

❖ The world would be a dull place without boys.

Chapter 11

Spiritual Intelligence Unplugged

"Spirit is the innermost quality of being. It is that part of us that is unstained, the primordial beauty from which we derive every inspiration, an inborn reservoir from which we can draw every jewel of excellence, the source of universal love and compassion, the clear radiance from which wisdom is born."

Geshe Lobsang Tenzin

Director of the Deprung Monastery in North America. What is Spirit: Messages from the Heart. Lexie Brockway Potamkin 1999

The word spiritual has strong connotations. Over the last century the gap has widened between two ways of interpreting the world and reality in general, intellectually and spiritually. In writing about spiritual intelligence I run the risk of alienating the more intellectual reader who perhaps has a strong background in academia and science. Many perceive the 'spiritual camp' as irrational and ungrounded at times and in opposition to the intellectual way of thinking. It is time to be more open-minded and to broaden our understanding of life. We can do this by revisiting previously challenging beliefs. Rigid thinking limits us all and creates divisions between people, cultures and global systems. Consciousness is evolving, whether we like it or not, and a balance between the two worlds of thinking would serve to be a positive shift. In many ways I have seen myself as a bridge between them. John Miller PhD writes in a similar vein about education.

"The holistic curriculum attempts to restore a balance between linear thinking and intuition." And " the focus of holistic education is on relationships – the relationship between linear thinking and intuition, the relationship between mind and body, the relationship between various domains of knowledge, the relationship between the individual and the community, the relationship with the earth and the relationship between self and Self."

John Miller PhD. The Holistic Curriculum 1996, p86

Spiritual intelligence is as important as emotional intelligence. I feel strongly that by building spiritual intelligence in young children we can help them understand themselves, others and the world. We can better prepare them to manage life. Yet spiritual intelligence is hard to explain and to explore. It is impossible to measure quantitatively and that makes it hard to evaluate. It has also been perceived as 'fluffy' as it cannot be discerned logically or with reason by scholars and members of the academic world. Spirituality places us in a constantly developing and evolving journey that requires life experience to activate natural questioning and searching. It is not determined by study or by research and rarely follows a linear path or direction.

How can we tell if a person is spiritually intelligent? And how can we help our children to become spiritually competent? Tobin Hart considers,

"One of the things we usually associate with 'spiritual people' is the quality of their moral and ethical choices. This usually means choices guided by care for others (relationships) and for what is right and just (universal principles)".

Tobin Hart. The Secret Spiritual World of Children 2003, p74

Deepak Chopra offers another explanation.

"A child raised with spiritual skills will be able to answer the most basic questions about how the   universe works; she will understand the source of creativity both within and outside herself; she will be able to practice non-judgement, acceptance and truth…..and she will be free from the crippling fear and anxiety about the meaning of life that is the secret dry rot inside the hearts of most adults….."

Deepak Chopra. Seven Spiritual Laws for Parents (1997) p 6

Now you can understand why the subject is a challenge both to explore and to teach to others! Rather than be led off up the many pathways that explore spirituality, some ancient and some contemporary, I would like to focus on ways that we can help build spiritual intelligence in children starting from an early age.

Universal truths that reflect core values about living with respect of self, others and our world are an excellent place to start. They give us a template to use at any age as we navigate life experience. Take, for example, the following.

The Native American Ten Commandments

- ❖ Treat the Earth and all who dwell thereon with respect
- ❖ Remain close to the Great Spirit
- ❖ Show great respect to your fellow beings
- ❖ Work together for the benefit of Mankind
- ❖ Give assistance and kindness wherever needed
- ❖ Do what you know to be right
- ❖ Look after the wellbeing of mind and body
- ❖ Dedicate a share of your efforts to the greater Good
- ❖ Be truthful and honest at all times
- ❖ Take full responsibility for your actions

These Native American commandments are a valid and worthwhile set of guidelines on how to live positively, regardless of which cultural group we belong to. Having such guidelines for children to follow or aspire to is essential in the building of spiritually mature and competent adults. The Bible's Ten Commandments offer another set of guidelines that can help parents and families to raise spiritually competent children and young adults. It is not so much what set of guidelines you adopt as ensuring that you have a strong template for your children to determine positive choices about how to behave.

A core aspect of healthy spiritual intelligence is awareness of the difference between the inner world and the outer world. Being able to interpret the events and experiences of life with a healthy balance of mind and spirit is a good indicator of having good levels of emotional, social and spiritual competency. My work as a teacher and counsellor has shown me that the children and teenagers most at risk were those who were unaware of the inner world of their being. These young people were at the mercy of powerful negative inner critic voices. They often had an absence of consciously aware, loving and caring people in their lives. The result was a complete lack of connection to their inner wise counsel, or human spirit.

Many people have no knowledge of spirituality yet they have a place in their lives that nurtures the inner world. Men who love to spend time in their sheds just tinkering around are accessing their inner world. People who love to spend time in nature by themselves, whether bush walking, fishing, surfing or swimming, are accessing their inner world. Creative people who love to play music, paint or knit are also accessing their inner world.

Accessing your inner world is not complicated. It is rarely a struggle and can happen spontaneously. Living with a pattern of connection is natural for children. They love to drift between their real world and their imaginary inner world where they can seek meaning and understanding without obvious parental influence. Children dream and imagine possibilities for the future that are positive and expanded. This is incredibly healthy for them. Being questioned or interrogated about their inner world is a sure way of shutting it down. Without a doubt children have a secret spiritual world. Tobin Hart writes:

> "They have spiritual capacities and experiences – profound moments that shape their lives in enduring ways. They are sometimes stunning, often tender and reveal a remarkable spiritual world that has been kept largely secret. From moments of wonder, from asking the big questions about meaning and life to expressing compassion and even to seeing beneath the surface of the material world, these experiences serve as the touchstone of our lives as spiritual beings on Earth."

Tobin Hart, The Secret Spiritual World of Children 2003, p1

It is an honour and privilege to share moments of enlightenment with children. One occasion will always hold a very special place in my memory. I once met a young boy I will call Benny who was struggling at school. He was about to be medicated for attention deficit hyperactive disease (ADHD) in the hope that it would help him concentrate better at school and be less 'hyper'. We chatted for a time and there were a few things about this nine-year old boy that left me in awe. Firstly, I did not have to build a rapport with him so that he could feel safe, he knew straight away. Secondly, he wanted to know about my work and why I made CDs and tapes for children. He then went on to share with me his view of separate realities and that he could be in more than one space at any time. Benny was very concerned about the social injustices in the world and he was most concerned with those that affected young children and babies. His insights about how to access his own inner-self, his wise counsel within, and how to help others were well beyond his years. Benny talked about how he saw God, or the Divine presence as he called it, and how he worried about people who lived without a Divine presence in their lives. His connection to nature was very strong and he used it as a way of grounding him and helping himself to calm. Benny had created his own mini meditations to help when he couldn't sleep; he wished his Mum would do them because she was much stressed and not sleeping well. The final part of our amazing discussion was on life purpose. He knew he was here to help others – he just wasn't sure how to do that best. We chatted about our natural gifts and the gift of free will that God has given us all. He became instantly at peace with being able to find his life purpose and getting on with his destiny. My heart still fills with warmth as I share this because of the huge impact this wise old soul in such a young body had on me. His presence and openness made my heart sing. I hope that our paths cross again one day so that we can chat some more.

I have another example of a wise young one with a high level of spiritual competence. She was a seven-year old girl who was brought to see me because she was sad and depressed. Angelique came into my office, sat down and said, "I have been looking for someone like you for ages". When I questioned how I might help she said, "Tell me why I am with my family...they are so alien to me. They smoke and drink excessively, they swear, they shout awful things at each other. They have no respect or love for nature and they have no God. Why am I with them?"   This little girl was struggling with being in an 'un-spiritual' family.

"Maybe you have come to teach them another way of living and being? Maybe you have been given this family to learn how to love unconditionally and you are in the perfect place for you to discover your gifts of compassion, empathy and patience", was my response. Immediately she brightened up. I gave her some reframing strategies to change her view of the world, some soul-strengthening activities, a CD and reassured her lots. She kept a strong spiritual practice in her life that was completely secret from her family. I often wonder how Angelique is today as she will now be thirteen years of age.

Spiritual competencies built together with emotional and social competencies give our children the tools for healthy, happy lives. One's capacity to form deep meaningful relationships, with oneself and others, and all areas of life are challenged without these tools. The number one key to resilience is connectedness to self, others and our world. Life challenges us from time to time and our capacity to get up from a knock and back into living is a product of the three competencies. Without a doubt, people with spiritual intelligence and a faith in the Divine bounce back quickly and probably don't fall as far.

I have found the following to be helpful for building a strong spiritual base with young children. These attributes are all part of what I loosely call spiritual intelligence, however, no one is definitive or more important than another. The key areas help build a strong connection to a child's inner world, where the gifts of the human spirit are born and nurtured.

Wonder

The unique childlike quality of wonder has a beautiful potential to bring joy and hope into our lives, easily and quickly. At any moment we can view something through the eyes of wonder and when we bring wonder into our everyday lives it adds sparkle and vitality. Enthusiasm is a key quality of wonder – it is infectious. As Daniel Goleman explains, "Emotions are contagious". The states that are evoked by them infect others – positively and negatively, intentionally and unintentionally. Being enthusiastic about nature, the sky, clouds, the moon or the stars on an inky dark night all help find wonder. Natural phenomena and places of beauty and majesty are also great for opening children to wonder; even having large posters or photographs of natural beauty throughout your home or classroom can help remind them of the 'wow' factors of nature.

Wonder works with the minute as well, like watching a cell split under a microscope, ants at work or a kitten being born, and is not always about the big aspects of life. Discovering knowledge and wisdom in beautiful books and archives can open to wonder. I believe the fast pace of life has helped to damage our sense of wonderment, especially in schools. Today's children are less likely to walk around our libraries in a sense of wonder than children of days gone by. Nowadays we tend to seek quick or ready-made answers instead of exploring wider possibilities with the mind's natural inquisitiveness and curiosity. While we cannot turn time back, I agree with Tobin Hart,

"We can begin to change this from the inside out by nurturing the natural openness in children, encouraging their big questions and making time for pondering."

Tobin Hart. The Secret Spiritual World of Children 2003, p104

Wonder has a transcendent quality to it. It allows us to expand beyond our ordinary waking state to something wider and 'more'. Rachael Kessler writes,

"Creating opportunities for students to transcend the barriers of gender, class, race, and belief not only nourishes the spirit but it is also the key to a civil society."

Rachael Kessler "The Soul of Education" 2003, p124

New knowledge and new learning that stretches us and excites us is also transcendent. Finding solutions to tough problems or resolving a conflict all have a sense of wonder and expansion about them. Wonder comes in many guises and forms. What is important is that we adults need to model an openness to it, and then our kids will keep their natural ability to find wonder in the world.

Awe

A closely related aspect of wonder and nurturing a spiritual intelligence in children is 'awe'. By this we essentially mean the capacity to see things as though for the first time, through a beginner's eyes. If you have ever witnessed a toddler see a dog or a cat for the first time you will know how awe can be expressed.

The natural capacity for awe seems to be diminishing as our modern world's fascination with technology and gadgets increases. Creating opportunities for children that they have not experienced before helps keep the gift of awe. Another way to help is to use the imagination. I have a clear memory of a class of six-year old children who, in the midst of creative visualization travelling to the moon on a magic cloud, reached out their hands to touch the moon. The looks of awe on their little faces were priceless.

Awe will stay alive and well only if we have that intent and we create time to assist our children to experience it. Take a moment and see the next wet day through the eyes of a child – kick your shoes or boots off and go and have fun in the puddles! Experience birthdays as moments of rare celebration and treat your child within with an ice-cream cake or maybe your favourite sweets. Otherwise, we will become desensitised to the awe of new things and happenings. Once again, the modern world does not place awe in a place of high priority and that may be why children need more and more frightening and challenging films to 'excite' them. Maybe this is another reason why Harry Potter is a runaway success; it fed the starving awe inside our children.

Listening with the heart

This aspect of emotional intelligence has been covered in the chapter on Building Intuition and Inner Guidance. Helping our children to sense with the heart and to be empathetic and compassionate is what listening with the heart is all about. Learning about it comes from many different sources. The main source is from living with adults who listen with their hearts, and who are truly loving, caring and understanding. This attribute is not something we are born with and **the sooner** a child is able to experience these qualities the better. The **more often** they experience listening with the heart the better. The **more varied ways** they experience emotional safety and consistency the better. This is the environment that helps a child create patterns of emotional self regulation and a healthy self concept, which are essential for emotional and social wellbeing later in life.

Daniel Goleman writes that our society needs to make it a priority to teach emotional literacy to our children,

"By leaving the emotional lessons children learn to chance, we risk largely wasting the window of opportunity presented by the slow maturation of the brain to help children cultivate a healthy emotional repertoire."

"Shouldn't we be teaching these most essential skills for life to every child — now more than ever? And if not now, when?"

Daniel Goleman. Emotional Intelligence 1995, p286, p287

Natural empathy is an interesting phenomenon. If a child fell over beside you what would your instinct be to do? Research shows that we are losing our natural empathetic tendencies; we are more likely to walk past someone in genuine need, to avoid 'getting involved'. Sad but true. Researcher Martin Hoffman argues that the roots of morality are found in empathy. He believes that one's capacity to empathise with a potential victim determines behaviour. Empathetic people are likely to help and those who are not are more likely to not assist. Rapists, psychopaths and child molesters are classic examples of people with a complete lack of empathy. It is important for children to be given guidance and encouragement to develop empathy in their lives at as young an age as possible.

Empathetic families are important in the development of a child's empathetic abilities and so too is the presence of empathetic carers and teachers in the early years of a child's life. Two of my sons were blessed to have a warm-hearted empathetic year-one teacher who sowed seeds of emotionally competent solutions to social challenges. Both sons loved her and this empathy extended to the parents of her students as well as her students. Even today both boys get a glazed look of happiness when they recall this special teacher.

Respect and reverence

Now more than ever before we are experiencing societies with little reverence or respect for others, for property or for ourselves. In recent newspaper reports there were accounts of the following.

❖ Elderly defenceless people being bashed

❖ Bus drivers being spat on by teenagers

❖ Graffiti on the increase

❖ Increasing numbers of incidents of road rage

❖ More brawls and violence at soccer and football games

❖ More violence on public transport

❖ Swans being bashed to death in a local park

❖ Dog tortured and killed by teenage boys

- ❖ Trees in parks killed by people seeking a better view

- ❖ Youths killed in a stolen car chased by police

- ❖ Welfare fraud cases increasing

- ❖ Illicit drug use continuing to rise

- ❖ Teenage pregnancies still on the rise

- ❖ Binge drinking, the new culture among teenagers especially in Australia

These are all examples of lack of respect and reverence that have been fuelled by emotional and social illiteracy. The result is situations of low or non-existent personal responsibility, complete disregard for anyone but self and poor moral fibre in the character of the people concerned - a recipe for trouble and crisis.

Teachers are very concerned about the absence of respect in classrooms and the impact this has. Bullying has become chronic all the way through our Western school systems, even in pre-school. These are signs of the appalling lack of respect that exists in today's world. My sense around the perceived lack of respect is that it is closely linked with emotional illiteracy. If a person is unable to manage their impulses, has low empathy and is unable to manage anger well, then they are likely to demonstrate a lack of respect in situations of challenge. Are such people capable of taking a small emotional pause during conflict to consider other possible solutions than punching someone they are annoyed at? Maybe all that person did was unintentionally cut in front of them on a roundabout? If a person is totally drunk and hurt in a fight what are the chances of them waiting patiently in a busy emergency department without becoming impatient and possibly aggressive?
Combining emotional illiteracy with a poor concept of self in an individual who may feel unloved and under valued increases the chances of these behaviours many fold.

Self acceptance and appreciation is an emotionally strengthening process that builds a person's ability to feel respect for self and for others. My experience in schools and communities is that a caring relationship must exist in some way before someone can have respect. Teachers who lack self respect also find it difficult to model this attribute for their students. It is impossible to fake respect for students and fellow staff if you have none for yourself and the life you are living. Students tell me that their capacity to respect their teachers is influenced by the following attributes of a teacher.

- ❖ Sense of Humour

- ❖ Fairness

- ❖ Mastery of the subject they teach

- ❖ Passion for their subject matter

Students are open to respecting a teacher if at least one of these characteristics is consistently present. If a teacher cares about how a student grows and develops, then that is the icing on the cake.

We have lost the ancient ways of honouring and valuing in today's world. Many indigenous people had patterns of reverence where one honoured the source of all life before each other. The elders were honoured, as were the children. The tribe saw the raising of children as everyone's responsibility and in this way respect and reverence was a part of living and breathing. This reverence extended to animals, waterways and the sky. Today, the pressure is to create wealth, comfort and speed, often at the expense of good health - physical, emotional, mental and spiritual. We cause severe harm to our environment and have senseless battles of power that erode basic human decencies. How can we expect respect from our children?

- ❖ We pour pollutants and chemicals into our drains and ultimately our oceans

- ❖ We cut down old growth forests and over fish our oceans

- ❖ We treat our elderly as nuisances and stick them into old people's homes that are horrid and sometimes unsafe for them

- ❖ We throw billions of tonnes of plastics away each year

- ❖ With globalisation, big corporations squeeze primary producers more and more and destroy country communities

- ❖ We seldom know our neighbours

- ❖ We have students in government schools with classrooms that have disgusting carpets and peeling paint on the walls

- ❖ Many families don't even share one meal a day together

- ❖ Colour and cultural prejudice exists in almost every society on earth

- ❖ Illiteracy is still high in areas of poverty even in developed countries

- ❖ Women and young children are raped and beaten often in countries experiencing civil unrest

- ❖ Indigenous kids are going deaf and blind because medical care is inadequate in remote areas

- ❖ Corruption prevents food, shelter and medical aid getting to sick and starving children

We have a global need for respect. Grass roots change is needed first, however, to heal our communities. Many decent people are doing their best to make these changes and they are really our only hope. People hold the key to building communities that are both safe and productive places to live. They can create a better tomorrow for our kids. Communities in cities and in country areas can begin to rebuild 'positive tribes' that allow children opportunities to grow and develop with autonomy and freedom. That way real respect and reverence can return. You could start right now. Today say hello to your neighbour or drop off some cookies to the local old people's home. Offer to help a young Mum by watching her children while she does the shopping.

Opening your heart to care for others builds connectedness and a sense of belonging, elements that are being lost. Respect can then come home where it belongs.

Relational Spirituality - Spirit of relationships

The attribute of spirit of relationships follows on from respect and reverence and includes the four Cs.

- ❖ Community
- ❖ Connection
- ❖ Compassion
- ❖ Communion

The essence of spirit of relationship is that communities practising the qualities of connection, compassion and communion build healthy individuals. The children they are privileged to help raise grow up to become healthy individuals. Connectedness is the result of people feeling they belong and that they are accepted unconditionally. No matter their age, young or old, and whether they are ill or vulnerable, their community watches over them. The story about the bushfires that I shared with you demonstrated how a community came to heal from the tragedy.

Communities can help each other conquer the tough parts of life. Vince Calleja, a local friend and funeral director in Albany, creates an opportunity each year for families to gather at Christmas to remember departed loved ones. This takes place early in December as Christmas approaches. People from all faiths attend and at the conclusion of the ceremony they share a cuppa and a home baked biscuit. The following words are taken from the community Christmas memorial ceremony held in Albany in 2002.

Christmas Memorial Ceremony

We have all gathered here at this special time of year to pause from our hectic and busy lives, to remember and reflect on loved ones who have left our physical world. Christmas is a time of celebration with loved ones, a time of making extra effort to thank people, to acknowledge people and to express our love through the giving of gifts and the sharing of friendship and fellowship. The ones we love who have left us are still part of all the memories over all the years, and that is why we have created this time to pause and remember in the company of others who have also lost loved ones. We do not grieve alone. One person's pain is mirrored in everyone else's - we need to draw comfort from the shared respect and love that is being felt here tonight.

I would like to share with you a poem about the art of remembering.

A Litany of Remembrance

In the rising of the sun and in its going down
we remember them.

In the blowing of the wind and in the chill of winter
we remember them.

In the opening of buds and in the rebirth of Spring
we remember them.

In the blueness of the sky and in the warmth of summer
we remember them.

In the rustling of leaves and in the beauty of autumn
we remember them.

In the beginning of the year and when it ends
we remember them.

When we are weary and in need of strength
we remember them.

When we are lost and sick at heart
we remember them.

When we have joys we yearn to share
we remember them.

So long as we live they too shall live for they are a part of us
As we remember them.

May we always remember them.

Roland B. Gittelshorn

Our world is in turmoil at this time. We all yearn for
      compassion. We all yearn for joy. We all yearn for world
      peace.
Yet above all the peace we yearn for most is within ourselves
      inner peace.

Over 2000 years ago a child was born with the aim of bringing
      peace to all mankind - regardless of our faith or absence of
      faith. The Christ child is the core reason we celebrate
      Christmas.

I would now like to invite you listen and to take a minute of
      silence as we allow our thoughts of remembrance to join
      together as one.

In silence, gentle silence.

The tide recedes but leaves behind
bright seashells in the sand.
The sun goes down but gentle warmth
still lingers on the land.
The music stops and yet
it echoes on in sweet refrains.

For every joy that passes
something beautiful remains.

Source unknown

Community fete and festival days are great opportunities to build spirit and to celebrate together. In rural Australia there are tulip festivals, jazz festivals, flower festivals, agricultural shows, wine and food shows, craft shows, antique shows, olive fairs, school reunions, country music shows and even 'dog in a ute' gatherings! All of these are opportunities for special interest groups to coordinate visitors coming to their communities to have fellowship and fun. They are very successful spiritually, financially and socially.

Strong, positive-thinking communities come together in times of need and tragedy, as well as for celebration. Indeed, it often takes a crisis to re-awaken a community to the importance of being connected. Recently a farmer and his wife had to relocate from their local community to the city so that the farmer could have treatment for a brain tumour. The younger son returned to the farm to run it while his Dad was away. Not only did the son's friends turn up to help with the sheep work, without being asked, others came and tended to the garden, pruning the roses and weeding. No debt or pay back was attached. On the son's birthday, his friends and other family friends turned up and put on a birthday barbeque. For his parents who were unable to be there this meant more than any words can express. Real communities know that what goes around comes around, and that one day the goodness will be returned even if in a very different form.

Remember that strong communities raise healthy, resilient children. Crime is reduced because people value and respect the environment in which they live. People are valued and in turn they value others. Here are some suggestions and recommendations that can help to strengthen communities.

Building communities that create resilient people

* ❖ Demonstrate care-giving environments in early childhood

* ❖ Address low literacy at as early an age as possible

* ❖ Encourage play and sporting activities in childhood

* ❖ Provide parent education for new parents and the parents of adolescents

* ❖ Make treatment available in the community for mental illness, addictions and domestic violence

* ❖ Create employment opportunities

* ❖ Have mentoring programs both inside and outside of school

* ❖ Encourage cooperative, collaborative teacher practice in schools

* ❖ Strengthen natural kinship networking – sibling and grandparent care

* ❖ Create opportunities for meaningful tasks and activities in the community, so that mastery experiences are possible

* ❖ Build community links between schools and the community

* ❖ Have a shared positive vision that values connectedness and demonstrates hope for the whole community

* ❖ Build networks and share ideas with other communities - give and share, learn and grow

* ❖ Have community celebration days

* ❖ Make the town or area welcoming

Build genuine linkages

Human development is a

"question of linkages that happen within you as a person and also in the environment in which you live,...our hope lies in doing something to alter these linkages, to see that kids who start in a bad environment don't go on having bad environments and develop a sense of impotency".

Bonnie Bernard

A story from the worldwide web shows the power of community. It is from a truck-stop restaurant manager and is an inspiring tale.

I try not to be biased, but I had my doubts about hiring Stevie. His placement counsellor assured me that he would be a good, reliable busboy, but I had never had a mentally handicapped employee and wasn't sure I wanted one. I wasn't sure how my customers would react to Stevie.

He was short, a little dumpy with the smooth facial features and thick-tongued speech of Down Syndrome. I wasn't worried about most of my trucker customers because truckers don't generally care who buses tables as long as the meatloaf platter is good and the pies are homemade. The four-wheeler drivers were the ones who concerned me; the mouthy college kids travelling to school; the yuppie snobs who secretly polish their silverware with their napkins for fear of catching some dreaded truck-stop 'germ'; the pairs of white-shirted business men on expense accounts who think every truck-stop waitress wants to be flirted with. I knew those people would be uncomfortable around Stevie so I closely watched him for the first few weeks.

I shouldn't have worried. After the first week, Stevie had my staff wrapped around his stubby little finger, and within a month my truck regulars had adopted him as their official truck-stop mascot. After that, I really didn't care what the rest of the customers thought of him.

He was like a 21-year old in blue jeans and Nikes, eager to laugh and eager to please, but fierce in his attention to his duties. Every salt and pepper shaker was exactly in its place, not a bread crumb or coffee spill was visible when Stevie got done with the table. Our only problem was persuading him to wait to clean a table until after the customers were finished. He would hover in the background, shifting his weight from one foot to the other, scanning the dining room until a table was empty. Then he would scurry to the empty table and carefully bus dishes and glasses onto the cart and meticulously wipe the table up with a practised flourish of his rag. If he thought a customer was watching, his brow would pucker with added concentration. He took pride in doing his job exactly right, and you had to love how hard he tried to please each and every person he met.

Over time, we learned that he lived with his mother, a widow, who was disabled after repeated surgeries for cancer. They lived on their Social Security benefits in public housing two miles from the truck stop. Their social worker, who stopped to check on him every so often, admitted they had fallen between the cracks. Money was tight, and what I paid him was probably the difference between them being able to live together and Stevie being sent to a group home.

That's why the restaurant was a gloomy place that morning last August, the first morning in three years that Stevie missed work. He was at the Mayo Clinic in Rochester getting a new valve or something put in his heart. His social worker said that people with Down syndrome often had heart problems at an early age so this wasn't unexpected, and there was a good chance he would come through the surgery in good shape and be back at work in a few months.

A ripple of excitement ran through the staff later that morning when word came that he was out of surgery, in recovery and doing fine. Frannie, head waitress, let out a war whoop and did a little dance in the aisle when she heard the good news. Belle Ringer, one of our regular trucker customers, stared at the sight of the 50-year old grandmother of four doing a victory shimmy beside his table. Frannie blushed, smoothed her apron and shot Belle Ringer a withering look. He grinned.

"OK, Frannie, what was that all about?" he asked.

"We just got word that Stevie is out of surgery and going to be okay."

"I was wondering where he was. I had a new joke to tell him. What was the surgery about?"

Frannie quickly told Belle Ringer and the other two drivers sitting at his booth about Stevie's surgery, then sighed.

"Yeah, I'm glad he is going to be OK" she said. "But I don't know how he and his Mom are going to handle all the bills. From what I hear, they're barely getting by as it is."

Belle Ringer nodded thoughtfully, and Frannie hurried off to wait on the rest of her tables. Since I hadn't had time to round up a busboy to replace Stevie and really didn't want to replace him, the girls were busing their own tables that day until we decided what to do. After the morning rush, Frannie walked into my office. She had a couple of paper napkins in her hand and a funny look on her face.

"What's up?" I asked.

"I didn't get that table where Belle Ringer and his friends were sitting cleared off after they left, and Pony Pete and Tony Tipper were sitting there when I got back to clean it off" she said. "This was folded and tucked under a coffee cup."

She handed the napkin to me, and three $20 bills fell onto my desk when I opened it. On the outside, in big, bold letters, was printed "Something for Stevie".

"Pony Pete asked me what that was all about," she said, "so I told them about Stevie and his Mom and everything, and Pete looked at Tony and Tony looked at Pete, and they ended up giving me this".

She handed me another paper napkin that had "Something For Stevie" scrawled on its outside. Two $50 bills were tucked within its folds. Frannie looked at me with wet, shiny eyes, shook her head and said simply, "Truckers".

That was three months ago. Today is Thanksgiving, the first day Stevie is supposed to be back to work. His placement worker said he's been counting the days until the doctor said he could work, and it didn't matter at all that it was a holiday. He called 10 times in the past week, making sure we knew he was coming, fearful that we had forgotten him or that his job was in jeopardy. I arranged to have his mother bring him to work, met them in the parking lot and invited them both to celebrate his day back. Stevie was thinner and paler, but couldn't stop grinning as he pushed through the doors and headed for the back room where his apron and busing cart were waiting.

"Hold up there, Stevie, not so fast" I said. I took him and his mother by their arms. "Work can wait for a minute. To celebrate you coming back, breakfast for you and your mother is on me."

I led them toward a large corner booth at the rear of the room. I could feel and hear the rest of the staff following behind as we marched through the dining room. Glancing over my shoulder, I saw booth after booth of grinning truckers empty and join the procession. We stopped in front of the big table. Its surface was covered with coffee cups saucers and dinner plates, all sitting slightly crooked on dozens of folded paper napkins.

"First thing you have to do, Stevie, is clean up this mess", I said. I tried to sound stern. Stevie looked at me, and then at his mother, then pulled out one of the napkins. It had "Something for Stevie" printed on the outside. As he picked it up, two $10 bills fell onto the table. Stevie stared at the money, then at all the napkins peeking from beneath the tableware, each with his name printed or scrawled on it. I turned to his mother.

"There's more than $10,000 in cash and checks on that table, all from truckers and trucking companies that heard about your problems. Happy Thanksgiving".

Well, it got real noisy about that time, with everybody hollering and shouting, and there were a few tears, as well. But you know what's funny? While everybody else was busy shaking hands and hugging each other, Stevie, with a big, big smile on his face, was busy clearing all the cups and dishes from the table. Best worker I ever hired.

Source unknown

Contemplation

The capacity to ponder and wonder about something is a valuable part of spiritual intelligence. This contemplation encourages a deep exploration of life and the endless search for meaning and purpose. Rachael Kessler believes that the search for meaning and purpose is one of the seven gateways to educating the soul as it deepens our relationship with ourself. It also enhances our understanding of life as we know it. Mindfulness allows us to be considerate and compassionate toward others – and it helps build relational spirituality, covering the four Cs.

A key attribute of contemplation is prayerfulness and the practice of prayer. This is covered in an earlier chapter.

Increased quiet time in classrooms and the opportunity for contemplation give students more time to think and to be more creative in their problem solving or searching around a question in my experience. The more they contemplate the more comfortable they become with it and the deeper and more insightful are the results. Qualities that can improve with time and space for contemplation include cleverness, positive leadership, and being thoughtful towards someone in need. Students with low levels of literacy find quiet time a great experience because there is nothing impeding their capacity to think, contemplate and express themselves verbally. You may remember from the earlier chapters that the pre-frontal lobe of the brain is where key problem solving and emotional resolution are based. It takes time and an absence of stress or conflict to access these processes.

Calmness, stillness and quiet

These qualities expand the potential for contemplation so that it can be beneficial in the lives of children and adults. Silence and stillness have a magic to them! It doesn't matter where, in your home, your workplace or your classroom, when you have silence and stillness something magical happens.

Our children are more troubled than ever before in the history of mankind. Those in the Western world live in a rapid world that is full of noise, activity, visual over-stimulation and many electronic screens. They live busy lives filled with activities and with enormous pressures to achieve and succeed, right from pre-school! This way of living creates stressed unwell kids, teenagers and adults!

Dr Fiona Stanley, a world authority on child health, expressed her concern at a recent conference in Australia.

"Health and behaviour problems among children have reached frightening levels and a national campaign is needed to avert a looming social crisis."

West Australian, November 9th 2002

Why is this happening to our children and in such epidemic proportions?

We have sped up the pace of life and living. We live in a world that is instant, we expect everything NOW. Communication, food, pain relief, results, well-behaved children; you name it, we expect it instantly. This expectation works silently and unconsciously. It creates stress when things do not happen like that. Children take all of childhood to grow – to learn how to think, learn, process information, behave appropriately, manage their lives, dress themselves, find their way home and learn who they are! We cannot rush this growth.

We all need to calm down – to simplify our lives and spend more time committed to being a positive part of our kid's lives. We need more quiet, less noise, less rush and more moments of exquisite stillness.

Our children now want to be the driving force behind their own learning. They need time to think and question the way they learn and make sense of the world. Many of today's kids have less desire than their parents to be rich and materially successful. For the new generation this may mean that they want to live effective lives with quite different attitudes and ways to their parents; they are more environmentally aware, socially accepting of cultural differences, against war, aware of their own responsibility for their health and wellbeing. The other alternative is that they lack responsibility, and many young people are in a spiritual void where emptiness, a lack of meaning in their lives and disconnection from society are part of their reality.

As an independent counsellor and educational consultant I see the broken spirits and damaged minds of children raised without love and awareness and without correct information. My special interest is in emotional literacy and human resilience and I know that our children's worlds can be made better. This can be seen in some homes and schools where the emotional wellbeing of children comes first. Research has long informed the belief that happy children learn best. A safe environment where differences are accepted and even welcomed allows children to learn both social and academic skills. Humans are programmed to be social animals. Social behaviour is not inherent and develops through the constant interaction of people with people over a long period of time. The capacity to develop coping skills and to be able to adopt a positive temperament can also be encouraged in our children, from birth.

Jenny Roberts from Western Australia is an occupational therapist with an extensive background in working with troubled children. She believes that we are crowding our children's lives with noise, too many toys, too much talk and too much parental direction. The behaviour of many children improves by simply creating space for them to be themselves. The same goes with being too 'loving' or caring; meaning leaping to every need, every cry and every moment of mild distress. By doing so we are preventing a baby from finding its own ways of soothing itself. The human brain is adaptive, which means that it is constantly making choices in response to situations. If one thing does not work it has a natural capacity to find a different solution. The Kids CODE that Jenny has developed allows parents to unlearn a lot of their preconceived assumptions that do not work. These parents 'let go' and allow their children to simply be children. So much of our fear and anxiety as parents is about what is right or normal. We are more attached to the outcomes rather than the process of growing and simply being. Calmness, stillness and quiet are really important parts of healthy family harmony.

The magic of silence and stillness is something that helps shape the developing child in a positive way. While there are many cognitive (left brain) benefits from teaching the magic of silence, there are even more emotional and social (right brain) benefits. The inner world of children today is in turmoil and the outer turmoil of the world that we have created contributes to that. I believe that children who can build a doorway to their own sense of value and worth will be better able to manage this chaotic, rapidly changing world. The doorway is found on the inside rather than the outside. John O'Donohue explains.

"We need to return to the solitude within, to find again the dream that lies at the heart of the soul. We need to feel the dream with the wonder of a child approaching a threshold of discovery. When we rediscover our childlike nature we enter a world of gentle possibility. Consequently, we will find ourselves more frequently at the place of ease, delight and celebration."

Anam Cara. Spiritual Wisdom from the Celtic World 1997

First open yourself to the magic of silence and stillness. Show your family calmness and stillness and create homes that honour peace and quiet. If you wish to read more, go to my first book Saving Our Children from Our Chaotic World: Teaching Children the Magic of Silence and Stillness (2003). Teach your children the magic of silence and stillness so that they can take it and use it as a skill that sustains them during life's challenges in the world and in adulthood. In this way they can hold hope, optimism and enthusiasm, and our world can be a better place than it is now. Teach it before we lose any more of our teenagers to depression, mental disorders, drug and alcohol abuse, and suicide.

Benefits of relaxation, silence and stillness

- ❖ Building emotional intelligence skills
- ❖ Giving students the time and opportunity for rest and renewal
- ❖ Providing the brain with opportunities to download or downshift
- ❖ Giving people the chance to think more effectively
- ❖ Encouraging the practice of reflection and 'wisdom in hindsight', especially for boys
- ❖ Settling the energetic fields of individuals and building group synergy
- ❖ Creating opportunities to open to creative expression
- ❖ Resting highly stressed nervous systems
- ❖ Building emotional and spiritual intelligence
- ❖ Nurturance of the human spirit in our children
- ❖ Assistance with building intuition
- ❖ Improving memory retention and facilitating optimal performance - cognitively, emotionally and physically
- ❖ Management of stress, confusion and anxiety

❖ Preparation of the whole person to focus on new information

❖ Creation of a safe place for the imagination to play - away from the ready-made, fast-paced and highly stimulating electronic images that bombard them daily

❖ Encouragement of the practice of healthy breathing and intention, to help in times of fear, stress and worry

❖ Improvement of the classroom environment

❖ Opening a space for the Sacred

Calmness, silence and stillness are good for everyone. They improve sleep. With good sleep we are healthier on all levels. Sleep is one of the most important essentials that our rapid modern world is making harder and harder to achieve. If you need a pill to get some sleep then maybe learning to relax or meditate could be a valuable consideration. Inner calmness, silence and stillness cost very little, are transferable and benefit all areas of your life.

Tenderness

The qualities of gentleness, kindness and thoughtfulness, elements of tenderness, are all part of spiritual intelligence. There is not enough in the world! Our fear-driven world has made normally tender people wary of using gentle touch and being kind. I have found that kindness and thoughtfulness tamed disruptive students. Nothing was more appreciated by a troubled child or teenager than a safe hug, preferably without words. Nothing supports a family losing a loved one than quiet thoughtfulness and gentleness – sometime in silence.

Some of the most amazing healing has happened in my consultation room when a young client has sobbed in my arms, without restraint. At one of my women's retreats a lovely lady with postnatal depression who had been unable to cry found that she could in the safety of the circle of women. She cried so much that she used an entire tissue box! Her husband was a bit surprised to see her afterwards and jokingly asked, "How come you have to pay to look that awful?"

Children who have experienced tenderness as a child are more likely to be capable of tenderness as adults. Simple opportunities to experience tenderness and kindness are important, whether in the home, at school or in the wider community. Remember, it is the small things that open children to understanding kindness. Tenderness is very powerful and does not require intelligence or physical strength!

Gratitude is also part of this attribute of spiritual intelligence. By helping our children to develop gratitude we encourage them to keep their minds away from the negative considerations of life. At the end of every day we can choose to reflect on the good, or the bad. With a focus on gratitude, over time we build a memory bank of blessings and moments to be thankful for.

"Gratitude unlocks the fullness of life. It turns what we have into enough, and more. It turns denial into acceptance, chaos to order, confusion to clarity. It can turn a meal into a feast, a house into a home, a stranger into a friend. Gratitude makes sense of our past, brings peace for today, and creates a vision for tomorrow."

Melody Beattie

The following poem also shows how gratitude helps us.

A Grateful Heart...

A grateful heart is one who's lived
through trials along the way...
then found the strength to look ahead
and face a brand new day.

A grateful heart is one who knows
that sorrow does not last...
and morning brings a ray of hope
to chase away the past.

A grateful heart will always be
much stronger than the rest...
for they have weathered every storm
and conquered every test.

Source Unknown

May the coming years see us all grow in our capacity to
show tenderness, kindness, gratitude and thoughtfulness to
ourselves, others and especially to young children!

Simplicity

By simplifying the way we live we can increase our
quality of life. We can relieve and reduce the stress in our
lives if we slow down and do less. We are seldom effective
when we work with an overloaded mind or are feeling
scattered. We have been seduced into believing that fast is
better - and the good news is that it rarely is; maybe if you
are an athlete, a car or a horse!

Carl Honore has written a beautiful book in
response to the 'disease called affluenza', where we are time
sick, constantly under pressure and working long hours.
Honore writes of slowing down and savouring life. This book
review by Larry Dossey explains why it is important.

"The speed of life borders on insanity for an increasing number
of us, and the price we pay is the erosion of our happiness and
health. If you sometimes feel engulfed by the mad pace of
modern life — and who doesn't?

Carl Honoré. "In Praise of Slow" could prove life-saving

—Larry Dossey, MD, author of Healing Beyond the Body and Reinventing Medicine

I am staggered how many 'quick' meals we have, that just need heating in the microwave. We do not benefit from the fast food and fast living pressures that come from endless advertising! Being raised on a farm, over twenty miles from shops, we grew up experiencing preparing everything from scratch. We ate our own sheep and Mum cooked soups, pies, casseroles and cookies with the real ingredients. When we had cows we made our own butter! The herbs like parsley, mint and rosemary to put into our food were from our own garden. We had an orchard and bottled fruit in summer to last throughout winter. Mum made our jams and marmalade. She also made lemon cordial from the lemons and tomato sauce from any excess tomatoes. We could eat passionfruit straight from the vines, pesticide and herbicide free. One of our favourite times was when the mulberry trees were full of ripe black mulberries. We loved to have mulberry fights after we had picked enough for Mum to make her delicious once a year mulberry pie! We also had chooks that ate the scraps and gave us eggs.

Modernism continues to speed up. We must resist kneeling at the altar of speed and look beyond being consumers to being economically sustainable. It is important for children to learn how to sustain themselves with their own resources, even if for only a short period of time. Many parts of the world have experienced natural disasters over the last two years. How would we survive if the shops were closed and our easy meals gone? Maybe we would recognise how precious water is and how dependent we are on food sources that are brought into our communities. We can help our children develop respect and reverence for our natural world and for the people who work in our rural areas. Big corporations continue to squeeze more and more out of the farmers' back pockets. We have our 'back pockets' too. When we realise what is happening it may be too late!

Young children only need simple things to learn and to grow – fulfilled with unstructured play in the natural environment and as little parental supervision as possible. Children need dirt, water, sand and paint. They need trees, pets, puddles and buckets to make sand castles. They need to be able to crawl into the cupboard full of plastic containers or the pot cupboard and have things that bang and make a noise. Fresh fruit, wholesome food and water nurture their growing bodies and they need to eat when they are hungry, not only at family meal times. Young children need to be hugged, tickled and sung to by the people they love the most. They need games like hop scotch, skipping, marbles, clapping, playing with frisbees and flying kites. These are ways of allowing children to learn naturally, without pressure and in an unforced way. Raising children is not a competition. It is a natural process that has been happening since man began. Remember that we have only had TVs for 50 years, computers for 15 years and mobile phones for around 10 years.

Preparing a meal can involve the whole family. Everyone can take on a task – peeling vegetables, setting the table, clearing away, washing and drying up. Involving children in helping to make homemade pasta, pizzas and bread are all really positive ways of teaching simple, meaningful involvement in home life. Our children learn to be responsible and helpful and it shows that meals take time to prepare. Eating is just one aspect of coming together as a family. Sharing friendship and fellowship are important components of family life. Many families eat in front of the TV and seldom allow meal time to be an opportunity to create positive connections with each other.

Lingering over meals is a learned behaviour. It only takes place when people are comfortable with a level of conversation that is respectful. To reach this needs time and happens when children have been really listened to over dinner, afternoon tea or at snack time after school. To be heard and to listen properly we must be fully present, not just with our bottoms on the seat! Lingering over meals allows people to be comfortable with slow food – an international movement that I am very much in favour of encouraging. Slow food builds connections between people and families.

Picnics also require time and effort and can be wonderful experiences. If the environment is beautiful it does not matter if the food is simple. It is great to gather families with similar aged children together for picnics and barbeques. Making enough time to linger, have a game of cricket, kick a footy or throw a frisbee is really important. I have learned that the washing does wait until you get back!

Slowing down and simplifying life helps create spaces in busy minds for moments of inspiration and insight. There is no doubt in my mind that I am more inventive, creative and effective after I have had quiet time. I have discovered that if I focus on one or two things at a time I am more successful than if I tried to do six things at once! Yes, I could be on five committees, work fulltime and run a family of four sons – but you know what, I worked out after I backed my car into a parked car that was behind me one night, it was unhealthy. I have now reduced my non-essential commitments and allow others to step up to the plate. That is how it is meant to be, we all take turns at being helpful citizens. My health is better, my family is happier, my dog is slimmer and my garden looks loved!

Simplification is not a problem of huge 'Einstein' proportions. Pause for one moment and think of one thing you can do to simplify your life, which will improve your health, your relationship with your husband or wife and costs nothing! Now do it. There is nothing more powerful than taking action. Procrastination can really scramble your head. Nothing is sweeter than enjoying a little less pressure and stress in your life. Eat slower! Clean your teeth slower! Savour your next mouthful of food! Enjoy taking a sip of your next cup of tea – pause, slow down, and enjoy!!

Laughter and Lightness

It may seem unusual to include laughter and lightness here. However, I have discovered that laughter can bring complete strangers together and it definitely helps children feel happy and safe. People without a sense of humour struggle in life; it is a key protective factor in resilient individuals. Laughter is also very much about the heart and soul.

Patch Adams, the American doctor who promotes laughter in helping healing, firmly believes it has unique potential to stimulate positive effects in both the healer and the person who is unwell. In my experience in the funeral industry and in counselling, laughter and lightness are undervalued. Laughter is present in friendships, positive relationships and also around disasters.

Laughter and its power

- ❖ Transforms emotional states
- ❖ Creates endorphins and a sense of wellbeing
- ❖ A key coping skill, especially for boys
- ❖ An anti-bullying strategy
- ❖ Encourages lightening up for the serious
- ❖ A bonding experience when shared in groups
- ❖ Builds inclusivity and connectedness
- ❖ Releases tension and stress
- ❖ Is a key element in effective communication, especially with close relationships

❖ An antidote to violence

A loving parent or teacher has the responsibility to help children learn how to use laughter and humour appropriately. Making fun of others or other cultures can be offensive and insulting; laughing at people rather than laughing with people is also insulting. Laughter is another learned behaviour that takes time to mature. One of my sons learned the hard way over the years yet he now has a rich and funny way of using humour that makes for great conversations. He has also bounced back from some serious life challenges by using his witty sense of humour. In his primary school years he made some disastrous mistakes that distressed other students and his teachers.

Do remember that it takes years to develop a mature sense of humour and that children need help. A good way to start is with introducing children's joke books when they are learning to read. Storytelling and joke telling are key components of human conversation and children need practice to be able to master these life skills. Start simple. Here are a few to enjoy!

A little girl runs out to the backyard where her father is working, and asks him, "Daddy, what's sex?"

Her father sits her down, and tells her all about the birds and the bees. He tells her about conception, sexual intercourse, sperms and eggs. He goes on to tell her about puberty, menstruation, erections, wet-dreams...and he thinks, what the hell, and goes on to tell her the works. He covers a wide and varied assortment of sub topics and by the time he's finished, his daughter is somewhat awestruck with this sudden influx of bizarre new knowledge.

Her father finally asks: "So what did you want to know about sex for?"

"Oh, mommy said to tell you lunch would be ready in a couple of secs..."

Children on what is love?

"Love is when Mommy sees Daddy on the toilet and she doesn't think it's gross." Karen, age 7

"Love is when Mommy sees Daddy smelly and sweaty and still says he is handsomer than Robert Redford."
Chris, age 7

"Love is when Mommy gives Daddy the best piece of chicken." Elaine, age 5

"When my grandmother got arthritis, she couldn't bend over and paint her toenails anymore. So my grandfather does it for her all the time, even when his hands got arthritis too. That's love." Rebecca, age 8

"When someone loves you, the way they say your name is different. You just know that your name is safe in their mouth." Billy, age 4

"Love is when a girl puts on perfume and a boy puts on shaving cologne and they go out and smell each other."
Karl, age 5

"Love is when you go out to eat and give somebody most of your French fries without making them give you any of theirs." Chrissy, age 6

Worldwide web

Being comfortable with laughter is a sign of emotional wellbeing. People who can laugh at themselves usually have a healthy sense of self and have a high degree of self acceptance and positive regard. It took me years to be able to laugh at myself and when I learned coincided with my personal growth. Our lives are sadder and less enjoyable without laughter. When couples stop laughing, their relationship is in need of healing. Children are the same. The shining eyes and giggles of a happy child are a sure sign that their lives are safe and full of healthy living.

Patterns of sadness can become unconscious over time. That is why encouraging children to laugh at funny stories or picture books is really important. The children who are most comfortable with laughter and lightness generally have significant people in their lives who model these ways for them. Significant adult allies are important in children's lives because they can help light the fire of laughter if it has been smothered by a challenging experience in a child's life.

Laughter builds bridges and connections between people and can turn a dull moment into something memorable. It also is deceptive with its healing and protective qualities. Laughter and lightness help everyone to feel better and are food for the soul. I hope you are blessed with moments of spontaneous laughter that fill you with joie de vivre every day of your life.

Spiritual intelligence can now be seen as something that underlies all of life. It encompasses all ages and every moment of our physical existence living as human beings. Spiritual intelligence is both inclusive and expansive. When a person walks a pathway of deep darkness they have lost their connection to spirit. They also show an absence of many of the qualities and attributes that make up spiritual intelligence. Being able to find a balance between our logical rational mind and our emotional and spiritual domains is the challenge of being human.

Essentially, our life journey presents us with experiences that allow us to grow in our understanding of ourselves and others. Rather than think "Look what the Universe has done to me........" reconsider and restate it as "Look what the Universe has done for me.....". A healthy balance between the head and the heart allows us to live from a place of unconditional regard, with acceptance and love of all things. We secretly yearn for this place and search for it; what an irony that it lies hidden within us. People with a strong spiritual intelligence access the place of 'bliss' or nirvana often in their lives, both by choice and sometimes spontaneously. They are unable to 'stay' because being human means being present in our bodies. We have the unique qualities of existing in a human body surrounded by others in social matrixes and living on a planet called Earth.

The pull of living with opposites and dualities calls our attention to the act of living, rather than the act of being. A high level of spiritual intelligence allows us to make choices about creating less suffering and pain for ourselves and others. We can experience the exquisite joy of deep connection and the love of others. Spiritual intelligence allows us to be beacons of light that help others find their way in the darkness. Finally, it allows people to fulfil their life purpose, or sacred contract whatever that may be, and to ensure they leave the world better than they found it. In my mind, spiritual intelligence allows the soul to express its divinity and wisdom in an honest and beautiful way while surrounded by the chaos and confusion of life.

> It is one of the most beautiful compensations of life that no man can sincerely try to help another without helping himself.
> Ralph Waldo Emerson

Key Points

❖ Spiritual intelligence can help young children to understand themselves and others, and to better prepare them to manage life

❖ Spiritual intelligence is nonlinear and difficult to measure

❖ Universal truths that reflect core values about living respectful of self, others and our world are an excellent place to start

❖ An awareness and understanding of the inner and outer worlds of being human is key to spiritual intelligence

❖ Spiritual intelligence includes:
1. wonder
2. awe
3. listening with the heart
4. respect and reverence
5. spirit of relationships
6. contemplation
7. calmness, stillness and quiet
8. tenderness and gratitude
9. simplicity
10. lightness and laughter

❖ Spiritual intelligence helps individuals to live lives with less suffering, more fulfillment and peace

❖ Spiritual intelligence enables a person to achieve their unique life purpose, or sacred contact, and to make the world better in some way because they were there

Chapter 12

Making the Sacred Welcome in Our Children's Lives

A little girl was busy drawing a picture. Her Mummy asked her what she was doing. The little girl replied, "I am drawing a picture of God". Her Mummy replied "but darling no-one knows what God looks like!"

The little child replied calmly. "They will when I finish my picture".

Source unknown

Around the world today, many people have walked away from traditional religions. Fewer children have Christian or faith-based schooling and many have very little positive education about the sacred in the early years of their life. Government schools walk 'on egg shells' by trying to avoid offending any faith or religion represented in our multicultural society. The result is a trend to removing ALL spiritual practices and activities, no more Christmas carols for preschoolers or the much loved nativity play, in some schools. The adult world has made decisions around religious festivals that children have little attachment to other than having fun. Children enjoy special activities and the religious festivals helped them feel safe and protected. Could they be bad for them, inappropriate or unsuitable? Why didn't we simply add the celebrations of others faiths in with the Christian ones?

Children would have loved it and would have been able to share the experiences.

We have made the Sacred, The Divine or God, unwelcome in our Government schools. I firmly believe this contributes to the huge number of alienated, depressed and disconnected teenagers that exist in our world today. They have not had the opportunity to be connected to 'the sacred'. These are disenchanted young people, mainly teenagers and young adults, who are seeking a sense of spirituality in their lives. They are doing this through modern avenues like movies, the internet and books. The incredible popularity of the classic good versus evil blockbuster movies such as Star Wars, The Matrix, Lord of the Rings and Harry Potter may very well be the product of children brought up by a generation who raised their children at a time when they were disillusioned with the mainstream churches. The Jedi Knight movement may very well be an expression of the natural seeking of young people for the mysterious and the mystical and a form of expression of the human spirit that they inherently understand. The popular culture may be seen by many to be soul-less, because of the technological and consumerist nature of what drives behaviour today.

Fortunately my experience is often very different. I meet young adults who enjoy music that has positive messages of the importance of love, friendship and of finding that which is good and beautiful in life. I encounter friendship groups that are gender friendly and culturally much more open and accepting than when I was a teenager. Indeed, in my work as a celebrant I see men and women playing different roles in a bridal party. For one wedding recently the groom's 'best man' was his sister and the bride's 'maid' was indeed a mate! Many young people are seeking something indefinable in their lives to fill the yearning to belong, to feel connected and to help them make sense of this chaotic world.

I have worked with suicidal young people and introduced them to deep relaxation and gentle touch, which can be very healing.

Sometimes all that is needed is for a person to be really heard, a few words shared with a genuine caring, concern and with a safe touch. In this way, young people receive reassurance that they are not alone in their struggle with life. All of us have moments that challenge us, when we call for added life skills and support if the challenges are to be overcome. This may sound simple to provide, however:

I have found that non-judgemental acceptance and unconditional compassion are two of the most powerful and rare gifts anyone can give to help another. This is not to rescue, smother or invalidate another person's journey – it is more about sharing the journey so that a person can move forward in making their own decisions and choices. In the past this was a role of religion.

A basic underlying similarity exists between the religions of the world. Caroline Myss is a theologian. She wrote the best selling book An Anatomy of the Spirit that links the human body to three spiritual traditions, to show the symbolic links. She compares the Hindu chakra system, the Christian sacraments and the Kabbalistic Tree of Life and finds enormous similarities, even though semantically they are very different. Caroline studied theology and the mystics of old to discover for herself the full power of the human spirit as it is awakened. She affirms:

"the mysterious spirit that lives within all of us and that needs to be nurtured and cared for, no matter whether or not we are outwardly religious. Children yearn to have practices and language that allow them to feel there is a benevolent power greater than themselves -albeit God, in their life - somewhere."

This belief in a benevolent being helps to build positive mind patterns and protective mechanisms that can support us in life. The higher being is powerfully linked into the development of a child's imagination (as explored in the Chapter on The Gift of Imagination).

Making The Sacred welcome in our children and our lives in this modern age invites us to widen our perceptions of God and the Divine. Quite simply, the word God has become contaminated with actions in the name of, or under the cover of, religion and the Church, including sexual abuse and zealous pronouncements of extremists who glorify atrocities 'in the name of God'. Children and teenagers are exposed to obscure behaviours of cults and mass suicides in the name of God as exposed by the media. Children do not have the maturity or intellectual discernment to process these happenings, which is difficult even for us. Extremists do not represent the majority of God-faring people that live in our world and who show compassion and goodness.

Maybe we all could expand our view of what God means in the lives of people right around the globe. Does it matter that He or She is known as Yahweh, Sacred Spirit, The Creator of the Dreamtime, The Source of All That Is, Allah, Buddha, Blessed One, Holy Father, Holy Mother, Holy Spirit or Mother Earth? Does it really matter that people seek to meet the sacred in ways that work for them? They may attend the same church every week and enjoy the sense of a faith family, play the didgeridoo, drum, chant, sing as a chorus or be part of music, sit silently or spend time in Nature, gather in satsang, meditate in groups, pray silently and alone, read or take themselves on a vision quest. I have shared many of these pathways to the Divine and have found my "God" every time. Some pathways to God require much effort and commitment, others little other than a willingness.

The search and yearning to find that place within us where sacredness lives, where the wise counsel resides, is so very important, much more so than how we find it.

Freedom Prayer

God is not foreign to my freedom.
Instead the Spirit breathes life into my most intimate desires,
gently nudging me towards all that is good.
I ask for the grace to let myself be enfolded by the Spirit.

Source world wide web.

For example if we really follow the wisdom of Jesus, or Buddha, or Allah, or the Dreamtime and allow ourselves to love all children, maybe even our enemies and those who are still asleep, then we will really help our children. Through practising unconditional love instead of judgement we become more accepting of other people's search for the Divine. Words of wisdom from all mainstream religions are expressing the same universal truths. Seek out the good within all instead of the differences and our children will benefit.

"Do not judge others, so that God will not judge you, for God will judge you in the same way that you judge others, and he will apply to you the same rules you apply to others."

Matthew 7:1-2.

Children respond to an open heart, regardless of who it belongs to. Our capacity to love one another demonstrates Goodness and sacredness to our children.

Father Bede Griffiths was a Catholic priest who for many years ran an ashram in India. He came to see God as 'that which is the further shore'. For him the palm of the hand represented the God essence with each of the five fingers portraying each of the major faiths of the world, including indigenous spirituality.

Essentially Fr Bede saw that faith and spirituality flowed from the same source and at the core of each belief was a system of truth that can be recognised as universal truths. The teenagers I have shared this concept with agree it makes sense and acknowledge that is allows finding The Sacred in different ways.

A very special spiritual mentor and friend, Catholic priest Father Hugh Galloway, once shared the following story with me. A lady in his parish was looking very disappointed one Christmas as she said to him, "Father Hugh, you remember my son? I have some bad news about him, he has become an Anglican". Hugh unexpectedly replied, "That's wonderful!" The mother was surprised at Hugh's reaction until he explained, "If he could not find God in this faith and he could in another, then that is wonderful news. It is finding God that is most important!"

Dr M. Scott Peck author of the best seller "The Road Less Travelled" also pondered on this question of which Christian hat to wear when he chose to become baptised.

"I couldn't decide if I wanted to be baptized as an Eastern Orthodox, or as a Roman Catholic, or an Episcopalian, or a Presbyterian, or a Church of Christ, or Methodist, or an American Baptist, or Southern Baptist, and that complex denominational decision was obviously going to take me 25 or 30 years of research to figure out. But then I finally realized that baptism is not a denominational celebration, and so when I was drowned on that morning, 18 years ago yesterday, it was by a North Carolina Methodist minister in the chapel of an Episcopal convent in a deliberately non-denominational celebration. And I have very jealously guarded my non-denominational status ever since. If one were to believe that somebody had to have a certain denomination or particular church to be a Christian, by that definition, I suppose I would not."

(from his web site www.mscottpeck.com)

If you are a committed Christian then your children may witness you participating within your faith community as something predictable and normal; similarly so if you are of a different religion or spiritual pathway. If circumstances make it possible, your children will attend a Christian or faith school that models your belief system and your spiritual and religious practices. A pattern of religious expression that your child sees is important for life. Children may reject much of it for a time, as in adolescence, but it serves as a rich fertile soil for renewed spirituality later in life. Thomas Moore in his book Care of the Soul terms this spiritual backdrop an 'inherited religion'. Moore writes that anyone can become a 'reformer', a Luther or a Buddha in relation to their own family religion (Care of The Soul 1992, p212). For parents, the most important message is to live and practice your faith so that your children have a language and a model on which to shape their soul's search for the Divine when they are ready.

Recently in Australia, Christian religions have come together to coordinate the teaching of religious instruction in our public schools. Teaching is all under one umbrella so that the program embraces the understanding that welcoming God into children's lives is far more important than which faith gains the most parishioners. How wonderful! This also means that churches share funding to support these school chaplaincy programs that provide a wonderful support to our high schools. Bringing Christian (or other) values and prayerful practice into the lives of our children is what is really essential. I am a huge supporter of school chaplains, especially in our high schools. They are a safe ear, a neutral place to go for a cuppa and a chat and, when chosen well, they impact positively on the lives of many students. Our children need that pastoral care more than ever before.

A word of caution, it is essential that both chaplains and scripture volunteers are trained and chosen carefully. Children are alarmed by well meaning scripture teachers who tell them that people who don't go to church 'wail and burn in hell'. Fear levels are already at disturbing levels in our world today and saying things like this is a serious threat to the mental health and wellbeing of our children. It also turns children away from God. We can keep God welcome in their lives by focusing on Divine unconditional love and its presence in their lives. Remember it was Jesus who said:

"Let the children come to me and do not stop them, because the Kingdom of God belongs to such as these.
Remember this, whoever does not receive the Kingdom of God like a child will never enter it."

Luke 18:15-17.

Neale Donald Walsch writes:

"Half of the world's people believe God is out to "get them" if they are not good. Fundamentalists of many religions strike fear into the hearts of their followers. You can't do this. Don't do that. Stop it or God will punish you."

Friendship with God 1999, p12.

Maybe the fundamentalist mindset comes from seeing God as the angry parent. I believe that to improve God's presence in our young children's lives we need to focus more on angels , mysticism and exploring faith in a global way., Maybe, instead of asking for God's help or guidance try encouraging children to be more familiar with the presence of angels and their strength and ability to assist. This is a little like asking God's helpers, as God may be busy; many of us have talked about Santa's elves that help make toys and goodies for all the children of the world. Leaving it to the helpers may help a child to accept the sacred into his or her life. When my youngest son was still young and I needed to travel overseas, I was able to comfort him by telling him how the angels are always with us. As he grew older I would ask him to take care when he went surfing; he would often whisper to me, "don't worry, Mum, the angels are with me looking after me".

The same approach works with teenagers. Beautiful angel cards can be used to gain insight into ourselves and our lives. If we choose to use these cards with the purpose of obtaining guidance on how to manage our personal lives, and we are aware, we are open to a positive message that has a God-centred answer. One such message that may opportunely reveal itself is:

"A quiet mind hears the voice of the angels more easily. This card is your angels' way of asking you to quiet your mind so that your angelic communications are loud and clear.......Tell yourself that receiving angelic communication is natural for you and that it is an everyday experience. The more you relax your mind, the easier it is for you to hear the answer."

Doreen Virtue. Healing With the Angel Oracle Cards.

It is better that our teenagers are reading positive messages than receiving advice from others who may not be aware of divine consciousness or spiritual being. The angel cards are specifically designed to express divinely guided messages and to help direct troubled minds away from fear to love. They help to fine tune the intuition and can help those who have no faith or religion to allow a consciousness, a language and a presence into their lives. The messages work to dis-empower our inner critic, which is very loud during the adolescent years. The messages are reassuring and comforting. We could all do with more of these messages when the going gets tough.

To help build an angelic pathway to the divine I recommend Maureen Garth's books. They have meditations for children and she introduces young children to the concept of a guardian angel, one that especially looks after them. In this way, the feeling of separateness and distance from God or the Divine is reduced. A sense of safety and inner protected-ness establishes, which reduces a child's fear and discomfort, especially so for those with sleeping disorders and anxiety. Our children want to feel loved and that they belong. Visualizations of a guardian angel are wonderful. They also introduce and encourage fantasy, which is so important for imagination and growth. The brain cannot tell the difference between what is vividly imagined or real, so their guardian angel feels like it is standing by them at night and keeping them safe – wouldn't you sleep better!

A Guardian Angel

"You take a wounded soul
and hold it in your hands
You teach us how to love ourselves
and to cope with life's demands

You teach us how to use our minds
And fill us up with love
You truly are a gifted angel
Sent from God above.

You build us up with confidence
To face each brand new day
And to recognize the power
In the things we have to say.

You trample on our phobias
And chase away our fears
And we know you'll always be there
To dry up all our tears

You've opened up our hearts
In a very special way
What an unexpected gift we've found
We have learned how to pray!"

Shell Towns, September 1996

My experiences in schools over the last ten years have shown me that many young people find the word <u>God</u> intimidating. For them it is full of connotations that practising Christians would find hard to understand. That is why I am offering suggestions on ways to open these young people to finding their own goodness, God-essence and the Divine to include within their lives. Using angel terminology in my everyday language was one way of bridging this gap. The use of ritual and ceremony was another. Young people relate to their own music and the vibrations of group energy. By being able to create their own liturgies that combine the traditional and modern interpretation of the sacred they open to staying 'on line' with the highest expression of themselves. We prayed together in classes, often with a lit candle or an incense stick.

A beautiful resource found its way to me last year from a place called Geraldton in Western Australia. It is a booklet written by an exceptional teacher called Sister Anthony. It is called "To God on a Magic Carpet." Sister Anthony discovered the value of creating 'pools of stillness" in children's lives and this lead her to create visualizations with a Christian focus. The ideas are so simple and easy for parents or teachers to use with children, especially children under ten. This allows the imagination of the child to create the spiritual templates for prayer and contemplation through out life.

Fran Dobbie, a passionate educator and self-esteem facilitator in New South Wales, brought ritual into every day of her primary school classes. They used Eastern terms like 'namaste' – which essentially means may the divinity within me recognise and celebrate the divinity within you; and they used Native American prayers and creation stories to create an environment rich in sacred and meaningful expressions. Her students undertook short meditations, silent prayers, yoga to open and expand the breath and activities to connect with the earth. Their altar had symbols of Christianity, Buddhism and Mother Earth on it. In subsequent years parents wanted Fran to teach their child. In her class the children learned to love themselves and they developed a Sacred consciousness. Fran now runs her not-for-profit organization called Essere in Sydney and now runs seminars and programs for kids, teenagers and parents to build resilience and self esteem.(go to www.essere.com.au) She is an amazingly gifted woman.

Blending beliefs and openings to God consciousness creates many potential pathways to the Divine that children can use as they journey through the confusing teen years and life.

Teachers like Fran take action to bring the sacred into their classrooms, introducing that place of mystery, experience and exploration. They teach the value of silence and stillness in the search for the Divine, and they teach the value of prayer. The seeds of symbolism are sown into children's consciousness so that maybe one day when the Divine comes calling they will recognise that essence. Rather than provide only one language, one way and one religion these teachers reveal how people have discovered the Divine over the centuries. Essentially we are all one; using our God-given gift of free will we can choose to express the Divine within us in ways that allow our soul to sing.

Helping children to find their own pathway to God, by showing them how people from the beginning of time have found the same sacred source, helps them to find themselves.

God bless all that I love

God bless all those that love me

God bless all those that love those that I love

God bless all those that love those that love me

This poem comes from a CD called Prayers of the World - created by the very special wise woman of peace Judi Weisbart Santa Barbara, USA.

Richard Tichnor and Jenny Smith wrote and illustrated a wonderful creation story for children called The Spark in the Dark. This is a very special story that introduces the spiritual concept that 'all is one'. We all have a star within our hearts that came from the source of all creation. This star shines brightly when we know we are loved and special and we feel connected to the creator. As we read this picture book to children we combine the power of storytelling, imagery and ancient wisdom, all in one amazing experience. I notice how powerfully this story affects indigenous children.

Another way to welcome the Divine into the lives of ourselves and our children is through ritual and ceremonies. This may include baptism and other religious ceremonies. Thomas Moore writes of the importance of rituals:

"Ritual maintains the world's holiness. Knowing that everything we do, no matter how simple, has a halo of imagination around it and can serve the soul enriches life and makes the things around us more precious, more worthy of our protection and care." (Care of the Soul, p226).

Rituals such as baptism are essentially rites of passage that symbolically and formally acknowledge the importance of children in our lives. As a civil celebrant I have performed many name-giving ceremonies, which are equivalent to christenings within Christianity. I once had a committed Catholic express his concerns to me when he was invited to his grand daughter's name-giving ceremony. At one point in the ceremony the parents acknowledged that they have chosen a civil ceremony so that their daughter could choose her own spiritual pathway, when old enough to do so. The ceremony itself is sacred because it is a ceremony with symbols of blessings, beautiful readings and often a candle ceremony. I silently pray before and after every one of my name-giving ceremonies, for the baby and their family, and I firmly believe that when one or more are gathered with intentions of goodness then the Divine is certainly there. The committed Catholic grandfather sent me a card following the ceremony congratulating me on a very blessed and beautiful ceremony that he found deeply meaningful and very personal. The main purpose of a baby's naming is to celebrate the baby's birth, the sacredness of life and the gratitude we feel at being given such an amazing gift. How can God not be present?

Ceremonies, funerals included, need to be part of our children's lives. When families have pets, like guinea pigs and goldfish, they are exposing their children to death in a way that makes their earliest experiences of death less challenging than when a family member dies. When a pet dies the family has a funeral and, when burying the pet, prayers are spoken that talk about that pet going into God's safe keeping and returning to God. Children are able to send the deceased pet their love and mentioning them in their prayers is normal and comfortable. This gives children a template that sets the way when a person close to them dies. The notion of going home to God or to heaven is comforting. I remember being asked by one of my boys about his Grandfather's journey after he died, "So Mum, is heaven as far as London?"

My experience as a funeral civil celebrant has shown me that the civil ceremony for a deceased loved one has a sense of dignity, closure and completion. Ritual creates this as it does in religious ceremonies. The template is similar but instead of prayers we use poems and readings that reflect on love and life. We follow the same sequence of honouring life, farewelling that person and committal.

The traditions of the past shape our interpretation of today. Where will we be as a civilized race in the years to come without a religious or spiritual tradition of any kind for our children?

Finally, I come back to a most important way of making the Sacred welcome in our children's lives. First learn to accept and love yourself so that you can truly love others, without either domination or submission.

"We cannot love another until we are at peace with our own self....I suspect that in the depth of our being, we all know that 'only love redeems', that love alone makes life worthwhile and gives it purpose and meaning. Without love, all our scientific, artistic and spiritual achievements are as straw. Time, tide and entropy will carry them all away."

Bruce Wilson. Reasons of the Heart, p192.

To live our lives as close as possible to the principal truths of all the major religions of the world is the best way to make God welcome in our children's lives. Do you really listen with compassion to your children and your teenagers as they search for meaning and understanding in today's confused world? Do you practise wealth sharing and tithing in your life? Are you a person of truthfulness and integrity in all your relationships - or do you occasionally try to beat the tax man or the social security system? Do you treat women and men in your life with the same level of respect and validation? Do you hold judgements of others that are unkind and without empathy? This is the basis of really walking your talk. Our children learn from what you do rather than from what you say – modelling is the most powerful teacher.

The most important message from this chapter is to be the person you want your children to be. Live from your inner spirit, that is the Divine within, and you cannot go wrong.

"Lord make me an instrument of your peace
Where there is hatred let me sow love

Where there is injury, pardon
Where there is doubt, faith
Where there is darkness, light
And where there is sadness, joy."

St Francis of Assisi

Key Points

- ❖ God is less present in our children's lives today
- ❖ Provide children with practices and a language that allows them to feel they have God in their life
- ❖ Does it matter what God is called? Surely connecting to the Divine is what is most important
- ❖ Non-judgemental acceptance and unconditional compassion are two of the most powerful gifts any person can give another
- ❖ By practising unconditional love we are being more accepting of others and their search for God
- ❖ There are many possible pathways to the Divine. The important thing is the destination and the journey rather than the process
- ❖ World religions have common universal truths and symbols
- ❖ Our children are in need of pastoral care
- ❖ It is important to build a religious and spiritual background early in a child's life
- ❖ Angel imagery and prayer are powerful and positive ways to bring God's presence into the lives of children and teenagers
- ❖ Ritual and ceremony welcomes the sacred into children's lives
- ❖ To live our life as close as possible to universal truths is the most important thing

we can do - doing this will make God welcome in our children's lives

❖ Our children learn from what we do rather than from what we say – modelling is the most powerful teacher

❖ Be the person you want your child to be - live from your inner spirit, the God within, and you cannot go wrong

Remember

In the universe is
a Great Light made up of many,
many lights all giving out light together
and forming one Great Light
which is infinite, with no limits.
This Light spreads out
all over the world- evenly,
without discrimination of colour,
creed, belief or how anyone behaves.
this Light is totally loving.

One day, two special
people decided to have a baby which
they both wanted so much.
And into this baby from inside
the Mother came a little
light from that Great Light which
settled into the unborn child.
It waited so that it could feel what
it was like being Human!
And so a baby was born
and the light inside shone brightly.
With so much love from the parents,
the light grew brighter and stronger
and more loving, reflecting the
light of that Great Light,
which we call God.

Inside the little child,
the light shone brightly, growing
bigger all the time.
The child knew it was really
God-Light experiencing being human
and it was good.
As the child grew older and was more
involved in the things the world

had to do and offer, the Child-Grown forgot
it's light most of the time and only
vaguely remembered how
beautiful it was to be totally
loved and full of Light.

Gradually the light was covered
over by the distractions and delusions
of the world, with it's anger and fear,
stresses and pressures, it's expectations
and demands, it's performances and pretences.
The light remained always but was forgotten
except when something good happened
and then it shone and glowed brightly in
the heart of the Child-Grown.
It felt the beauty of a human being instead
of the ignorance of a human doing.
The light within was forgotten,
but it never gave up on its human form,
but continued to glow.

One day however,
The Child-Grown experienced
great hurt and sadness and called out
in vague memory of something once long ago
which had felt good always.
The light shone out and glowed
brightly in loving comfort and kindness
and the Child-Grown wondered.
"What was inside that felt so good and kind,
so loving and so peaceful?"

As the memory
stirred within the Child-Grown,
so the light grew stronger and brighter
with a radiance that shone out so brightly that
the Child-Grown felt great happiness and
peace inside, despite the
troubles and hurt.

This made the

Child-Grown look inside and ask:
"Who is this? Is it me?"
And the light shone brighter still and the
Child-Grown remembered that once long ago
there was always the feeling of love.
There was always a
glow inside.

The Child-Grown had
a round crystal hanging in front of
the window and when the sunlight shone through,
the crystal sent out rainbows of all colours,
which danced around the walls.
When the curtains were drawn,
the crystal hung dormant, waiting for the curtains
to open and let in the light.
The Child-Grown watched the crystal
one day and saw how it came alight and alive
when the curtains were open
and the light streamed in.
A memory stirred.
The little facets of the crystal shone out,
each creating its own light,
yet still a part of the one
big crystal of light.

The Child-Grown
remembered that there was a
little facet of light inside the heart which
has glowed and radiated brightly when the child
was young and free of the curtains that humans
put up around their hearts.
And the Child-Grown
remembered that the Divine purpose
here on earth was to see what it
was like to be human.

The curtains were
opened and the light glowed
and shone brightly.
With love and attention

from the Child-Grown,
the Light grew brighter and stronger
with a brilliance and radiance
which was breath-taking.
The God-Light remembered
it was also part or a Light which was
greater than we can imagine!
Brighter and more radiant than
we can see... but we
can 'feel' it.

If we sit quietly
with our curtains opened,
our light, our God-Light
reflects and shines with infinite light
and dances with the Source
from whence it came.
The Gold-Light which we are
shines forth into the world,
reminding other people that they
too have a God-Light glowing
behind the curtains
of their hearts.

And when we die,
the Light does not go out.
It is indestructible and eternal
and returns to the Great Source of Light.
It takes with it great love
and infinite respect for those brave souls,
"being human", who have experienced
life's challenges and adventures.
The God-Light remembers the frailty
and courage of the Human, the laughter
and the joy and sorrow of the Human,
and takes these experiences
back to the Source with unlimited love
and understanding of
being Human.

And the great Source

of Light and Love shines ever
more brightly and radiantly as our God-Light,
the brave little light which is in us,
returns to tell a story and becomes once again
with the whole source of Light, which was
never separate and always loved us and
kept us, the invincible God-Light,
glowing even behind the
darkest curtains.
"Remember!"

Written by Joan Terry at a Tibetan Buddhist Monastery, India,
1997 - Dedicated to her grandsons Jordan and Henry.

Chapter 13

The Power of Prayer

Dear Lord

It's me again. Hope you have a spare moment to listen to
me 'cos I need a friend...and I know from the poem
"Footprints" that you are always with me, and that
sometimes you carry me......

Thank you for being there.......where ever 'there' is...

I remember being taught as a small child to pray every
night before bed. Yet few of my prayers were answered and so
what was the point? I prayed that God would help me to be
good and not to make my Mummy angry. I prayed that He
would help me to stop wetting the bed and would make those
scary nightmares go away. When these petitions were not
granted my faith was shaken, at about six years of age! This
was with prayers of intercession, asking for something for
others, as well as prayers of petition, asking for something for
myself.

Dear God

Please bless Mummy, Daddy and baby Ben. Please help me to
be good and can you please look after Granny cos' she's sick
right now.

Amen

Then there are prayers of confession, repentance and asking
for forgiveness.

> Dear God I have been naughty. I have stolen sweets from my friend. I am sorry and ask that you still love me and forgive me.
>
> Amen

Then there are the prayers of lamentation, crying in distress and asking for vindication.

> Dear God
>
> Why did you give me such a mean Mummy?
> When she hits me for being
> noisy I get scared and I wish you could make my Mummy happy so she can be kinder to me.
>
> Amen

And there are prayers of adoration, invocation and thanksgiving.

> Dear God
>
> I love you and ask that you keep watch over me and my family. Thank you for all that is good in the world including the sun and the sky,
> and my dog Butch.
>
> Amen

Theologian Richard J Foster describes twenty-one separate categories of prayer! Essentially, "Prayer may be individual or communal, private or public. It may be offered in words, sighs, gestures or silence." (Larry Dossey, Healing Words, p6).

It is unnecessary to complicate prayer in the lives of our children. We can teach them exact words and the way we believe is the best way to pray and in the process we take away that magical quality of a child talking to God as he or she sees fit. A child's relationship with God is shaped by the concepts and constructs that are formed during the teachings from their family and their faith community. If a child has a concept that God is all knowing and all powerful, and that he listens to church leaders and adults ahead of children, then the child may be less likely to engage in spontaneous prayer and also less likely to use prayer as a natural and regular part of his or her life.

Encouraging children to express their own messages to God, as well as possibly using more formal prayer, is helpful to them.

Children's Prayer

Now I lay me down to sleep
I pray the Lord my soul to keep
Safely through both day and night
Wrapped in God's Divine White Light.

Now Dear Lord,
I pray, Bless the ones I Love
with your unconditional Love,
Let us see with clear sight,
and be guided by the Angel's Light.

Atira Hatton, Seattle Washington, USA

My experiences as a child created for me a God who judged every moment of my life. I was a sinner every week because I was unable to follow his rules about going to church and worshipping. My Mum was Catholic but she did not drive and we lived twenty-five miles from the church! I struggled nightly to pray.

Fortunately for me I found God in nature. He became my friend as I played in his playground. I escaped my troubled world by playing in the bush with the quietness, the natural beauty of trees, rocks, flowers and the sky. This opened up a different channel to God and I found him to be loving, understanding and caring, and my prayerfulness flowed. This connectedness continues in my life. I am spontaneously drawn to prayer when in nature - in God's garden. I also find a sense of connection within places of worship, in sacred gatherings when a Buddhist monk chants, during a didgeridoo ceremony, a drumming ceremony or an evangelical song and dance event.

I believe that the intention of people gathered together to celebrate their expression of the Divine helps to open others to the experience. All present can reach a transcendent state as they are gathered to celebrate the ritual and ceremony. Maybe it just shows 'that when two or more are gathered in my name........"

I chose for my sons to attend a Christian primary school so that they could have the values and morals of home reinforced and modelled everyday. It was also an opportunity for them to become familiar with prayer from an early age. At preschool, simple, loving gestures build safety and concern for others in the classroom. This 'familiarity' with God allows their unconscious mind to open to accepting prayer and liturgy later in life. It is now that the boys are almost adults that I feel reassured by their comfort with my prayerfulness and my God-centred ways of seeing and interpreting the world. They tell me that they find the Divine out in nature, especially when they are surfing. The pause between the waves is a great place for God to come and share their thoughts. The inherent strength of nature and of being at its mercy gives an edge that helps them to remain respectful of forces beyond themselves and that can shape and change their lives in an instant. My Dad used to have a motto about God and adversity; it was, "There weren't too many atheists in the trenches during the war!"

I cannot imagine a day without prayer. I believe very much in the power of prayer. I believe that prayer deepens my relationship with the Divine and that it deepens my ability to positively influence the lives of others. I pray deeply for those I love, for those I meet, and for those on our earth who have no-one who prays for them. I also believe in the power of prayer when we have loved ones who are ill, lost or in pain of some kind. I teach others the potential that lies in the power of prayer so that they may experience the same wonderful feelings and to show them that we are not powerless. We can help others even if they live on the other side of the world and even when they have left this physical world.

"In the silence of my innermost being, in the fragments of my yearned-for wholeness, can I hear the whispers of God's presence? Can I remember when I felt God's nearness? When we walked together and I let myself be embraced by God's love. Could God really be watching over me? Maybe."

Source world wide web.

People may never know that we have prayed for them. When teaching in a Christian college, we were asked to pray every morning. At first I was reluctant as many of the students were not Christian. Then my own passion for prayer took over and I spoke with the students about what it meant for them. Those among them who were willing to pray did not have a strong concept of prayer or of the Divine for that matter. We gathered and used prayers from a number of prayer books, different religions and sources and from the students themselves. It was easy for those without a faith to 'do a prayer for us each day'. One such boy, who had said to me at the beginning of the year that he did not believe in God at all, came up to me at the end of the year to say, "I just want to tell you I am not so sure anymore about God not existing......" That is the power of holding a passion about the sacred, something bigger than us that can influence our lives!

Consider how else prayer can be a part of a child's life? How else can we share divine intentions and good intentions that bring light and goodness into our lives? A very special person who was a mentor of mine when I first began to work in palliative care taught me the value of creative prayer. This is prayer with symbols rather than words. A ten year old boy, Shane, who spent his days with us, had a brain tumour. He was incredibly wise with a great sense of humour. He spent his days cheering up the other older people as they struggled with their life-threatening illnesses. When he became sicker my mentor taught him how to send rainbows of love to his parents, other family and his friends. He drew them and gained enormous comfort from seeing himself sending rainbows of love from his heart. As he was dying, we gathered around him and sent him the same rainbows of love. Not only did it feel like the right thing to do, it was comforting and meaningful. Whenever his loved ones see the rainbows in nature now they open their hearts to Shane's love, because of this symbolic experience. To me this is prayer.

Young children know how to draw and paint how they feel before they are able to express their feelings through language. I believe we can teach children this form of prayer early in life so that they have it forever. I wish I had had this gift when I was small. I may not have been so disappointed with my first experience of God through prayer. I may not have felt so powerless in the midst of a world full of adults. Creative prayer also provides a tool to send healing energy out to those in need, like when Granny is sick or for the starving children seen on TV.

Many children are raised in homes where prayer is absent. Creative prayer becomes a less threatening way of introducing prayer to them. The intention of sending goodness, love and compassion is what makes prayer most important. Larry Dossey tested the power of prayer and found that "love, compassion, caring and empathy catalyse healing events and that this power operates at a distance" (Healing Words, Larry Dossey p117). The intention of prayer is what is important rather than the form.

> "Here I am Lord
> Here I am Lord - body, heart and soul.
> Grant that with your love,
> I may be big enough to reach the world
> And small enough to be at one with you."

> Mother Teresa

In one maximum security prison I am aware of, prisoners spend the first hour of their day sending healing energy into our earth so that others may benefit. They do this in a deeply meditative state. Does this mean it is more or less effective than those who say their rosary in churches across the world? Or those who pray novenas in groups to seek a special intercession, for example for a person to heal after a serious accident? Do extroverts pray better than introverts? Once again, let's take note of Larry Dossey's findings.

"The most important lessons are that prayer works and that there is no formula, no 'one best way' to pray that everyone should follow."

(Healing Words, p100.)

What can improve the effectiveness of our prayers? As we become more comfortable with silence and stillness our ability to pray improves. The quietening of a busy mind, the moving 'inward' and connection to our inner being brings us to a closer connection with God and the Divine presence in our lives. If we can build a pathway, a form of ritual that pre-empts prayer, we deepen the prayer experience. Bringing our hands together, offering a blessing, sitting in silence and stillness and keeping a pattern of behaviour, like kneeling (what some people call genuflecting) all help open to the moment. Attending the same church, religious or spiritual place is helpful for many on the journey. By having these patterns of prayer we are also making imprints on our children's lives. That is only if the habits are pleasant and provide positive life experiences. Remember, the unconscious mind follows our movements as well as our frequent thoughts.

A well worn path in my psyche means that I am able to find a place of deep inner stillness in the midst of a crowd. This is very helpful to me. When we are confronted with anguish or emotional pain the immediacy of the moment makes the power of our prayer deepen and it does not matter HOW and where we pray.

"When we are miserable prayer is no longer a dry rote repetition. It becomes a living and vibrant cry for help. It becomes authentic. In pain we forget the "thee's" and the "thous" that keep us separated from God, and reach a new level of intimacy that comes from talking to God in our own way, saying what's in our heart."

Joan Borysenko, Guilt is the Teacher, Love is the Lesson 1990, pp181-182.

My recent experience of overbalancing on a six foot ladder certainly validated this. I plummeted towards the floor praying for help from God with the simple words, "Oh my God I need help right now!" Thankfully I was only bruised and shocked; my bones and ribs were fracture free. My doctor was pretty incredulous that I didn't have any cracked ribs and I KNEW I had been assisted, surely that's what matters.

On the other hand, Larry Dossey expressed that our prayers need to be more focused on gratitude and thanksgiving than praying incessantly for 'things'. This way we are acknowledging "that the world at heart is more glorious, benevolent and friendlier than we recently supposed" (Recovering the Soul, 1989, p207). This shift in focus is also in alignment with the concept that we create our own lives – what we focus on we create. What this means is that by focusing on the good that exists in our world we are expecting *more good*. A spiritual principle of gratitude is healthy as it keeps our minds in the direction of optimism and hopefulness and we move on from the disappointments of life. Such a focus is especially helpful for our children and helps reduce the fear saturation that has enveloped our world. As a Christian this means that we are grateful for Jesus' life and all that he came to teach us. We are grateful that he lives within our hearts and helps us to be more like Him.

My final comment on prayer is that I believe it helps build connectedness both with ourselves and with others. Prayer helps us connect to our inner world, our higher self, our God consciousness and in this way to make decisions that aid rather than hinder our lives – or simply make decisions that cause less suffering. With increased quietness and prayer, I believe we create space for God to reach us, to speak with us, guide us and to encourage us to be the best person we can be.

Prayer is simply the best food imaginable for our hearts and souls. This is why I encourage you to model positive prayer in children's lives, as early as possible. Prayer helps children to cope with the chaos, the confusion and the uncertainty of life.

"One night my grandson, David, was spending the night. When he went to bed I noticed he sat up and put his hands in the praying position.

When he finished his prayers I said, "You sit up when you say your prayers?"
And he said, "Yes Grandma."
And I said "How come?"
And he said, "Because you are closer to God, and it helps."

David (6 years old), Graham, Washington (World Wide Web)

Key Points

- ❖ Use simple prayer for children

- ❖ Model prayerfulness at home and in schools - sharing prayer in groups positively influences all

- ❖ Symbolic prayer is powerful

- ❖ Prayer enhances healing

- ❖ By improving our comfort with silence and stillness we improve our ability to pray

- ❖ Prayer works regardless of form or method - as the intention ensures its success

- ❖ Early habits of quietness and prayer help children find prayer later in their life

- ❖ Prayers of gratitude can improve our perceptions and concepts of life - by focusing on the good

- ❖ Prayer is food for the heart and the soul

- ❖ Prayer builds human connectedness

- ❖ Prayer allows the Sacred more space to reach us.

Chapter 14

Nurturing Kids' Hearts and Souls in our Schools

Streemin

Im in the bottom streme
Which means Im not bright
Don't like reading
Cant hardly write

But all these divishns
Arnt reely fair
Look at the cemetery
No steemin there

Roger McGough. "The Glassroom"

This chapter has been challenging to write, causing me concern and sleepless moments in the darkest part of the night. I have decided I could write a whole book on schools and education, it's a big subject. I will allow the next chapter 'Magic Moments: Heart and Soul Stories from Schools Around the World' to show you what it means to nurture kids hearts and souls in school, from the point of view of well respected and well-loved teachers.

When I began teaching in 1977, new teachers were usually given the worst classes, worst classrooms and often the worst timetables - maybe it was a rite of initiation. You either sank or swam. From what new teachers tell me today little has changed except that students are even more challenging, oppositional and difficult to teach. Yes, schools are full of wonderful technology, terminology, and psychology; more assessment, more pressure and more chaos. The rapid pace of living has impacted on our students in many ways. Many live with their minds overstimulated by 'things'; fingers on a mobile phone and an ipod plugged into their ears. In the pressures of this modern world with its consumerism, technology and speed we have more teenagers than ever before suffering from failed traditional schooling, eating disorders, addictions and suicide.

These kids and teenagers still need committed teachers who help them learn and grow. Even better, they need teachers who help them think, problem solve and develop socially, academically and emotionally. But what do the students want from us as their teachers? Imagine for a moment that a student wrote the following.

Memo from your student

❖ Don't be afraid to be firm with me. By doing this you make me feel secure.

❖ Don't let me form bad habits; I rely on you to warn me of their existence.

❖ Don't nag as this takes power from me when I am learning to be responsible for my own actions.

❖ Don't let my mistakes devalue me as a person; they are merely indications of how I can improve.

❖ Don't make me feel smaller than I am, my defence will be to make you feel small too.

❖ Don't correct me in front of my peers or other teachers unless you can do it with compassion and it is a lesson for us all to benefit from. I would prefer you to correct me in private.

❖ Don't concentrate on my imperfections; it may lead you to overlook my strengths and talents.

❖ Don't question my honesty too much; I am easily frightened into telling lies.

- Don't be inconsistent as it confuses me and threatens my faith in you as a teacher.

- Don't put me off when I ask questions or I will stop asking them. Also, I sometimes ask questions for those not brave enough to ask.

- Don't suggest that you are perfect, infallible or better than me as a person; knowledge of facts alone does not make a person superior. Please try to be honest and real as these qualities encourage me to be the same.

- Don't tell me my fears are silly. They are very real to me and reassurance and loving support will help me to conquer these fears and to grow and understand things better.

- Don't treat boys and girls differently; we admire those who see us each as unique and valuable regardless of gender.

- Don't bribe me with rash promises as that threatens my trust in you and I feel hurt when I am let down by broken promises.

- Don't assume you know how I am feeling or what is happening for me. That is nothing but arrogance even if well intentioned.

- Don't pressure me to reveal anything I do not feel comfortable to share. Trust is a personal choice.

- Don't judge me on account of knowing my parents or my siblings. I am a unique human being and I deserve the right to create my own relationship with you, free of preconceptions.

- Don't jump to conclusions on appearances when resolving conflict. Check both sides of the story before attempting to help us solve the problem.

- Watch my body language; it may tell you something I can't tell you.

❖ Remember that learning from experience can be messy, especially with paper, glue, clay, sand and paint, and the biggest lesson may be the cleaning up!

❖ If you recognise my pain or hurt show me you care, preferably in a small private way. I don't need a public viewing and it only adds to my anxiety.

❖ When all else fails please keep a sense of hope that I am still a worthwhile person, especially when I don't deserve it.

❖ **My final message to you is this:**

"You are very important in my life right now. You play a unique role in the formation of me as a whole person. Be careful when you share in my intellectual, physical, emotional and spiritual growth that you don't concentrate too much on any one area. I am grateful for your support and guidance in my developmental years. Thank you."

Maggie Dent. 1993

Our students need people around them who are consistent caregivers, who are able to care and respect students where-ever they are in their development. Now that we know how the brain develops maybe we could be more empathic towards students who have been deprived of essential nurturing in the early years of their lives. As Bonnie Bernard, the mother of resilience, suggested let's focus on what works for these students instead of what doesn't and what they struggle with. Let us help students learn about themselves, others and how to live in our world in safe environments amongst committed educators.

The way of tomorrow is definitely education that takes into consideration the whole child. Over emphasis of assessment and reaching benchmarks is a drive that often shuts authentic learning down for life. It sucks away creativity, student directedness and enthusiasm for cooperative collaborative unfolding of curiosity and intuitive learning. Accountability and results are seldom able to give measures of the social, emotional and moral growth of students; yet, surely these are equally as important. The giving of awards for academic and sporting success also creates a sense of failure - for the 99% of the school community who never receive that public accolade. The year after year progress of students who are graded according to these two main yardsticks does much to crush the spirit of our emerging generations. Is it any wonder we have such huge issues in the Western world around illicit alcohol and drug abuse, violence, obesity, teenage depression and youth suicide figures that are simply outrageous. Essentially classroom teachers know what can improve schooling and yet politicians continue to make decisions about education based on intellectual and fiscal directives!

"The body of a child will not grow if it is not fed; the mind will not flourish unless it is stimulated and guided. And the spirit will suffer if it is not nurtured."

Rachael Kessler. The Soul of Education (2003) p 34

What does 'soul of education' mean? How does it work and where is it happening? Essentially 'soul' attends to those areas neglected in our schools – the recognising, valuing, encouraging and nurturing of non-academic and non-competitive qualities in education. This means:
- ❖ commitment to being respectful of diversity in our schools – of colour, age, gender or culture;
- ❖ building connectedness between and within all those who attend a school, which can be achieved through building genuine relationships between and among all who share in this amazing journey called education;
- ❖ we can celebrate the ancient ways of 'actualisation' or personal growth through songs, dance, art, storytelling, poetry and ritual;
- ❖ the vocational and academic programs can have equal valuing, where craftsmen and women are also seen to be valuable and incredibly worthwhile in the fabric of our communities;

❖ having balance between the individual and group activities that show that self, unity and cooperation all have value;

❖ making learning fun and valuing the role of laughter and lightness in building emotional competency, safety and interpersonal bonding in groups;

❖ helping children learn how to think and how to use their own minds to interpret the world and to find that elusive thing we all search for, MEANING;

❖ teaching children life skills and values that help them form effective loving relationships and to be able to contribute positively to our world;

❖ we care deeply about our role in the development of every child who comes to us.

Finally it means that parents and teachers work together with the same agendas, the same intentions and the same positive commitment to 'bring forth the greatness within each child'. It is important to acknowledge and really listen to our young – to the students in our schools. When their autonomy is threatened they have little choice but to be resentful.

Our children's search for involvement and autonomy starts much earlier in life than ever before. The old model of schooling has it roots in times of punitive punishment and discipline, where respect was often gained through fear alone. This approach no longer works. Respect goes both ways and must be earned. Today's young value teachers who are passionate about the subjects they teach, enjoy their work, care about their students and know how to laugh. The students especially respect those teachers who practise fairness in all their classes. There are more and more of these teachers finding their way into education, because they want to be there. The positive education of our children will continue to rely on those amazing teachers who turn up everyday with passion for their career, their students and the schooling system. The teachers have a genuine affection and commitment to young children, teenagers and love their job.

There are thousands out there who are doing all of the things that build 'soul' in a schools, maybe without knowing it. Daily these teachers give hope to kids and their parents that what matters most is the gift of life. They make a positive difference everyday and, thankfully, they make our world a better place to be in.

When a school community embraces a new vision of creating a safe environment that supports the unique growth and development of all students, including those with special needs, many things change. Firstly, communities look at the physical environment and study ways to improve it. How can students look forward to coming to schools that are in a poor state of repair – with torn, vomit-coloured carpets, peeling paint and disgusting toilets. Eco-therapy is a new field of study that explores the way our physical environment enhances or diminishes our wellbeing. Tired, depressing schools could very well be contributing to student un-wellness, more than we have previously thought. Many schools in the government sector have given up waiting for government funding and begun fundraising and making the physical changes themselves. Students get enthusiastic when positive things are done to make their schools look better.

The spirit of school can be sensed very quickly by an outsider who comes into the school. I have seen some wonderful examples of landscaping and outdoor settings that have been built by the parent bodies. This has created pleasant places for students to eat and play. Staff rooms that have plants and couches and are painted in bright colours also lift the spirits of staff. These steps not only create positive school environments they build community spirit, which is doubly beneficial, especially in rural and remote communities. Students spend so many hours at school it makes sense for the physical space to be pleasant and have a positive energy.

I am very passionate about many of the philosophies of Maria Montessori, Rudolf Steiner_and Reggio Emilia, among others. These people insisted that education should be understood as the art of cultivating the moral, emotional, physical, psychological and spiritual dimensions of the developing child. The notion of holistic education is based on the premise that each person finds identity, meaning, and purpose in life through connections to the community, the natural world, and to spiritual values such as compassion and peace.

Holistic education aims to bring forth an intrinsic reverence for life and a passionate love of learning. This is achieved, not through an academic curriculum that condenses the world into instructional packages but through direct engagement with the environment. While few public schools are entirely committed to holistic principles, many teachers try hard to put many of these ideas into practice – more and more as the years go by. By fostering collaboration rather than competition in classrooms teachers help young people to feel connected. Teachers use real-life experiences, current events, the dramatic arts and other lively sources of knowledge in place of textbook information, to kindle the love of learning. By encouraging reflection and questioning, rather than passive memorisation of 'facts', teachers keep alive the 'flame of intelligence' that is so much more than abstract problem-solving skills. By accommodating differences and refusing to label children, for example as learning disabled or hyperactive, teachers bring out the unique gifts contained within each child's spirit.

Holistic education is more concerned with drawing forth the latent capacities and sensitivities of the soul than with stuffing passive young minds full of pre-digested information. It is an education that prepares young people to live purposefully, creatively, and morally in a complex world."

Ron Miller editor. The Renewal of Meaning in Education: Responses to the Cultural and Ecological Crisis of our Times (1999)

As the human species evolves further the need to embrace a more holistic approach will become even stronger for development of the pre-frontal brain. My concern here lies with the changing paradigms and pressures to abandon the old and leap 'off-ship' to embrace the new. Such abandonment happened twice in my teaching career and caused my students and myself much angst and confusion. Change is inevitable as we evolve in response to new knowledge and learning. However, let change be negotiated and explored and let decisions on the process of change have respect for all stakeholders. Experienced teachers feel invalidated by change that is mandated and that discredits former preferred ways of learning, saying they are now outdated. Even though I am a passionate advocate for student-centred holistic learning I still value clear structure and building blocks. I like rote learning of times tables, especially with singing and chanting, and certain grammar conventions. Don't throw the baby out with the bath water!

The essential elements in evolving education are that the art of teaching is honoured and that caring relationships be placed above academic pressure. It is important to honour the whole range of human experience in our schools, to prepare us for life. We learn how to manage challenging people by spending time around them. We learn how to manage criticism by experiencing it. We learn about freedom of speech and its consequences when we are made to accept responsibility for any pain we may have caused another with our words. A teacher in the US explore this a little more,

"When I think of the list of teachers who really taught me, I wouldn't describe them all as caring and loving. My favourite teachers were caring and loving, but the ones who really pushed my academic edges wouldn't get the loving title... and yet without a doubt, I know they cared about my success, my growth, and my learning. They were tough and I was never quite sure how the *felt* about me although I knew they believed in me.

I think that it is important for teachers/educators to recognize and KNOW what their own personal style of connecting and relating with other people is.... for them to know their strengths in relationships, what types of people they connect with easily, and their weaknesses, who they have difficulties connecting with, who finds their style distasteful (thus resisting). I see great value in a teacher who is capable of 'seeing the possible' and is able to see 'what is' in the relationship and respond from there. I can believe in a student indefinitely, however, if I can't find a way to connect with them, then my powers as a guide are much weaker."

Turnaround Teachers. WorldWideWeb

Remember that all life experience stimulates the brain to grow and evolve. Human adaptability is the key to survival and if we create school environments that prevent challenge on any level we may very well be holding back the full development of the individuals that exist within it.

No matter what philosophy we follow as teachers we must strive to enhance the art of our teaching each year. As teachers and educators we need to keep growing in our ability to engage learners and to create the opportunities for richness and variety that create mild challenge without creating stress in our students' brains. In this way we stimulate optimal conditions for learning, for all students not just the gifted or the average student. These pathways honour the multiple intelligences and preferred styles of learning of all students.

Take this wonderful visualisation from James Dakin of Teaching Freedom in the UK as an example.

Maths Lesson: Understanding millimetres, centimetres, metres and kilometres (in shorter form than the lesson itself):

The children closed their eyes and, after our initial Journey to relax and centre them all, were transported to a far away land where there was a queen, who reigned over a wonderful country and was fascinated by measurements.

She greeted us warmly and when we said that we didn't understand measurements, she asked if we'd like to spend the day with her chief measurers. The children all agreed willingly!

So we were sent off into the garden with a magnifying glass to look for Mr. Millipede. Looking through the grass we soon found him beavering away measuring the blades of grass. His role, he told us, was to measure the blades of grass in the Queen's garden to ensure that everything was looking good and, as each step he took was 1mm long, it made him the perfect person to do it.

Shortly, we met up with Mrs. Mouse. Mr. Millipede, tired after measuring lots of blades of grass, climbed up onto her back for a rest and introduced us to her. She explained that her role was to measure the flower beds and, as each step she took was 1cm long, she could do it very accurately. Sometimes, she told us, if the flower bed was a tiny bit longer or shorter than her step then she'd ask Mr. Millipede to walk underneath her so they could give accurate measurements such as 55cm and 3mm - good teamwork!

All of a sudden the ground began to shake and we became frightened until Mrs. Mouse told us that it was Nellie the Elephant coming to say hello. Nellie slowly put her trunk onto the ground and invited us to go for a ride with her. Wow, what a view we got from on top of her. Nellie explained that her job was to measure the borders of the Queen's gardens and as each of her strides were a metre long, this meant that she was perfectly qualified to do this. Sometimes if her stride didn't match the distance around a garden perfectly, she'd ask Mrs. Mouse and Mr. Millipede to walk underneath her so that she could deliver an accurate measurement such as 78m 12cm and 1mm!
Even better teamwork we thought.

And it was at that stage that they all thought we should go for a rest by the sea for some time out. As we got onto the beach we heard a big booming voice coming from one of the caves underneath the cliff. We listened carefully and heard this enormous voice repeating over and over the following phrase:

"I don't kill everything, I just kill Ometres. I don't kill everything, I just kill Ometres!" Puzzled, and a little scared, we decide to go and investigate. As we walk into the cave the voice gets louder...

"I DON'T KILL EVERYTHING, I JUST KILL OMETRES!"

Inside the cave there was a huge cavern, in the middle of which was a huge giant. "HELLO" his voice boomed at us as he looked at us with a friendly smile, "I'm the Queen's intercity measurer, would you like to come for a walk with me?"

We say yes please and before we can move he's picked us up in the palm of his hand and placed us on one of his shoulders and, stooping until we get out of the cave, we set off towards the horizon. As we walk he tells us that each of his strides is a kilometre long and that his job is to measure the distance between cities so that the road signs can always tell drivers how far they have to travel.

Later, when we are back in the garden giving Mrs. Mouse a lift back to the palace, we meet the Queen who asks us if we've had a lovely day and what we've learnt. We tell her that we finally understand how measurements work with millimetres being the smallest, measured by the smallest employee we've ever seen, Mr. Millipede, who was responsible for measuring the length of the blades of grass in her garden. We now know that centimetres come next,
they were measured by Mrs. Mouse who was responsible for measuring the flower beds. Metres came next with Nellie the Elephant measuring the boundaries of her gardens and finally kilometres, which was the responsibility of her giant who didn't kill everything, he just killed Ometres, in other words, he just measured kilometres! And with that we went
back into our classroom to practice all of our new found knowledge.

This was created during one of our training courses and when she spoke it to the audience they gave her a spontaneous

round of applause, such was its
brilliance. And guess what, her children all understand
measurements now, they are 8 to 9 years old.

James Dakin. Teaching Freedom www.teachingfreedom.com

Innovative teaching practice stimulates classrooms
and all who sail in them! Teaching to Learn by Christine
Ward is an excellent resource for teachers interested in
creating more success in their classroom. It is packed with
the latest knowledge around brain-compatible learning,
accelerated learning and how to direct mental imagery and
mental rehearsal. After all these years I still have students
who stop me to tell me they still know how to turn their
brains on, how to visualise the success they want and how to
challenge their brain to think smarter! The 'new' knowledge
from NLP, educational kinesiology, brain research and brain-
compatible learning has completely changed the potential for
learning environments. When this knowledge is coupled with
heart-centred passionate educators – the sky is no longer the
limit.

Another excellent resource is The Thinking Learning
Classroom by Glenn Capelli and Sean Brealey. This
innovative and unique resource challenges how you think
and remember; and its beautiful poetry inspires you.

"Yes we were born to learn
and we were born to teach
as we were born to love
and we were born to breathe
we say yes in all that we do
in our message for me and for you."

Glenn Capelli and Sean Brealey. The Thinking Learning
Classroom 2000, from Born to Learn, the chorus p15

Chick Moorman explores the potential of teachers to be 'way
showers'.

"They show us that real education has nothing to do with covering content, but is now and always has been a drawing out of what already exists within the student rather than a putting in of what we see necessary to fill perceived deficiencies."

Chick Moorman. Spirit Whisperers, back cover.

This refreshing book validates the challenging place where teachers find themselves today. It also validated much of what I had discovered to be true in my own teaching career. Teachers are in-between the old, "the shame based, right/wrong, competition, fear, punishment, rescuing, judgement, demand for compliance and obedience to outside authority form of teaching" (p207) and the edge of the new paradigm. Teachers are aware of the changing consciousness; he or she understands the need for students' growing autonomy. In this new paradigm the student has input into their learning that they also direct and evaluate. The emotional, spiritual and social growth of students is supported and encouraged with shared respect for diversity and difference. This journey into uncharted waters allows our children to grow up with a better opportunity to realise their full potential than ever before in the history of mankind.

We may very well need to re-consider how our schools are designed and built. There may need to areas for vegetable and fruit gardens so that students can explore eco-sustainability. There may also be a 'Calmness Centre' where children can retreat to for some time out, to rest in a calm safe place where they can receive pastoral care. This same centre may run relaxation activities including children's yoga, contemplation and visualisation sessions and provide bean bags to catch a nap. Such a centre would be a place for children who are experiencing family trauma to come and be supported, freely. The heart-centred teacher who ran such a centre would be skilled as a teacher, counsellor and resilience specialist and would be able to help students with their schooling as well as offering life skills and pastoral care.

The same centre could be a resource centre and run seminars for new parents; parents with children with special needs, literacy problems and emotional and social problems. It could run programs for gifted children and have the ability to create social programs that bring the community closer to the school, such as singing to the elderly or reading to toddlers. I would like the centre to have a teacher trained and comfortable to use safe touch, so that touch-deprived children are able to be soothed and nurtured. The school chaplain and other parent volunteers, with appropriate training, could also help, to ensure that children receive additional support. Specialist care could be available with referrals would made through the school.

Children from homes with low emotional literacy would be able to experience care and support over a period of time, instead of just the twenty minutes every now and again that they receive now. This way they may be able to build emotional, social and spiritual competencies that allow them to move beyond the generational patterns of dysfunction. Childhood stress is beneath much poor behaviour and low achievement. This proposed model could be the best way to support tomorrow's children to cope better as they grow in our less than perfect world. The essential focus would be on building a network that supports the healthy raising of children, within school and the community.

In closing this brief overview on schooling I must express my faith in what is currently happening in classrooms around the world. There are many excellent and committed teachers, more than those who are less than competent and disinterested. The new teachers coming through are passionate about teaching and are really keen to make a difference. A more holistic approach is occurring even within highly structured school systems. With this, everyone wins – students enjoy learning better and teachers are renewed in their enthusiasm for education.

My humble suggestions to improve schooling, especially in government education, are as follows.

- ❖ A less cognitive approach to schooling - value the trades, musicians and crafts people.

- ❖ Place a priority on building emotional intelligence and social and moral competencies so that kids can form more effective relationships and life skills, most important for being resilient and happy in life.

- ❖ Create safe, quiet and small schools where kids can be happy and thus learn better. If not smaller schools, continue to work towards smaller classes.

- ❖ Improve school environments to reflect respect and valuing of the school.

- ❖ Teach thinking skills, accelerated learning techniques and memory strategies so that all students can become smarter, not just the bright ones.

- ❖ Lighten up in schools - have more laughter and fun so that kids can feel connected and that life really is worth living; this is especially beneficial for boys.

- ❖ Keep a good balance between work and play in primary school – no homework before 10 years of age.

- ❖ Ensure all students have creative pursuits, every year of schooling – increase opportunities for the arts.

- ❖ Allow kids to be kids for as long as possible. Have more play-based, non-competitive and competitive physical activities to encourage our kids to be more active and to help reduce the obesity problem at the same time as they learn how to lose, to cooperate and share.

- ❖ Introduce more 'out of classroom' real activities like bush walking, growing vegetables, creating school cafes that provide the many levels of 'real' experiences from growing food, preparing and cooking food, serving food, and running a business. Recycle old computers to needy families, decorate and paint tired toilets or classrooms, learning the benefits of volunteering and community help, learn first aid.

❖ Teach stress management early in life - relaxation, breathing, yoga, stretching and personal fitness.

Real-life skills can be learned in schools to impact on the rest of students' lives. With their understanding of technology and information technology (IT) students can create their own DVDs or CDs. They can use these to teach others. Tomorrow's schools will be dynamic and like no other.

I recently noticed an article in the paper about someone who had been in my oldest son's class at school. He had been considered a bit of a 'nerd' as he was small, shy and largely invisible. He has just turned over $1 million in his first year of business, selling products online. In the coming year that figure is likely to be $1.5 million. Everyone has the opportunity to become successful in today's rapidly changing world, without necessarily following the old models of university and career. It is an exciting time as well as causing confusion. That is why life skills are more important than ever to help our young cope with the unpredictable chaos, unexpected change and instant financial success!

Always remember teaching is the second most important job on the planet. Dedicated, effective teachers change today and the future, everyday. They make a positive difference, sometimes with just a smile or a word of encouragement. Of course the absolutely most important job on earth is parenting.

This song sums up exceptional teachers.

Thank you Super Teacher

A song by David Koutsoukis and Glenn Capelli

Well there's no nicer words to hear
Than after many years
Someone comes along and says
I remember you

You taught me in Grade 2
And I'd like to say "thank you"
Because you were,
A Super Teacher

Or what about the day
An ex-student comes to say
I'm glad that you're still here
After all these years

Now there's more learning to be done
Coz here's my little son
And he knows you are
A Super teacher

Hey thank you Super Teacher
I want you to know
The difference you made
Hey thank you Super Teacher
I'm a lifelong learner,
Because of you

Imagine sitting home alone
When from the blue there on the phone
Comes a distant call
From a former student

I just had to call and say
I started teaching school today
Because of you
Super Teacher

Hey thank you Super Teacher
I want you to know
The difference you made

Hey thank you Super Teacher
I do what I do,
Because of you

Yeah, think about your life
And who you'd like to thank
For the attention and direction
They've given you

For their constant love and care
Yes, they were always there
Because they were
A Super Teacher

Hey thank you Super Teacher
I want you to know
The difference you made
Hey thank you Super Teacher
I am who I am
Because of you

Hey thank you Super Teacher
I want you to know
The difference you made
Hey thank you Super Teacher
I'm a lifelong learner,
I do what I do,
I am who I am
Because of you
(Available via their web sites)

Key Points

- ❖ Students need teachers who help them think, problem solve and to develop socially, academically and emotionally

- ❖ Teachers need better training in emotional intelligence and how to build it

❖ Our students need consistent caregivers who are able to care for and respect students, where-ever they are in their development

❖ There needs to be more soul in education

❖ Students' search for involvement and autonomy is much earlier in life than ever before

❖ The school physical environment impacts on the wellbeing of everyone

❖ Holistic education aims to call forth an intrinsic reverence for life and a passionate love of learning

❖ Teachers need to be consulted and heard when major change is being planned

❖ Innovative teaching techniques increase student engagement and interest and are transferable in life

❖ Education is between the old and the new paradigms

❖ Real-life experiences in learning environments keep our 'new students' engaged better

❖ Life skills as a conscious part of school curriculum to help build resilience

❖ New models of schools are coming

❖ Teaching is the second most important job on the planet.

❖ Choose to be exceptional

Chapter 15

Magic Moments: Inspirational Stories from Schools around the World

Heart centred teachers who show compassion, kindness, and a clear intention of being a positive part in students' lives do make a difference in ways that are very hard to measure. Sit back and enjoy these stories. Some of the names have been changed. There are contact details at the end of each story for each author.

Magic Moment One

Letter from a Year 12 student on Retreat

This is a letter to all those that made this possible. When I am talking about this, I am talking about the year 12 Retreat at Nanga Bush Camp. I am one of your pupils whom went on this trip wanting excitement and fun in sport and recreation. I was disappointed to put it mildly at how boring I found it to be. With all this mambo jumbo about yourself and the life around you I thought it was going to be a long week.

I soon found that it was not going to be so. On the second day we began talking about our families. I found that unluckily I was in a group that did not discuss anything private. This was not teachers or pupils problem but instead my lack of courage to speak out and discuss my story/ problems.

It amazed and inspired me when a small group of students stood up and told their story. They were so courageous and open to a whole year full of fellow pupils. I am a boy whom grew up never ever showing emotion and find it extremely difficult to let my feelings out. Thus I did not stand up and tell my story.

I found though that this program actually had meaning and was further implicated when I received my letter from my mum. It was the first part in my life that I and my mum have ever discussed our feelings towards me and I have actually listened. I read the note shaking as I am now doing writing this letter and observed for the first time in my entire life at how beautiful, courageous, loving, caring, beautiful, and yes smart my mum is.

I have never understood my mum until now and it disappoints me that I know that I will not return a letter too her because of my sacredness and shyness to express my feelings to anyone. One day it will backfire on me that I was not so open and sharing of my feelings, but my personality cannot do it.

I hope that the teachers involved understand that this camp no matter how boring it gets from here on in have in fact changed my life severely and I believe for the good. You should continue this course no matter how stressful and hard it is because although the pupils might not thank you too much I know that I will love your's forever for the great gift you have given me today. Thank you guys so much.

Years Sincerely

Scared Boy   XXXXXX OOOOOO

Footnote: One of the traditions on our Year 12 retreat is to give the students a letter written by their parents. They then reply to it. This letter was addressed to the staff instead. It is reproduced here, complete with original spelling and grammar, with the permission of the student.

James B DE PIAZZI
A teacher at MacKillop Catholic College, Busselton, West
Australia

Magic Moment Two

The Circle of One

A serious shock awaited me when I returned to mainstream schools in Scotland as a supply teacher, after ten cushy years abroad. Previously, I had been warned by my employers that I'd never find another permanent contract because there was a glut of teachers in the Central belt. Yet now there is a distinct shortage of teachers in certain areas and in certain subjects and the result led directly to my meeting a disaffected class of 12 year olds who'd listed a tally of twenty-two temporary English teachers over the first four months of their high school careers. It was an ignominious start.

Standing in front of the rows of desks that first day, I made no impression at all and was simply ignored as the class carried on chatting to each other, throwing bags and books around in an atmosphere of general mayhem. I
was invisible – they had become inured to strangers and had no recent history of a working relationship with an English teacher as guide or mentor, having received instead a succession of caretakers. As a supply teacher moreover, I was regarded as fair game. Over the next couple of weeks, I came to understand that they felt abandoned and angry, but right then, instead of care or compassion, I experienced a real sense of powerlessness. It was hard going, pulling every stunt from my armoury of 'interesting one-off lessons', and rapidly learning that no-one had much respect for the 'assertive discipline system'. In retrospect, it seems to me I held my breath till Easter then collapsed with relief, planning not to come back.

Yet the Easter holidays provided an unexpected resurrection in my vocation. At a conference, I was hugely inspired by Jenny Mosley's entertaining presentation about Circle Time and how she had devised this method during an earlier teaching career dealing with wildly reluctant detainees of the ROSLA years, whose attitude and behaviour bore a distinct resemblance to that of my own recent clientele. The strategies she had devised to bring interest and relevance to her classes were obviously tailor-made for mine, too. Better still, her infectious enthusiasm and self-disparaging humour had the audience in tear-streaked fits of laughter, so I knew for sure I was being shown how to bring in that all important element so often sadly ignored in education – fun!

After the 'show' I immediately moved fast to the stage and nabbed my new heroine, breathlessly asking about training in the Circle Time approach. She gave me the contact details but stressed, "There needs to be authenticity in your method – keep a journal of what works and doesn't work for you personally."

On the way out I asked a total stranger what time it was and that was the way I met and subsequently befriended, incredibly, the mother of one of my most difficult students. A delegate who could not attend at the last minute had given her a ticket, that's the only reason she was there, but what a startling coincidence. She asked me about Circle Time and whether I would use it with my classes, and I promised I would.

So there I was, armed with the barest of plans and the noblest of intentions. The very first day back in school, a boisterous army of third years (hormonally fired 14 year olds) exploded into the classroom unexpectedly, their exam having been cancelled due to an absence. Of course, I had no lesson prepared. "This is it, then", I thought and, pretending utmost confidence, proceeded to arrange them in a circle and announce the beginning of something new....

An hour later, the bell rang for break and nobody moved. "That was great, Miss, can we do it again next time?"

Revelation!
How had it worked?

First of all, putting everyone in a circle removed the arrangement of hierarchy with teacher at the head of the class, in one fell swoop. By putting myself in the circle, I became part of the group and played as an equal. Suddenly everyone was equally visible and equally audible, and in games where everyone took a turn to play, sequentially, it became quickly obvious that if even one person didn't play ball, the whole group suffered – immediately. Then spoken or unspoken peer pressure operated to make any rebels conform. What a powerful method! Immediately, I had the interest, attention and participation of the group – a radical behavioural shift.

Secondly, although I had some rudimentary ideas of how to operate the circle, I certainly did not have much more. My most overwhelming contribution to our success that the day was the depth of my ignorance. I had zero knowledge, zero experience and zero expertise. So when I asked the group to volunteer games they knew themselves from Primary, great delight ensued as they vied with each other to reconstruct 'old favourites'. Then, as the pace quickened, these were elaborated and we moved to another stage – co-creation. "Let's do it like this", someone would say, or "let's have a rule like this to make it work better."

Collaboration, co-creation; a new order was developing in the room. You could hear a pin drop between games and catch a palpable new emotion. anticipation. When I found a point where it could work we moved out of the games entirely and into a process of discussion, with each person taking an equal turn. We talked that day about what things could make it better to be a student in that school, and soon they were off and running, sharing sensible, zany, creative ideas in a supportive atmosphere with attention for each individual at an all-time high.

It was a revelation for me in that job. Here was a versatile tool for getting to know every brand-new class I got landed with, whatever the subject. I could ring the changes with a variety of preambles: "Well, I know you're disappointed your PE teacher is off today, but I'm sure you'll enjoy these MENTAL games ...." or "We're going to do a different sort of drama today...."

I discovered that when it came to any subject in the humanities, Circle Time had a valid and useful role to play. It didn't just get me out of a tight spot; it was genuinely educational AND an entertaining experience. No wonder I would get stopped in the school playground; "Miss, can you do that thing with us, that you did with so-and so's class?"

For me personally, the most valuable aspect of the process was that it could be a short cut to finding out about the inner lives and the personalities of those individuals I would go on to teach in various other subjects, and this certainly brought in a more considerate and caring approach in my relationships with students in various environments around the school. It was a quick way for me to get to know them, and vice-versa. The process raises self-esteem, awareness, emotional literacy and transparency.

I also know now that if any pupil is experiencing anything unpleasant, unhealthy, negative or damaging, whenever there is a Circle Time process, eventually it will be raised in the group, as nothing can hide in an atmosphere of openness and mutual support. Extreme sensitivity, tact and discretion are the qualities which require to emerge in the group in these cases, and it can be surprising, and almost unendurably touching, to witness how healing this group-inspired empathy can be.. Clearly, the age-old tradition of sitting in a circle of entertainment and story-telling and personal sharing is a precious part of our culture still, one which creates an opportunity for bringing much more than mere harmony to a group. You can gather together a disparate group of fiercely individual adolescents who may be out looking for a fight, but sitting them down in a circle and creating harmonious frequency by using circle time games has an extraordinary alchemy – it creates what Oleta Adams sang of as "A Circle of One".

Dorota Reising <u>dorotareising@hotmail.com</u> England

Magic Moment Three

Heart First

I first walked into a classroom in 1974 and was blown away by the response of young people. What an amazing job and to think I would be paid money to have this much fun! Later years have brought challenges but one thing has remained the same, the love of my subject, the love of children and finding ways for them to connect through positive learning experiences. As I embark on my last term of full time teaching in Mathematics in 2005 before I commence training as an Anglican priest, I reflect from a place deep within on the students who have touched my heart. Students can spot insincerity from 500 paces and I have always remembered the words *'I don't care how much you know, until I know how much you care'* and I have always had a strong pastoral theme in my contact with young people that fits comfortably with my personal mission to serve others with love and energy.

When students have been deeply troubled through mental illness, depression or feeling suicidal and they have turned to me for help, I have been humbled and touched but also saddened. One boy described his struggle with mental illness that seemed to come out of nowhere in Year 9 as 'wishing that he had a drill to make a hole in his head so that all of the new found turmoil in there could simply drain away and he could have his life back'. As we sat in the sunshine we both started to cry at the same time. I could not help him in any way except to just be there with him at this scary and difficult time.

Another student wrestling with her sexuality was often sucked into a vortex of depression where suicide seemed the only rational option in a time of extreme irrationality. I encouraged her to see the wonder of the universe around her, how precious she was and how many gifts she had to share in a rich and fulfilling life ahead. She was one of the brightest students in my teaching career, her brain would run at one million miles per hour and she was always asking interesting and creative questions and sharing evaluations and new ideas. She wrote the following:

Dear Ms C
I guess everyone over there is pretty worried about me, well don't be because I'm fine, in fact better than I could ever have dreamed.
I've enrolled in a school for the 'creative, gifted and independent student' and I'm loving it. I'm doing the equivalent of the top Maths; a writing course (I'm in the process of publishing my play); I take art, computers and 'philosophies of the revolutionist' which is a very provocative course. I'm a boarding house mistress for the juniors, which is great because I get accommodation and a bit of pocket money.' I'm seeing the school shrink bi-weekly and I'm feeling much more positive and confident. I'm so happy here!I write to you not only to communicate my happiness and safety, but also to thank you for offering me a non threatening audience for my thoughts. You know if it wasn't for you I doubt I would have continued to write, and it was because I liked and respected you very much that I continued to work in maths and my other subjects when at times all efforts seemed so pointless. I'm glad I did because it helps me do the work here.
I miss you, but not with an ache but with a special warm feeling. I guess that's because you're special and warm to me! To you and your family I send my love.

In my teaching career I have been given wonderful opportunities and professional recognition through awards and promotion but it will be the responses of students and families in crisis that I will take away with me as the most important accolade.

Gail Costello former deputy principal , amazing Maths teacher
gailcostello@hotmail.com

Magic Moment Four

Matthew

In my first year of teaching as a high school English teacher I met a wise teacher in one of my classes. His name was Matthew. He was thirteen and he was illiterate. I can still remember clearly his cheeky smiling face and the most beautiful brown eyes peering out from under his long fringe. Matthew was always restless and found it hard to concentrate.

One afternoon after helping him with some work I offered to drop him home as it was really hot. When I arrived at his home he asked if I would like a cup of tea. His manners and his courtesy took me by surprise. Once inside he turned the kettle on and excused himself for a few minutes and soon returned with the washing off the line—neatly folded. Anyone who has sons will know this is pretty unusual. Washing brought off the line usually still has the pegs attached!

Then Matthew said, 'I am home first and so I help Mum get things done as this is her late day and Paul, my brother, has basketball training. I just have to put a chicken in the oven and then I will make your tea. Is that alright with you?"

I watched as this capable young lad took a chicken out of the refrigerator and put it into the oven for his sole parent mum and obviously much loved brother. Then we had a cup of tea made with a teapot and a strainer. We chatted about many things from friends to pets and to his favourite foods. It was a very comfortable experience and I felt I was in the company of someone much older.

The following week I showed the class a video that was an introduction to a topic on tolerance. It was a symbolic presentation that simply showed different coloured dots that moved around with background music. When it had finished I asked the class what the video was about. There were many confused faces in the room and my A level students had no idea what the video was about.

Matthew put up his hand and said, 'Miss, it's easy. The video is about colour prejudice and shows how some people think they are better than other people because of the colour of their skins—and that's not true. We are all the same really."

The class was stunned and so was I. Here was the boy who couldn't read and could only write a few words showing us that wisdom, true wisdom, cannot be measured by grades or assessment. Matthew showed me that day something that all teachers need to know. Students cannot be judged by their academic performance, their dress, their hair or the way they behave. What is important is that we believe in the inherent goodness and wisdom that lie within, maybe dormant, but still present nevertheless. It's the character and humanity that quietly develop within us all as we progress through life that are really significant.

From that day on Matthew was respected in our class and that meant the world to him. He felt he belonged and that people cared. His behaviour was never a problem and the other students helped him with his literacy and always turned to him to listen to how he viewed the world.

Unfortunately having poor literacy skills meant that life outside of school was much tougher. Without a supportive network that cared about him Matthew struggled in life and numbed his pain of believing he was dumb and useless with drugs and alcohol. This journey took him into mental illness and deep depression and Matthew took his own life when he was 23 years of age.

I hold Matthew as one of the wisest teachers I ever met.

Maggie Dent maggie@maggiedent.com

This has been used with permission from "What My Favourite Teacher Taught Me - A collection of inspirational stories" selected by Robyn Henderson Sea Change Publishing Australia

Magic Moment Five

Learning From Children

I firmly believe it is a huge privilege to work or play with children! Do you remember, at school, coming across an over-used line from the ever-sentimental Wordsworth about children ... "...trailing clouds of glory"?   I never really understood it ... it used to make me think of fat little cherubs sitting pinkly on white clouds!

None of it! I now, through my long experience of working with children, truly understand what the great man was saying. Grubby, snotty, ear-ringed, spiky-haired, children are still trailing clouds of glory today!!! Children have qualities of honesty, forgiveness, kindness and wisdom which, if given the right sunny emotionally safe forum, will glint and gleam strongly at anyone who cares to notice. However, this vein of gold running throughout children can be dimmed, over a period of time if too many bickering, critical, dominating adults caste their cold shadows across it.

I, and thousands of other warm, enthusiastic teachers across the country, run circles for children.   It is a very humbling experience, not only do the children forgive the child who has called them names, ruined their games, pushed them out of the line or hidden their precious possessions ...

they go one amazing step further ... they help them. Take this true scenario. A very troubled child shuffled in his seat, looked down at the floor then, occasionally glancing up through hooded eyes he muttered quietly;

"I'd like some help 'cause I lose my temper too quickly".

Up go their hands to offer help. He points at different people to give him ideas.
"Would it help if you counted to 10 before you lashed out?".
"No, I can't get past 3, but thanks".
"Would it help if you walked away from the ones that annoyed you?".
"No, 'cause they keep coming after me!".

"Would it help if you told the teacher?".

"No, I have tried to tell her, but she keeps telling me to ignore it and I can't".
As I listened carefully I could see him batting away at all their offers. As useful as they were, they would have put more pressure on him to make changes. He had lost faith in himself, he believed he was bad. His hunched shoulders, under his thin top, spoke of the untold burdens he was already carrying. Looking around, I realised we would have to go on to another level of support – when children dig even deeper into their reserves of kindness and offer to do something themselves to help the situation.
"Has anyone here got a 'would it help if I' ...", I asked.

A few silent, motionless seconds descended on the brave little circle, and then, suddenly, a hand was raised. Looking directly into the eyes of the child concerned he asked;

"Would it help if I stopped calling you names?".

Electric silence. He sat up wide-eyed;
"Yea, that would help a lot, thanks".
And so the first stages of an important strategy began ...
Together, with goodwill and with a vision of what a happy class team would look like; tiny achievable, tickable targets will be agreed upon and rewarded by the whole class. They

will sign class certificates to each other and continue to ask, through the circle, what other ways they can support each other socially and emotionally.

But children don't just offer this energy and goodwill to their own kind! They also know that adults need a supportive hand. This next scenario again highlights their generosity of spirit.

A tired teacher whose turn it was to ask for help in circle time looked around at her circle of 5 and 6 year olds and said;
"I need some help because I get very cross and bad-tempered in the afternoon".
Nodding knowingly many children put their hands up to help her ...

"Would it help if you let us know when this horrible mood comes upon you?", asked one child.

Listening carefully to what her classmate suggested a little girl put her hand up.
"Miss, would it help if you had a special hat?", if you put the hat on we would all know".

When I went back later to the class I saw the teacher had a wonderful big silly hat hanging on a peg. She explained that whenever she was becoming too bad-tempered she would put the hat on and the class knew then that they must not speak to her. Watching them tip-toe around made her laugh and she was able to hang up her bad mood with a flourish.

You see, those clouds of glory are not just about children's generosity of spirit, but they are also filled with the sound of chuckles. Children laugh a lot, they make jokes a lot, they love seeing people smile, they bring us very close to seeing the joy we were always meant to know.

Jenny Mosley
(First appeared in Findhorn Foundation & Community's Global Network online magazine)
www.circle-time.com.uk

Magic Moment Six

Once upon a time.........

I took on a new middle management post in a large girls comprehensive school in the UK, and a huge workload to go with it, and something happened that really brought it home to me that the kids come before paperwork and tasks. I took on a large year 10 tutor group (32 15 year old hormonal girls) that were fairly unruly as they had so many temporary teachers, and I had to work quite hard and setting down my expectations regarding behaviour, routines, manners etc, in order to quickly make a difference with the class and not perpetuate problems for their last couple of years in school, so I was fairly strict and school "maaamish" with them, whilst feeling that I was being fair and friendly.

As well as my pastoral duties to the group, I had a new team of 12 teachers with whom I also had to establish a fairly rapid rapport, a department where lesson planning etc needed to be improved and to cap it all, a split site school with no classroom of my own - sometimes I was moving buildings every lesson thought the day. My coping strategy for this was to multi-task, and in retrospect, although it enabled me to keep up with organising everything, it affected my tutor group badly. After a few months, a couple of the girls in the group complained about me to the Headteacher, and their parents came in. The girls felt that I didn't care about them, was indifferent to them and over-strict. They were even a bit scared of me. I was shocked to the core by this, to the point where I had to go home for the rest of the day because I couldn't stop crying! I wasn't upset about the complaint, but about the way I had been perceived by my own tutor group. I had felt that as well as being strict I had made a real effort to get to know them and be friendly, but without being their buddies.

However, by multitasking in their presence (e.g. sorting out filing cabinets in the background over lunchtime whilst they used my classroom as their form room, or packing up a box ready for my next lesson in another building whilst they left the room to go to assembly) I had been perceived to be cold and uncaring. Wow - that really shattered my confidence. The Headteacher was brilliant about it, and explained to the girls and their parents that this was far from my intention and how upset I was. He showed me a quote he had pinned up on the wall in his office, that as given to him by his mentor many years previously before he became a head. It said "If only you could see yourself as others see you". I was seen as an intimidating suit in a whirlwind of efficiency, rather than as a human who cared.

The interesting thing about the incident, was that it brought us all closer together. The girls were shocked about how upset I was, which made them realise they had mis-read me, as well as my realisation about the mixed messages I was sending out. It was a hugely emotional experience where we all learnt that despite the pupil-teacher relationship, we are all really human after all! I have since taken much more care with children and my body language. I may feel inside that I care about them but now I try and make that overt. It was a painful and yet wonderful learning experience for us all.

Clare Smale Publishing Editor "Teaching Expertise"
Web: www.teachingexpertise.com

Magic Moment Seven

Being There

To build one's self-esteem only enhances their ability to learn and live more productively, happily, healthy and effectively in all areas of their lives. Having good self-awareness is the most important component an individual can have in life. It is the basis of what makes one who they truly are. "We are the true keepers of our own destiny'

As a primary school teacher I saw a need in the classroom environment that needed assistance. I felt that teachers on the whole were being overloaded with the expected extra-curricula activities and ever increasing workload. I decided through my implementation of my 'different' teaching style in the classroom, to develop it into a package that would 'take the load' off teachers and that our programs would enhance the teachers classroom environment in a more conducive manner, where the skills and strategies that students learnt from our one-day workshops would then be utilized in their everyday living, this including the classroom – so learning was simply about just that 'gaining knowledge and having fun'.

I have had many touching, amazing and uplifting experiences working with students. All powerful and some most definitely spirit-altering.

One young Year 10 student at a public school in the suburbs attended our Indigenous 2-day cultural living skills workshop. Kate was a thin, shy young woman, tackling the puberty conditions of acne, weight issues and simply trying to fit into her social age group. During the workshop these 17 year 9 & 10 students were taken through a journey of self & culture discovery. As part of the second day, linking their 'living Indigenous culture' and issues of self-esteem we explored ways in which one can release their worries and fears. The process we used after discussion and effective hands-on activities that they were physically able to demonstrate the release came a meditation.

We always explain every aspect of learning to them and how within their bodies, with practise, these skills actually affects mechanisms within the structure of the body, cells and thought patterns to create positive change and release of negativity from their body.

As the students lie separately and listen to the dialogue of the meditation, they take themselves to a place in their minds where it is safe, where they feel strong and are able to release any fears, worries or troubles they may have in their lives.

As they go to this place in their minds, they experience and see many wonderful positive things about themselves and their lives. Upon being present in the room after the conclusion of the meditation, we always share with each other. Some students share, others choose not too. Kate sat quietly and didn't want to share as did the majority of students on this particular day, which is usual. One lad asked was someone waving their hands above his head, he said he felt that the 'eagle' that was suggested in the dialogue was hovering above him. That left him speechless! The experience for this group left them all a little speechless – hence the room became calm. During the quietness and reflection that each embarked on, they were able to draw this place as a keepsake for them. (a cue to remind them to go here often prior to sleep) Kate sat quietly. I could see her withdrawing from her friends, as I walked over to her, she protectively was hiding her drawing. She looked up at me and asked with a small tear in the corner of her eye, 'I saw black head-stones, and a black tree and the grim-reaper, does that mean I am going to die?'. I took her aside, others heard her speaking, they all put down their pencils. 'No, Kate, it just means that there is so much blackness inside of you and you now have to colour it in!'

Kate was a self-harmer, abused!

Two days later I received an sms at midnight, from her telling me that she was using the skills learnt and was feeling for the first time in years 'nice inside'. She thanked me for bringing Essere to her school and that she would use these skills for the rest of her life.

Sometimes for me, the journey of Essere's growth can be challenging, and I too want to just walk! Then I meet another Kate or receive another sms or email and realise that I too am still colouring in.

I am a single mum, a teacher, an author, my heritage is Aboriginal from the 'Yuni' people (south coast of NSW), I am a mover and a shaker and I believe in moving forward. Most importantly I smile often and love to have fun.

To offer, educate and support individual's through preventive measurable processes will minimize, eliminate and promote awareness of the different kind of stresses that is caused by physical and emotional adversity.

We all need tools to equip us through life, continuous personal growth starts with a state of mind that accepts that there is always room to improve in everything we do.

Fran Dobbie Sydney NSW

Website: www.essere.com.au

Magic Moment Eight

Behind The Mask

I was surprised to see his name on my class roster. I wasn't sure why he signed up for leadership class. I thought maybe he needed the credit to graduate. As I walked down the hall to the classroom, I noticed he was leaning against the wall outside the classroom. As others entered the class, he waited until the last possible moment to join our group. He looked at the semi-circle of chairs in the middle of the room and he went to the opposite side of the room. I quietly walked over to his desk and asked him to join us. He replied, "No, I like it here!" I encouraged him to "play the game for one day". He reluctantly moved himself to the circle, yet kept his head down as I described the course activities.

Over the next few weeks, he slowly engaged in the experiences and started to interact with others. He sometimes wouldn't have his work complete and he sometimes took an opposing viewpoint from the common perspective. Then, one day it happened! We went on an outdoor adventure challenge course and the entire group was transformed. Leaders emerged that one day in the woods, but the one who held the group together was Jake, the reluctant leader.

With each challenging element, he shouted encouragement to peers who he may never have spoken to in the 4 years of his high school. When others became discouraged, he suggested unique solutions to the challenge and often his idea was the solid one that allowed the group to move to a new element. The final element required he and a partner to pull one another up a series of beams suspended from the tree. Each beam was further apart from the next. By coordinating movements and finding the inner strength to persevere, he led his partner, a rival in the classroom, up to the highest level. At times, his partner wanted to give up, yet Jake was not about to give up on this feat. "You are going to do this and you are coming now!" was heard from above. We laughed at the conviction in his voice. There was not going to be an opportunity to turn back. The only option was to succeed and his partner realized that very quickly as the two surpassed physical and emotional barriers and at the top, rang the bell!

The afternoon came to a close and his peers thanked him for his help. He never made eye contact with them and once again lagging behind the group, he appeared to be pondering the thoughts within his mind as he walked seemingly in need of his own space. I wondered what the next day in class would bring.

The students formed the circle of desks and chatted about the day's events even before I had arrived. Once I began prompting them with discussion questions, they shared from their hearts what they had learned. "I learned I can do more than I thought I could do; I learned I could trust people; I learned there are more ways to solve a problem than I realized." The ideas flowed. Kyle offered praise for Jake who was his partner in the challenging climb. "I know we haven't been friends and we have actually expressed opposing views, yet yesterday was a huge accomplishment for me and I couldn't have done it without you! You never gave up on me and I know you could have done it so much faster, yet you helped me succeed. I thank you for that." As if on cue, the room silenced awaiting Jake's response. "That's cool man, you did a good job." He made direct eye contact with Kyle and he seemed to be connected with all in the room. One day's lesson seemed to shift the hardened exterior of this young man. It was only the beginning of many more opportunities to share and learn from one another.

About a month later, we created a "gratitude project" as a way of thanking teachers who made a difference. Each student wrote letters of appreciation to every teacher and every employee in our district. The guidelines were "share a memory of when the person made a difference in your life." At first, there were a few grumbling of uncertainty of how it might be received by the teachers, yet within moments, the students agreed to participate.

Written to a study hall supervisor: "First, I want to apologize for the day that I shoved a desk in study hall. No one knew what was going on at my home and I didn't think anyone cared. This year I learned that people care more than I realized. I want to thank you for calling my coach instead of the principal. That told me that you believed in me. I want you to know it made a difference. Thank you." Signed: Jake

As I read his note, I wondered if that one lesson about human connection allowed his heart to open and his mind to remove some of the obstacles in his path. I wondered if the unconditional connections that he felt with his classmates allowed him to look into his past and find those who cared. I do know that the woman who received the letter was filled with tears of joy that a senior in high school would remember a moment in time when he was in grade 7. This young man was choosing to connect with another without expectation for how it would be received. He chooses to risk and connect. He chooses to remove his mask of "tough guy" and became real. Allowing his vulnerable side to show, he discovered his fullest potential and today proudly has reached his goals and serves his country as an U. S. Marine.

Teresa Huggins Teacher, Youth Leader and Inspirational Speaker Clinton, NY, USA
huggins@dreamscape.com

Magic Moment Nine

Blockers

Christian Miller didn't do substitute teaching because he needed the money. He did it because he enjoyed it. He was a former teacher, now retired, and sincerely liked being around children. "Subbing is one of the ways I stay young," he told many of his friends.

Recently assigned to sub in a third grade classroom, Christian was moving uneventfully through the day. Thankfully, no behaviour problems required his attention. He had followed the detailed lesson plans for math and language arts. Spelling appeared next on the agenda.

The directions for spelling were simple enough. Christian was instructed to announce a ten-minute study time and then give the students a trial test on their weekly list of words. Students spelling all words correctly on the trial test would be excused from the final test on Friday. At the conclusion of the short study time, Christian asked students to clear off their desks and take out a piece of notebook paper. Immediately, seven students sprang from their chairs and headed towards a bookcase at the back of the room.

"Whoa," announced Mr. Miller. "Where are you going?"

"We're going to get the blockers," two students answered simultaneously.

"Blockers? What are blockers?" asked the surprised substitute teacher.

"They're what we use to block our papers so that other kids can't see them," answered one eight-year old. "They block the other person's view," added another.

Constructed with two 8 by 10 sheets of cardboard and taped in the middle, blockers stand upright. They are designed to shield one student's paper from another's eyes.

"No, no, no," cautioned the substitute. "We don't need blockers."

"Yes we do," responded the third-graders.

"Why?" Christian asked aloud.

"Because we'll look on each other's papers," said one child. "Ya," agreed several others.

"You look at each other's papers?" asked Christian.

"Several of us," reported one student.

"No," countered Christian, "no one will look today. We don't need the blockers."

"We need them because some kids cheat. They look," warned a well-intentioned girl in the back of the room.

"Let me see a show of hands," challenged Christian. "How many of you are going to look on another's paper?"

No hands were raised.

"See, we don't need blockers today," Christian explained to the class.

"They say they won't, but they will," a student informed the substitute teacher. Heads nodded in agreement.

Undaunted, Christian asked,

"How many of you are just saying that you won't look, but you really will?'

Still no hands.

"See," he said again, "no one in this room is going to look."

"We always use blockers," shared one persistent student who wasn't buying into the--- we don't need blockers--- theme. "Mrs. Tattersall wants us to use them so we don't cheat. They block us from cheating," she explained, hoping to get this substitute teacher to finally appreciate the necessity of blockers.

"O.K. we'll use blockers," announced Mr. Miller, appearing to finally cave in to the perceived need to use an external object to protect one child's paper from another's need to look.

"We'll use blockers," he continued, "only this time we'll use our inside blockers. Looking or not looking at another's paper is an internal decision that each of you make. It's something that happens on the inside of you. If each of you chooses to use your inside blocker, we won't need outside blockers. Things like honesty, integrity, respect, and caring are decisions that each of us make on the inside. When you make an inside decision, the outside takes care of itself. Outside blockers are only needed when the inside blockers have not been turned on."

"How about if we play with using our inside blockers today and see how that goes?" Christian challenged the room full of eight-year olds. "Let's see how well your inside blockers are working. Are you willing to turn them on and see what happens?"

"Yes," several students responded, finally conceding to the relentless challenge of their substitute teacher.

"O.K. Number your papers from one to fifteen. Put your name in the upper right hand corner. Turn on your internal blocker. Here we go."

The spelling test proceeded without incident. Students practiced spelling words and they practiced using their inside blockers.

Following the test, Christian allowed students to correct their own papers. Papers were then collected and left for the regular classroom teacher to peruse. Later, he assumed, scores would be added to a grade book so that the learning could be appropriately documented.

No record was made of the 23 eight-year olds who successfully used internal blockers that day. No note was left for the regular classroom teacher to explain why blockers weren't used. No documentation of the learning experience was necessary. Perhaps that type of learning is best recorded the way it is used, on the inside, in the hearts and minds of the students who experienced it.

Chick Moorman is the an educator, parenting specialist and author in the US : www.chickmoorman.com .

Magic Moment Ten

Praise

My journalism class was busy working, typing in stories, talking in groups about ideas or advertising. One girl, Emma, grabbed a printout of her story from the printer and gave it to me. "What do you think?" She went back to her computer as I read it. It was for the first parent newsletter of the year. "It's good!" I said. The noise in the class stopped and heads swivelled around. Everyone looked at me. "But....?" said Kirsty "There has to be a 'but'."

I looked at her puzzled. "But nothing! It's really good, good exactly as it is, exactly what is needed. Emma has done a really good job in a difficult situation."

"But teachers always, no matter how good something is, always give a 'but' – 'but you could do this to improve it...' 'But you haven't quite used these words in the best way', I can't believe you are happy with it as it is."

Everyone was nodding. I had obviously broken a deeply entrenched rule of teaching. I thought it really sad that these students had obviously not been recipients of unconditional and unstinting praise.

I was reading at the time a book by Rupert Sheldrake and Matthew Fox called Natural Grace. I had just got up to the chapter on Grace and Praise. Grace is about unconditional love, and praise is an expression of grace. I read how they believed we had forgotten how to praise, had replaced it with criticism and cynicism. Praise is an expression of joy within, a recognition of what and who is good, celebrating the gifts of nature, significant moments. It's about changing your mindset so you can see the value in what surrounds you and what you experience, enabling you to express that. It really was a fundamental part of life, one that energized, kept the flow going, made you feel that things were worthwhile. Were my students living lives in a praise-free zone? What could I do about it?

I had my half hour weekly pastoral care class coming up with a mixture of students from journalism and physics. We met each week, sometimes I would choose particular themes which we would discuss or experience, other times we brought food to share, or had to deal with administrative needs of the school. We were gradually developing into a supportive group. I decided to do a session on praise and brought in my little bear. We were in the big physics room and I asked them to sit in a circle on the floor at the front of the class. "We are going to talk about praise," I said. I chose some snippets from the book to read and told them about my journalism class and my concern that praise seemed to be something of a novelty to them. I then asked them to think about how they felt about praise and what it meant for them. The bear was a talking bear – as each student wanted to say something they held the bear. Initially this drew a laugh, and then it became something fun – what it did was change the mindset. As the students talked the discussion got deeper and deeper, more anguished, then more hopeful and pro-active. At the end of it these students had decided to actively bring a sense of grace and praise into their lives.

I listened as Kirsty explained that her experience of praise was of someone praising her then asking her to do something - she now couldn't listen to praise without asking what the person wanted from her. She found it really difficult to accept praise and had a severe distrust of it. One boy, Robin, said how everything he did was criticized, that he just wanted someone to praise him, for himself, not to tie it to his achievements because he knew he never was going to be perfect or the best. Another said how important it was to understand when it was appropriate to praise and when it was important to criticize or suggest ways to improve – if everything she did was praised how could she ever learn? We discussed how could teachers tune into what students needed – how could you celebrate the person and the effort while still being helpful. Another spoke about how he had nothing to praise in his life – it just was so drab and grey. Other students were horrified and we discussed the darkness within that caused us to see the world this way.

I then asked what might it mean and feel like to have a sense of grace and praise within you. What could generate that sense of joy within, no matter how little? Perhaps we needed to learn to praise ourselves and things we experienced as well as other people. What might it be like to be active practitoners of praise? Kirsty asked for the bear and held it tightly as she spoke. "I guess I have such a sceptism towards praise that it would never occur to me to praise myself or someone else – it has never seemed like a meaningful thing to do. But now I wonder.... Maybe not seeing things as something to praise has affected the whole way I live my life, as if it is going to attack me!" Some students nodded. Robin said, "Here I have been wanting praise, but thinking about it I haven't really praised anyone else..." He looked thoughtful. Ian said "The problem is it just isn't cool to praise – people think you are weird or the teacher's pet or something." Robin said, "But why should we be confined by peer pressure, maybe we should be less cynical and sceptical and really say what we value." "Ooooh, too brave, too much emotion!" said Kirsty. "OK," I said "Who's feeling brave then? How about actively thinking and acting praise in the next week and see what happens. To start, how about each of you think of something here and now that you could be glad about or feel joyful about. Could we go around the circle and each person say "I am glad that..."" My students looked thoughtful. "Who would like to go first," I asked. "OK," said Robin, and took the bear. He looked everyone straight in the eye and said he was glad that he had so many friends. The next person took the bear, held it and looked at in then very sheepishly said what she would like to praise. And so it went on, each person getting more confident, the energy and positivity in the room lifting with each turn.

Students were smiling as we left. It was a start. I headed down the corridor. Behind me I heard Robin talking to a friend from another class. "We just had this really cool lesson on praise," he said, "and I just wanted to tell you what a good friend you are."

I smiled.

I then began to think about how much praise I was generating in my life. While I valued and acknowledged some things, how many other things were left unacknowledged. Although my classes were pleasant, cheerful and full of laughter I wondered if I was praising enough. How much was the notion of assessment restraining the way I praised or criticized students? That night I had a wonderful conversation with a friend and he said to me "Thank you for such a wonderful conversation… I feel so stimulated and full of energy." I just looked at him and said how wonderful I thought it was too, and it usually was and how remarkable that I had never really seen it has something to be thankful and glad about – that it was wonderful to acknowledge the way someone makes you feel. I was really thoughtful and in my classes I watched what was happening more. I realized so much was happening that was worth celebrating. When someone asked a question I would say "That is such an interesting question, it has really challenged me…" Or, "That was such a good discussion, you guys are really thinking well today." Or, "Gee, that was a great lesson, I really enjoy teaching you guys." My whole attitude changed and it seemed my whole life. In praising students or my peers I found that they became more energized and motivated, which energized me and made things easier to do. Meanwhile my pastoral care kids were practicing praise in my journalism and physics classes. It wasn't just me doing it – they were acknowledging others, their experiences. It took on a momentum of its own. In journalism one day a girl sat down a bit late and obviously really harried. "Hi Leah, it good to see you," I said really meaning it. She just looked at me and burst out laughing. "I really love this class, Sue," she said, just being here changes my mood from really really bad to feeling so good!"

Finally the journalism team were ready to assemble the many pages of the student magazine. We were armed with staplers, music and food brought in by the whole group. Everyone was busy folding, sorting and stapling over 300 copies. As we walked around the table, Kirsty suddenly said, "You know I just feel so proud!" We all looked at her, smiling. "Why, Kirsty?" I asked. "I just feel so proud of all of us, of our effort, of even myself, we have just done such a good job, we've really kicked ass!" She was highly emotional. I gave her a hug. "We've all come a long long way in doing this," I said, "Let's celebrate!"

Sue Stack educator Tasmania Australia. Co-founder of hen: holistic education network hen@edna.edu.au

Magic Moment Eleven

Real Honesty

My teaching career to date has spanned two continents and has included boys ages six to 16. I was fortunate enough to teach First Grade for eight years in Baltimore, Maryland, USA and then move to Perth, Western Australia, where I have taught Year 10 Commerce, Year 2 and Year 7 – albeit in boys' schools the whole time. I have many stories and memories of individuals encountered along the way: boys who have inspired me with their courage, their insights and their character, and educators who have shown unbelievable depths of compassion, devotion and commitment.

Some of my greatest joys as an educator have been teaching six- and seven- year- old boys the thrill and challenges of the classroom, but my story today is of another age group and, in particular, one group of boys who surpassed both my and their own expectations of themselves as thinkers and agents of change.

Picture the 'normal' 12-year-old boy at an independent all boys' school. Typically, he will be the one who is in the process of emerging from that age of carefree naivety and approaching the onset of hormones which will (riddle his face with acne and) give rise to the tumultuous mood swings of adolescence. This 'boy' perceives life through a television or computer screen akin to the cave wall in Plato's famous allegory. A 12-year-old boy is an interesting mix of innocence and adult who is not often known for his deep insight and reflection. Now imagine 28 of them in the class with a teacher who is often accused (by his beloved wife) as never having matured past 12 years of age himself.

'Gentlemen, I would like to introduce you to our next text. We will spend the next five weeks during Literature class reading and discussing abstracts from *This I Believe* by Australian writer, John Marsden.'

Several groans, two eager faces and the inevitable question as to how they were to be graded and what percentage of this total mark for Literature was to be assigned to this unit of work.

'Gents, this assignment will not be assessed, not marked in any way and will have no reflection on your grade for this class … (big pause as two boys laced fingers behind their head and started to put their feet onto a desk). HOWEVER … I will collect your final papers and publish them in a book. I will send the book to each one of you and to your family and they will be filed in the school's archives.'

I selected a few poignant abstracts from *This I Believe* and read them to this group of 12 year olds. As I read, more eyes came up, shoulders stopped sagging and the scene out of the window became less interesting. When the bell rang no one moved … silence. Then from the desk right near mine (you know the one, it is separated from all classmates, distractions and avoidance tactics), 'Hey, cool. When do we get to read some more?'

As part of our Literature class and our Religious and Values Education we all spent the next three weeks reading, listening and discussing aspects of what others believe. It was great ... the class was 'cooking along' and I had chosen a text that reached all the boys ... what a great teacher. But, just as these conceited ideas were beginning to form in my head, it happened!

'That's bullshit.' (Silence and open jaws on the faces of the rest of the class)

Now, before I go on, I should say that would have been the first time a boy had sworn out loud in my class and definitely the first time this particular individual had said anything in class in the last two weeks (mum and dad had recently separated in acrimonious circumstances). Before I could get my typical teacher reprimand out of my mouth he continued ...

'How can these people believe in this stuff and how can you all sit here and nod and agree? I don't believe any of this and ... my life sucks and ... this is just crap.'

Silence.

'Me neither', piped in another 'Some of this stuff is so 'not me'. Like this God stuff ... come on.'

'What about the God stuff?' another asked.

And then it began. Not for 5 minutes or for an hour, but for days. We did not open a book, touch a computer or use paper for hours some days. The boys stopped sitting at their desks, but organised chairs, tabletops and bean-bags to sit in a semblance of a circle. Discussions raged about almost every topic a twelve-year-old boy cared about (lucky ... not yet a factor)

I sat back - at times involved ... at others ignored - as they talked and listened to each other. There was no judgement about others, no fighting. It was an incredible experience to watch these boys forget about timetables, grades and me and instead to focus on themselves, their beliefs and, most importantly, to try to answer the question raised most often by their peers ... 'Why do you believe that?'

There was laughter (lots of it), tears and long periods of silence. I learned more about what I believe about myself and life, and about this amazing bunch of boys in a few weeks than I had all year.

There is so much more to this story and so many moments during those discussions, but I feel as if I would take away from the experience and, more importantly, detract from their beliefs and trust if I were to share them. It was beyond words...

However, I did have to limit the discussion because each boy was to write his own *'This I Believe'* with a paragraph about himself and then whatever he wanted to express about his own beliefs. We would carefully edit, but would not change any of the content or meaning.

The resulting book not only reflected a depth to these boys well beyond their tender 12 years, but also a collective maturity and clarity acquired as a result of their discussions. They wrote as 12-year-olds do. They did not instantly mature into great writers, but the core of their beliefs and the reasons they gave for these convictions were incredible and continue to inspire in me a belief in boys and in our future.

The following is my introduction to their booklet and it begins to express my gratitude to 28 boys in their journey towards reflection, understanding, acceptance and belief.

'This booklet contains a piece of personal writing from each boy and is a culmination of four weeks of intensive discussion, teaching and learning in our Religious and Values Education program and Literature class. These boys were asked to show compassion and courage, to listen without passing judgement, to accept others and their beliefs and, most importantly, to begin to discover who they are and what they believe.

Within the arts, modes of expression differ, but I feel writing can be a powerful tool by which people can share sometimes confusing, sometimes perfectly clear concepts and feelings with others. The writing within our own This I Believe reflects every point on the spectrum: every belief, every intention, every event and emotion imaginable. It is important to keep in mind that each piece is the voice of an individual, of a mind that needs to make sense of the world, of a heart that feels the effects of every moment in his life and perhaps, of a 'sense of self' that is striving to surface.

These pieces of writing are singular in their honesty, their reflection of youth and the inevitable emergence of boys into men. They are a reflection of the boys as members of their families, their school and as individuals.

I thank the boys for their honesty and for being true to themselves. I encourage them to always 'walk the high road' and show the acceptance of others, which they have consistently demonstrated the past year. I am proud of them for what they have accomplished this year, and forever grateful for the many lessons they have taught me.

This I believe.

Clark Wight, Father and Head of Junior School, Christ Church Grammar School, Perth Western Australia.

Magic Moment Twelve

Let the Diamond Shine

We all know the amazing way little children can melt our hearts and connect so easily with people who care about them. It seems that as children get older they become more reluctant to let the diamond within shine. I had one amazing incident a couple of years ago that brought both myself and my male colleague to tears and made me realize that maybe we don't give our older children the opportunity to shine.

I teach in a beautiful country school of around 100 children and this particular year our upper primary class had a large number of boisterous boys in the group. I was teaching the kindy, pre-primary, year 1 class of around 24 children. Being such a small school our Pre-primary and year 1 children played with the rest of the school during lunch breaks and were looked after by the older children. Unfortunately, the rough play of the older children was frightening the younger children, so-much-so that they had started coming back to class upset and scared to play in the playground. One afternoon after lunch break my children asked to be allowed to eat lunch and stay in the junior play ground.

That afternoon I spoke to the year 6/7 children and told them of the younger children's decision. When I left the room the children were silent. Later that day I got a message asking if the older children could speak to my class. Unprompted, these children had decided to apologise to my class and to take on a buddy so that the younger children would always have someone bigger looking after them. Each child stood face to face with a younger child and made a commitment to be there for them. The last child in my class to stand was a little autistic boy who the children had forgotten to include. When I asked the group who would stand for Joseph the children looked around at each other and one by one they stood up until the whole group of 11 and 12 year olds were standing and together said "I make a commitment to be there for you."

The whole time my colleague and I sat silently, in awe of the amazing love children can show. (I can honestly say that for the rest of that year we had no more playground heartache!)

Denise Dewar , Mother and Teacher from South West of West Australia. Facilitator of Safe Touch Education
email. dewarclan@hotmail.com

Magic Moment Thirteen

Happy Birthday

Courtney was developmentally and physically challenged, but I encouraged her to participate in gym class and to be proud of her efforts just like everyone else. Although she couldn't speak, her facial expressions and body language told me she liked being in my class. On the day of my birthday, during my second year of teaching, Courtney brought to my office a cupcake she made in home economics. While her assistant, Sara, sang Happy Birthday, Courtney smiled and held my hand. My surname consists of four syllables, Be-vi-lac-qua, and when it came time for Sara to sing my last name, she stopped after 'Ms.' Courtney let go of my hand and articulated the sounds, "uh-uh-uh-uh." She let go of my hand to offer me the cupcake. Then she reached up to give me a hug.

Patti Bevilacqua

Magic Moment Fourteen

With a Little Help

This is a wee story about a boy in my class last year. He was placed in ESC (Education Support) due to extremely low self esteem and confidence. His lovely father came to see me after Robert had nearly completed a year with me and said I had taught his son nothing! I have this to add.

Two weeks later we went on camp, and we were on the flying fox. We were a half hour over time but the instructors were committed to getting everyone through. I was aware Robert had already chickened out of the superman swing and so I was with him in line at the flying fox. I wanted him to achieve success as I knew it was fear that often stops him from achieving his goals. We were standing together on the high stand, half hour over time, lunch had started and two adults below were saying hurry up, the pressure was on!

Time kept ticking - I kept talking, reassuring and encouraging Robert - time ticking and then from somewhere moved forward. From somewhere very deep inside himself he gathered the strength and courage to do the jump. I screamed with joy, tears streaming and to this day (2005) I swear it was a huge turning point for Robert. He succeeded.

This is still a strong memory for us both. In a sharing circle on reflection of camp this was his and my highlight, this was not only ours but other children who were still at the tower witnessed this moment. They also named this as one of their highlights. Robert has been integrated since. Yes it had looked like I had I taught him nothing for two years. However over that two years he had come to trust me enough to take a big risk, to overcome the voice of fear within. Because he had tasted success that once, possibly for the first time in his life, Robert grew. With a little help Robert had been able to achieve and since then he has been different. Without the encouragement and support he may have let himself down. He would never been able to achieve this moment of success without a little confidence, self esteem and time.

From Trichelle Edwards teacher south of Perth, West Australia. Email: perthkiwis@hotmail.com

Conclusion

As I write the final pages to this book I have received three phone calls from desperate parents who have deeply depressed teenagers who do not want to live. Nothing is as frightening for a parent than to know that their child may take their life, despite the love they feel for their child. A parent's love is sometimes simply not enough to keep them alive.

Recent research from Queensland has indicated that a child's social environment may only have a very modest effect on whether children become depressed or suicidal. "This showed that extremely dysfunctional family relationships and poor communication styles have little impact on the observed mental health of children." (Professor Jake Najman, University of Queensland Schools of Social Sciences and Population.) This shows that depression and mental ill health can occur anywhere in any home at any time.

I recall walking beside many teenagers on this dark, cold journey. And many of them were from good, loving families with everything to live for and yet they wanted to die. Some had already cut and stabbed themselves because of the irrational pain of hating themselves. It is happening everyday in every part of our modern world. Professor Silburn of the WA Ministerial Council for Suicide Prevention writes

> "this is the first generation brought up on conspicuous consumerism. And they have no perceived guide to help them manage the new freedoms, cultural changes and technologies that have led to incredible individualism." (West Australian p8, May 25th 2005)

The pressures of the modern world are causing our young to struggle more with living. Many of these teenagers have clinical depression where the "happy centre" of the brain has stopped creating the chemicals needed to feel happy or positive. Many do not have depression and still want to leave this world. In my experience there is a severe disconnection to the human spirit, and that indefinable aspect of us called "soul". Life with its shallow, selfish and insecure way of living begins to overwhelm us as we lose touch of simple, life enhancing experiences. This happens over time and as each of life's challenges crushes or wounds us we crawl further and further down the dark hole of crippling fear. This paralysing fear numbs our thinking onto the eight lane highway towards negativity and apathy.

As we are mind- body-spirit the fear driven mind set inhibits the body's natural mechanism to nurture and protect itself. We become too exhausted to exercise the body – no natural endorphins. We avoid friends and people we love and avoid the natural endorphins of feel connected and loved. We sometimes reach for mind altering substances like alcohol and illicit drugs to numb our emotional pain - once again shutting down the body's natural mechanism for healing. This also means we block moments of laughter and lightness – also a source of natural endorphins. We will slowly avoid eating healthy food and we struggle to sleep and the body becomes more and more toxic. We stop spending time with our pets, our favourite places in nature and stop playing the songs and music that we love. We avoid intimacy and safe touch, and can no longer meditate and we close the door to our intuition and our inner wise counsel. The dark blanket pulls us deeper and deeper into the darkness until we seriously contemplate escaping from the pain permanently. We feel useless, powerless, worthless and too embarrassed to ask for help.

Much of my focus with this book has been about preventing the above cycle from occurring in our children's lives at any age. It is about giving more knowledge and information to the key carers of children, under ten, so that the unintentional and avoidable damage to children may be reduced. If we are able to build life skills that became second nature to children then maybe we can protect them from tumbling down the dark hole. If we learn ourselves, and then teach our children about emotional literacy, social norms and the importance of honouring the soul by feeding the human spirit often, I firmly believe we can reduce youth and adult suicide. If we are able to parent with spirit, with consciousness and with gratitude for the gift of a child's life, we can build a strong base of unconditional regard and acceptance that will support them in their journey through life. Our children will know that they belong and that they matter. Life is challenging and it will knock us to our knees – our capacity to bounce back, to be resilient is shaped throughout childhood and adolescence. Emotional literacy means we are able to empathise better, be aware of how others are feeling and we have better coping skills, and we lose the fear of showing how much we love those dear to us. We cannot overcome the challenges of life on our own and strong bonds between family and friends are what we all need to survive and then to conquer this thing called life.

At the darkest moments in the world over the last five years 9/11, Bali bombings, the tsunami, the hideous terrorist attacks, the war in the Middle East and the natural disasters around the world – what really matters to people is who comes home. Money, wealth, fame, material possessions amount to zit when the crunch comes – we want to be reunited to our loved ones. The matters of the heart are meant to come before the matters of the head.

This is what our troubled children are trying to tell us.

This is what our troubled communities are trying to tell us.

This is what our troubled earth is trying to tell us.

Clear the fear, the judgement and the shame.

Come home to the heart.

Clear the hate, the prejudice and the past

Come home to the heart.

Clear the jealousy, the neediness and the pain

Come home to the heart.

Come home to your own heart first.

Then allow others in.

Then our children can fee calm and safe.

Then our world can become a place of real peace.

Come home to the heart

Come home soon.

References and Bibliography

Andreas, S. & Faulkner C., (1996) "NLP: The New Technology of Achievement" London, Nicholas Brealey Publishing.

Arrien, A. (1993) The Four Fold Way - Walking the Way of the Warrior, Teacher Healer and Visionary." San Francisco: Harper

Bartlett, Jane (2004) "Parenting With Spirit: 30 Ways to Nurture Your Child's Spirit and Enrich Your Family's Life" Rider, UK.

Bennett, Barrie., et al (1991), "Cooperative Learning" Canada. Education Connections,

Bernard,B. (1991) Fostering Resiliency in Kids: Protective Factors in the Family, School and Community." Portland, OR. Northwest Regional
 Education Library.

Biddulph, Steve (1995) " The Secret of Happy Children" Sydney: Angus & Robertson.

Blackerby, Don, A, (1996) "Rediscover the Joy of Learning." Success Skills Inc, OK, USA

Bloom, William, (2001) The Endorphin Effect: A Breakthrough Strategy for Holistic Health and Spiritual Wellbeing. London, UK, Piatkus Publishers.

Boyd, Julie., (2000). (1998)"Creating Resilient Youth" www.workingfutures.com.au

Brendtro, L., Brokenleg, M & Van Bockern, S. (1990) "Reclaiming Youth at Risk: Our Hope for the Future. "Bloomington, IN: National Education
 Service.

Burns, E Timothy., (1991)"Our Children Our Future" , USA Marco Polo Group

Caine, RN and G., (1997) "Education on the Edge of Possibility." USA, Association for Supervision and Curriculum Development.

Canfield, J., & Siccone, F., (1995) "101 Ways to Develop Self –Esteem And Responsibility." Simon and Schuster, Mass. USA.
Canfield, Jack & Hansen Mark Victor,(1995) " A 2nd Helping of Chicken Soup for the Soul", USA, Health Communications Inc.
Capelli, Glenn & Brealey (2000) "The Thinking Learning Classroom." The True Learning Centre, Perth Western Australia
Carroll, Lee & Tober, Jan (1999) "The Indigo Children: The New Kids Have Arrived." Hay House, USA
Chapman, Gary & Campbell, Ross (2002)" The Five Love Languages of Children." Strand Publishing, Sydney.
Covich, Suzanne (2003) "A Circle in a Room Full of Squares" John Curtin College of Arts, Fremantle W Aust.
Dent, Maggie (2003) "Saving Our Children from Our Chaotic World: Teaching Children the Magic of Silence and Stillness" Dunsborough West Aust, Pennington Publications.
Dewar, Denise (2005) "Hands on Learning" West Aust
Dingle, Peter, Dr (2004) 'The Deal for Happier, Healthier Smarter Kids :A Twenty First century Survival Guide for Parents.' Perth WA.
Dossey, L., (1989) "Recovering The Soul", USA., Bantam.
Dossey, L. (1993) " Healing Words: The Power of Prayer and the Practice of Medicine." San Francisco, Harper San Francisco.
Falcone, Vickie, (2003) "Buddha Never Raised Kids & Jesus Didn't Drive Carpool: Seven Principles for Parenting with Soul." Jodere Group, USA.
Garth, Maureen,(1996) "The Power of the Inner Self: A Book of Healing" Australia, Harper Collins Publishers.
Garth, Muareen, "Inner Garden" , "Inner Space", Harper Collins Publishers

Gibran, Kahlil (2001) "Gibran," Axiom Publishing, South Australia

Goleman, D., (1995) "Emotional Intelligence." New York. Bantam.

Goleman, D., (1998) "Working with Emotional Intelligence." London UK, Bloomsbury.

Greene, Ross.W., (2001) "The Explosive Child: A New Approach for Understanding and Parenting Easily Frustrated, Chronically Inflexible Children." New York, Harper Collins.

Griggs, Dawn Emelie, (2003) "The Spirit of Learning" Jubilation Press, Vic Aust.

Grille, Robin. (2005) "Parenting for a Peaceful World." NSW, Longueville Media.

Hall, Janet, Dr. (2001) "Fear Free Children" Lane Cove, NSW. Finch Publishing.

Hart, Tobin, PhD(2003) "The Secret Spiritual World of Children" Inner Ocean, Hawaii.

Hartmann, Thom (2000) "Thom Hartmann's Complete Guide to ADHD; Help For Your Family at Home, School and Work." USA

Harvey, Janice (1998) "Mum it's nothing personal but I Want to Die." Nedlands, W.A. Awareness Publications.

Henderson, Robyn (2004) "What My Favourite Teacher Taught Me : A Collection of Inspirational Stories. Vol 1, 2, &3 " Sea Change Publishing, Kingscliff, NSW.

Hunt, Jan (2001) "The Natural Child: Parenting from the Heart" New Society Publishers, Aust.

Hunt, Valerie. V., "Infinite Mind: Science of the Human Vibrations of Consciousness", California, USA, Malibu Publishing Company.

Jackson, Paul Z and McKergow, Mark (2002) " The Solutions Focus: The SIMPLE Way to Positive Change" Nicholas Brealey Publications, UK

Joseph, John (2002) "Learning in Emotional Rooms; How to Create Classrooms that are uplifting for the spirit", Focus Education, South Australia.

Kavelin- Popov, Linda "(1997) The Family Virtues Guide,; Simple Ways to Bring Out the Best in Our Children and Ourselves"
Penguin, New York.

Kessler, Rachael (2000) " The Soul of Education: Helping Students Find Connection, Compassion and Character at School." ASCD Publications, VA, USA.

Kurcinka, Mary Sheedy (1991) "Raising Your Spirited Child: A Guide for Parents whose child is more." USA, Harper Collins.

Carroll, Lee & Tober, Jan (1999) "The Indigo Children: The New Kids Have Arrived." Hay House, Carlsbad, CA, USA.

Loomans, Diana (1994) "Full Esteem Ahead" HJ Kramer Inc, CA, USA.

Loomans, Diana (1994, 2003) "100 Ways to Build Self-Esteem and Teach Values" HJ Kramer/New World Library, Novato, CA, USA.

Miller, John. P.,(1996) "The Holistic Curriculum," Oise Press, Canada.

Miller, John. P., (2000) "Education and The Soul" State University of New York Press, New York,

Moore, T., (1992) "Care of the Soul; A guide for creating depth and sacredness in Everyday life. " New York, Harper Collins

Moorman, Chick (2001) "Spirit Whisperers: Teachers Who Nourish a Child's Spirit." Personal Power Press, MI,USA.

Moorman, Chick (1998) "Parent Talk : How to Talk to Your Children in Language that Builds Self-Esteem and Encourages Responsibility." Fireside, NY.

Moorman, Chick & Weber, Nancy "Teacher Talk: What it really means." (1998) Institute of Personal Power, USA.

Myss, Caroline (1996) "The Anatomy of the Spirit" Crown Publishing, New York.

Norman, Susan (2003) "Transforming Learning: Introducing SEAL Approaches" Saffire Press, London.

O'Donohue John, (1997) "Anam Cara: Spiritual Wisdom from the Celtic World" London, Bantam Press

Parry, T., & Gregory,G.,(1998) "Designing Brain Compatible Learning" Australia, Hawker Brownlow Education.

Pearce, Joseph Chilton (2002) "The Biology of Transcendence: A Blueprint of the Human Spirit." Vermont, Park Street Press.

Pelzer, D (2000) "Help Yourself: Celebrating the Rewards of Resilience and Gratitude. " USA, Penguin.

Pert, Candace (1997) "Molecules of Emotion: The Science Behind Mind-Body Medicine" USA, Scribner

Pinker, Steven (1997) "How the Mind Works" London, Penguin Press.

Polis, Benjamin (2001) "Only A Mother Could Love Him: My Story how I lived with ADD and Overcame it." S.A. Seaview Press.

Porter, Louise, Dr, (1994) "Children are People Too: A parents' guide to young children's behaviour." South Australia, East Street Publications.

Pytches, Mary (1990) "Yesterday's Child: Healing Present Problems by Understanding The Past." Great Britain, Hodder and Stoughton

Roberts, Jenny. (2005) "Freeing Noah: A Family Learns How to Calm and Heal Their Child " Jenny Roberts, Busselton.

Rosenberg, Marshall (2000) "Nonviolent Communication" CA,USA, Puddledancer Press.

Rozman, Deborah (1975) "Meditating with Children : The Art of Concentrating And Centering." USA, University of the Trees Press.

Sams, Jamie (1994) "Earth Medicine: Ancestors' Ways of Harmony for Many Moons" San Fransico, Harper.

Solter, Aletha, Dr, (1984) "The Aware Baby." Shining Star Press, Galeta, CA, USA.

Stanley, Fiona ,Prof, Richardson, Sue & Prior, Margot(2005) " Children of The Lucky Country: How Australian society has turned its back on its children and why children matter." Pan McMillan, Sydney.

Stern, D, (1985) (2000) "The Interpersonal World Of the Infant: A View from Psychoanalysis and Developmental Psychology" Basic Books, USA.

Taylor, Marjorie (1999) "Imaginary Companions and the Children Who Create Them." New York, Oxford University Press.

Thesenga, Susan (1994) "The Undefended Self: Living The Pathwork of Spiritual Wholeness." California, Path Work Press.

Thomas, Patrice,(2002) "The Magic of Relaxation." Pademelon Press, New South Wales.

Ward, Christine (2001) "Teaching To Learn: Your Guide to Success in the Classroom", N.Z. Accelerated Learning Institute.

Ward, Christine & Jan Daley (1998) "Learning to Learn: Strategies for Accelerating Learning and Boosting Performance." Caxton Press, Christchurch, New Zealand.

Wight, Clark (2005) "A Time to Connect: Being 10 and Moving Forward." Christ Church Grammar . Perth WA.

Woss, Melanie., (1992) "Melanie" Sydney, NSW, Pan MacMillan Publishing.

Youngs, Bettie.B. & Youngs , Jennifer Leigh(1999) "Taste Berries for Teens: Inspirational short stories and encouragement on life, love and tough issues." Florida, Health Communications.

Children's Resources

Bentley, Linda "Puppets at Large : Puppets as partners in learning and teaching in the Early Years." Positive Press UK

Edwards, Hazel (1980) "There's a Hippopotamus on Our Roof Eating Cake." Lane Cove, NSW, Hodder and Stoughton.

Fox, Mem and Argent Kerry (1995) "Wombat Divine", Gosford, Aust, Omnibus Books.

Fox, Mem and Lofts, Pamela (1988) "Koala Lou" Aust, Penguin Books.

Garth, Maureen (1993) "Starbright" "Moonbeam" "Earthlight" Meditations for Children. Australia, Harper Collins Publishers.

Lewis, Melinda (2004) " My Magical Story Journal" Westmead, Aust, Storyspeaks.

Lindamichellebaron, (2002) "The SUN is on: Poetry and Ideas," Harlin Jacque Publications, NY, USA

McGrath, Helen & Noble, Toni "Bounce Back: A Classroom Resilience Program." Pearson Education, NSW.

McLachlan, L & Kummer C ,(2004) "Kindayoga" Wild Journey Films, Sydney, NSW.

Milne, A. A. (1926) "Winnie-the-Pooh" Great Britain, Methuen Children's Books

Mosley, J & Sonnet, H "Wet Playtime Games" , "Clapping Games (with CD)", "More Clapping Games (with CD), "Skipping Games ,", " Playground Games", "Singing Games (with CD) *music by Caroline Radcliffe,*

Mosley, J "Here We Go Round" Wiltshire, UK, Positive Press.
Mosley, J CREATE HAPPIER LUNCHTIMES:
.Guidelines for Primary Midday Supervisory Assistants, Wiltshire, UK, Positive Press
Mosley, J "Circle Time" Wiltshire, UK, Positive Press.
Mosley, J "The Circle Book" Wiltshire, UK, Positive Press.
Mosley, J "Working Towards a Whole School Policy on Self Esteem and Positive Behaviour." Wiltshire, UK, Positive Press.
Mosley, J "All Round Success." Wiltshire, UK, Positive Press.

Jenny Mosley's Circle Time Handbook for the Golden Rules Stories
THE GOLDEN RULES STORYBOOK SERIES:
Stories by Donna Luck, illustrations by Juliet Doyle

1. We Are Kind and Helpful... we don't hurt other people's feelings
2. We Are Honest... we don't cover up the truth
3. We are Gentle... we don't hurt others
4. We Listen... we don't interrupt
5. We Look After Property... we don't damage things
6. We Work Hard... we don't waste time

McLachlan, Leonie and Kummer, Christopher "Kinda Yoga"

www.kindayoga.com

Rowling, J.K. (1999) "Harry Potter and the Prisoner of Azkaban" Great Britain, Bloomsbury Publishing.

Schimmel, Schim (1994) "Dear Children Of Earth" Minnesota, USA, Creative Publishing

Teel, Patti (2005) "The Floppy Sleep Game Book", New York, Penguin.

Teel, Patti (2005) "The Floppy Sleep Game Book: A proven 4-Week Plan to Get Your Child to Sleep." Perigree Books, New York.

Tichnor, Richard & Smith, Jenny(1994) "A Spark in the Dark" Nevada City, CA, Dawn Publishing.

Thorp, Georgia "Power of Puppets" Wiltshire, UK, Positive Press

Tozer, Marianne "Sing and Be Happy: Promoting Emotional Intelligence Through Song" , Perth WA, Fairsea Melodies.

Tremolada, Michelle (2002) "My Imagination Heals – Parents Workbook" Australia, Mind Image

Tremolada, Michelle (2002) "My Imagination Heals – Kayde and Sarah's Secret Adventure." Australia, Mind Image

Weise Jo & Wells, Steve (2004) "Rose and The Night Monsters" Inglewood, West Australia, Waterford Press. (www.eftdownunder.com)

Wroe, Jo Browning & Holliday, Carol(2004) "Forest of Feelings: Understanding and Exploring Emotions" UK, LDA.

Recommended Websites

1. Byronchild Magazine - the global family life magazine supporting the evolutionary imperative of conscious parenting.
www.byronchild.com
2. Fran Dobbie inspirational Australian educator, self esteem facilitator
www.essere.com.au
3. Amrita Hobbs author of Dare to Be Different a
www.amritahobbs.com

4. Thomas Hartmann
www.thomhartmann.com/addbooks

5 Kinda yoga website details Sydney Aust
www.kindayoga.com
6 Melinda Lewis creator of "My Magical Story Journal"
www.storyspeaks.com.au
7. Jenny Mosley UK dynamic educational consultant
www.circle-time.co.uk
8. Jenny Roberts Creator of Kids Code
www.parentswantinghelp.com

9. Robyn Henderson Sea Change Publishing – get the book out from inside you!
www.seachangepublishing.com.au

10. SEAL Society for Effective Affective Learning in the UK www.seal.org.uk

11. International Council for Self Esteem
www.self-esteem-international.org

12. Jack Canfield 's web site www.jackcanfield.com

13. Telethon Institute for Child Health Research in
Perth, West Australia www.ichr.uwa.edu.au

14. Patti Teel's web site is www.dreamflt.com

15. Dr Peter Dingle's web site www.drdingle.com

16. Lonny Gold's work via his web site
www.going-for-gold.net.]

17. The Wannabee Foundation is committed to
helping children and to assist parents to manage
the many challenges facing families who live with
young highly sensitive children.

www.wannabee.org.au

18. Wonderful natural products for babies and
toddlers www.natureschild.com.au

19. James Dakin and the team at Teaching Freedom
www.teachingfreedom.com

20. Vickie Falcone www.parentingwithsoul.com

21. Chick Moorman www.chickmoorman.com

22. Children of the New Earth
www.childrenofthenewearth.com

23. A US magazine www.parentingwithspirit.com

24. Youth Focus – a suicide prevention program for
youth www.youthfocus.com.au

25. Youth Care – promoting school chaplaincy across

West Australia www.youthcare.org.au

26. Most extensive resource for the early childhood field www.earlychildhoodaustralia.org.au.

27. Teaching Expertise excellent resource for teachers in the UK www.teachingexpertise.com

28. Glenn Capelli's web site www.**glenncapelli**.com

29. **David Koutsoukis** www.funman.com.au "Super Teacher"CD

Youth Care: School Chaplaincy

Chaplaincy is currently growing at a rate of 10 schools per year with significant growth in Primary Schools as schools recognize the integral role chaplains play in meeting the needs of children.

All Chaplains aim to provide sensitive Christian presence within a secular state school system. School chaplains work with student's families and staff in the school community to fulfil the following roles.

Social

The chaplain offers **strategic support** and **training** to develop leadership and citizenship skills for specific groups of students

emotional

The chaplain provides **pastoral care** through pastoral conversations with individuals and groups experiencing personal or social difficulties enabling them to **work through their difficulties** and adjust to change.

spiritual

The chaplain **stimulates** and **challenges** students to examine the big questions of life and meaning, helping them to formulate **their own beliefs and values systems** and works with staff to incorporate aspects of the core shared values into the educational program of schools.

mental

The chaplain **provides self esteem** and social skill enhancing programs for specific groups of students that will enable students to **participate more confidently and effectively** in the educational programs of the school.

physical

The chaplain creates **networks** between the school and welfare and community-based services. The chaplain informs students of the services that are available to them and enables them to **independently** access those services.

Chaplaincy

Chaplains work within the school as caring adults as part of a professional student services team by:

- ❖ Building relationships with students, families and staff.
- ❖ Offering pastoral care.
- ❖ Being a mentor.
- ❖ Providing additional practical help for teaching and administrative staff.
- ❖ Offering input into spiritual and "meaning of life" questions.
- ❖ Being a positive role model.

Providing a link between schools and local communities.

(c) August 19, 2005 YouthCARE

Telephone Counselling Services for Children and Young People

If you or someone you know is in crisis and needs someone to talk to you can call
Kids Help Line 1800 55 1800
From anywhere in Australia, available 24 Hours toll free
Lifeline 13 1114
Telephone counselling service, available 24 hours for the cost of a local call
Gay and Lesbian Switchboard 1800 631 493
Counselling, referral, information, available 6-10 pm weekdays, 2-10 pm Wednesday
Samaritans Suicide Crisis Helplines
- ☐ Perth: (08) 9381 5555
- ☐ Perth Youthline: (08) 9388 2500
- ☐ Toll free for country callers: 1800 198 313
- ☐ Sydney: (02) 9833 2133
- ☐ Launceston: (03) 6331 3355
- ☐ Tasmanian callers outside Launceston: 1300 364 566

The Samaritans are members of Befrienders International whose mission is to build effective suicide prevention services worldwide resourced by volunteers.

In the UK ChildLine is the free helpline for children and young people in the UK. Children and young people can call us on 0800 1111

Childhelp USA® National Child Abuse Hotline
Combating Child Abuse Across America 1-800-4-A-
CHILD 24 Hours a Day

Book Orders- Email to maggiedent@maggiedent.com

Orders at applicable rates

Nurturing Kids' Hearts and Souls

Name: _____

School/Organization: _____

Order N°: _____

Address: _____

Phone: _____

Quantity: _____

For full range of products, go to:

www.maggiedent.com